Storytelling Globalization from the Chaco and Beyond

NEW ECOLOGIES FOR THE TWENTY-FIRST CENTURY

Series Editors: Arturo Escobar, University of North Carolina, Chapel Hill

Dianne Rocheleau, Clark University

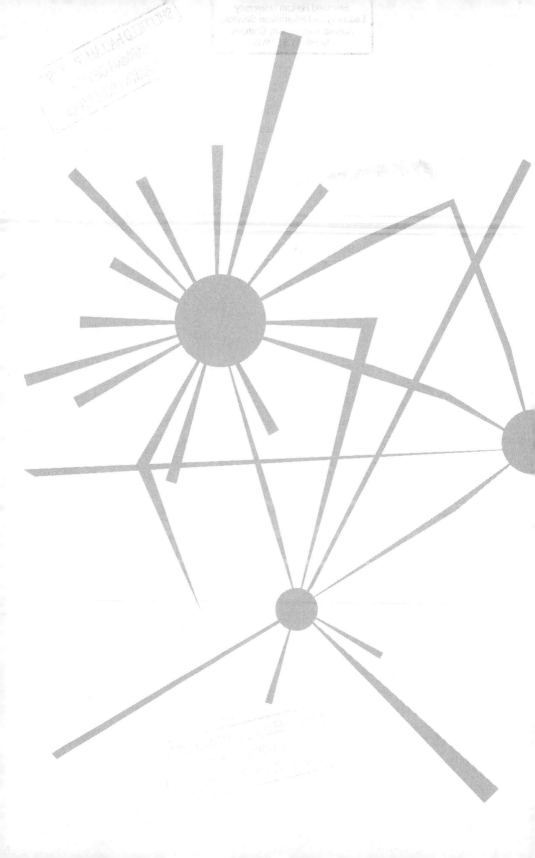

Storytelling Globalization
from the Chaco and Beyond

MARIO BLASER

DUKE UNIVERSITY PRESS
Durham & London 2010

© 2010 Duke University Press
All rights reserved
Printed in the United States of America on acid-free paper ∞
Designed by Jennifer Hill
Typeset in Arno Pro by Achorn International

Library of Congress Cataloging-in-Publication Data
appear on the last printed page of this book.

Duke University Press gratefully acknowledges the
support of the Dean of the School of Liberal Arts of Siena College for
providing funds toward the production of the book

A mis padres y a Milan
. . . por traerme y por llevarme mas allá

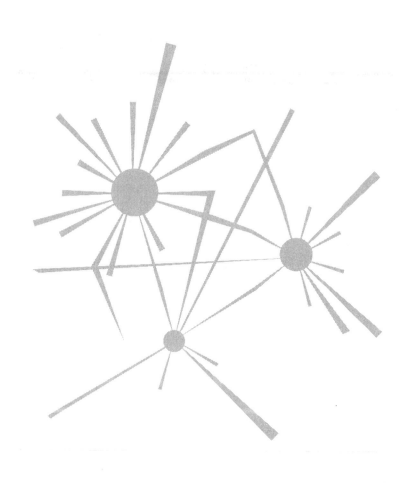

Contents

About the Series

This series addresses two trends: critical conversations in academic fields about nature, sustainability, globalization, and culture, including constructive engagements between the natural, social, and human sciences; and intellectual and political conversations among social movements and other non-academic knowledge producers about alternative practices and socio-natural worlds. Its objective is to establish a synergy between these theoretical and political developments in both academic and non-academic arenas. This synergy is a sine qua non for new thinking about the real promise of emergent ecologies. The series includes works that envision more lasting and just ways of being-in-place and being-in-networks with a diversity of humans and other living and non-living beings.

New Ecologies for the Twenty-First Century aims to promote a dialogue between those who are transforming the understanding of the relationship between nature and culture. The series revisits existing fields such as environmental history, historical ecology, environmental anthropology, ecological economics, and cultural and political ecology. It addresses emerging tendencies, such as the use of complexity theory to rethink a range of questions on the nature-culture axis. It also deals with epistemological and ontological concerns, building bridges between the various forms of knowing and ways of being embedded in the multiplicity of practices of social actors worldwide. This series hopes to foster convergences among differently located actors and to provide a forum for authors and readers to widen the fields of theoretical inquiry, professional practice, and social struggles that characterize the current environmental arena.

Maps

Preface

The truth about stories is that that's all we are.
—Thomas King, *The Truth about Stories*

In July 1999, Don Veneto Vera, a *konsaha* (shaman) of the Yshiro people of Paraguay, explained to me the chain of circumstances that had resulted in me being alive and working with his people. In short, it seems that Don Veneto, mobilizing a complex network of human and nonhumans, had saved me from a disease that would have killed me. These events had taken place beyond my awareness, as they had unfolded in a reality/world, the *yrmo*, of which I had only references through Don Veneto and other Yshiro elders and intellectuals.[1] Although I had known of it for years, the *yrmo* had had until that moment little personal relevance for me. What little I did know about it, however, was enough to make me realize that because Don Veneto had acted on my behalf, I had certain obligations toward him and the humans and nonhumans he had mobilized, which would involve commitments that I was not sure I would be able to honor. Among the responses I considered was to leave and never return. While I eventually decided otherwise, this event confronted me with a political and epistemological dilemma which had never before presented itself with such clarity and urgency, pushing me to reconsider my involvement with the Yshiro communities and, ultimately, to write this book in its present form.

I had been working for close to nine years on a variety of topics and projects with Yshiro communities when the incident with Don Veneto took place. At the time, I was engaged in a project commissioned by the leaders of the four communities of the Ebitoso, one of two Yshiro groups (the other being the Tomaraho). I had been asked to contribute to their efforts to create an organization that would federate the Yshiro communities by promoting, through group discussion and individual conversation, a critical awareness of what caused communities to be fractured along lines of religion, gender, political orientation, and age. In those meetings, people expressed their views about the issue, and I, as a good anthropologist trained within a critical tradition of analysis inherited from the Enlightenment, explained their different "views of the world" as particular events within larger economic and political processes, which, while not immediately accessible to them, were nevertheless the common ground from which their differences spanned and could be worked out. Producing these explanations was not a problem; the problem arose when I tried to share them, for my Yshiro interlocutors consistently refused to have their perspectives reduced to the terms of my analysis. I resolved the immediate, practical problem by working with the participants' own explanations in trying to bridge their differences (something that eventually happened, but not because of my "method") and reserved my explanations for an academic audience. However, I was left with a sense that there was something profoundly wrong with this solution. Although this feeling was not new, I could not readily articulate its source until the incident with Don Veneto.

If Don Veneto's story contained implicit prescriptions about how I should conduct myself regarding a whole series of issues, responding to these prescriptions in all honesty would require me to somehow accept his explanations of how things worked "in reality." I quickly realized that this dynamic was similar, albeit in reverse, to the one I had introduced in my interactions with other Yshiro interlocutors: for them to act on or think of their differences according to my explanations, they had to embrace my interpretation as their own. As I further pondered this realization, it dawned on me that this similarity was just apparent because there was a central difference between our explanations: the "colonial difference." In effect, my long-felt discomfort with the division in my anthropological practice, between an academic and an applied stance, stemmed from the significative difference that it signaled between the Yshiro's way of seeing and explaining the world, and my own. This difference was due not to the substance of these views and explanations, but to the fact that they were situated in unequal positions within a field of power.[2] In short, the division in my practice signaled the coloniality of knowledge that transmutes different knowledge practices into hierarchical differences.

In my applied incarnation I was engaging fully with the Yshiro peoples' views of the world because I was not able or willing, in the immediate moment, to impose my own explanations of the world on them. Thus, I had to argue, negotiate, and modify my stance vis-à-vis theirs. In my academic incarnation, in contrast, I could domesticate those different perspectives to make them fit into explanations that I would later present for discussion among scholars. My encounter with Don Veneto clarified for me that while I had the option of switching between these incarnations, my Yshiro interlocutors did not. In effect, I could have brushed aside Don Veneto's explanations simply by not returning to Paraguay, thus avoiding the uncomfortable situation of having to give a direct response to his interpellation. In a less dramatic fashion, this was what I was doing when I produced my analysis for academic publics; I was brushing aside my Yshiro interlocutors' views of the world without major consequences.[3] In other words, by switching stances I could circumscribe, to my convenience, the space in which I negotiated my views with those of the Yshiro. My Yshiro interlocutors and friends, however, could not seclude themselves from being subject to expert analysis and its repercussions. In the most obvious way, through a chain that links academic production and policymaking, scholarly interpretations have been a constant feature of the terrain in which the Yshiro have had to operate since the Paraguayan nation-state began to claim control over their territory and lives.

Becoming aware of this made exceedingly clear that academic production of knowledge—including my own—was thoroughly entangled with the politics of representation, which shaped, among other things, the divisions within the Yshiro communities. So, if I intended to understand how those divisions were produced in order to counter them, I had to account for the location of, or the significative difference between, both academic and Yshiro accounts of the world.

Yet, I wondered, how should I account for the differences between my explanations and theirs? Should I describe our differences by using the frameworks accepted in academia, or should I let such accounts emerge from the discussions I had with my Yshiro friends? While the latter possibility solved my immediate personal dilemma, it did not engage the problem in its wider significance and impact. In effect, I could refuse my position as expert and negotiate my views with my Yshiro interlocutors, but this would not erase the structural inequalities between the Yshiro and the experts. Even if I were to embrace Yshiro perspectives as my own, this would not automatically accord them the same standing as academic perspectives; rather, I would be accused of "going native." On the other hand, if I used accepted academic frameworks to criticize those inequalities with "authority," I would reinstate at another level the hierarchical relations that the Yshiro hoped to contest through the creation of their federation. I was in a dilemma.

Seeking to address this dilemma has taken me in directions that I could not have imagined at the beginning of this journey. Looking back, I can see that I began with a question (although at the time it was not as clearly formulated as it is here): how could I produce knowledge that would contribute to the Yshiro project, rather than unwittingly erode it? The challenge was how to avoid contributing to a long history, in Paraguay, in which modern experts try to "help" indigenous peoples by claiming ever-increasing accuracy in their depictions of indigenous reality, while in the process reinforcing the hierarchies between indigenous knowledges and their own. To prevent my work from feeding that history, I had to account for the conditions of possibility that would inform such an intellectual project. In other words, brushing aside self-flattering ideas of personal or epochal progress, what made it possible for people like me to ask these kinds of questions at this time? Pursuing this line of inquiry led me to academic analyses that characterize the present moment as one of globalization, and to their debates over what this concept might entail. As I gained familiarity with these debates I came to see them as the tip of the iceberg, intimating struggles over the meaning of globalization that reached beyond the academy. In short, the term *globalization* seemed to indicate the site of a generalized struggle to define or shape an emerging state of being: globality or the global age. Surprisingly, exploring the globalization debates, which in principle seemed to lead away from the immediate concerns that had driven the Yshiro leaders to create their organization, instead brought me right back to them. The Yshiro endeavor to defend and further the *yrmo* (Yshiro reality/world) is in fact an integral part of the ongoing, multiscalar, and increasingly better articulated struggle to define and shape the global age in a way which is profoundly antithetical to the dominant project of defining and shaping globalization as "modernity writ large."

My tour through the globalization debates and back to the Yshiro project did not leave my original question unscathed. Seen in the context of all-encompassing struggles, which manifest in different ways in different sites but nevertheless help to define and shape the global age, my dilemma acquired a different character. The problem was no longer how to produce applied and academic explanations that corresponded with each other; instead, it was how to perform, in the sites associated with these roles (i.e., the academy and the Paraguayan Chaco, where the Yshiro live), knowledge practices that would resonate with each other in their aim of articulating differences in symmetrical ways, rather than reinforce hierarchies in one site by contesting them in another. My applied experience was key in this regard for it was through this experience, and years of practical involvement with certain Yshiro individuals, that I had encountered a knowledge practice with such potential. At the risk of distorting its wider reach, a risk which I hope to dispel throughout this book, let me tentatively present this knowledge practice simply as storytelling. But, importantly, this book is not about narrative forms or oral literature; the concept of storytelling stands for a way of practicing knowledge.

As for many other indigenous peoples, storytelling has for the Yshiro profound performative qualities, that is, stories are not only or not mainly denotative (referring to something "out there"), but rather they help produce that of which they speak. Being aware of this, Yshiro intellectuals and elders would insist that storytelling always has a purpose (to produce certain realities) even if one is not aware of it, and that knowledge always connotes storytelling. Conceiving this ethnography as storytelling has helped me explore a possible way out of the dilemma. My argument is that storytelling globalization is one of the many grounded ways through which the present moment is being shaped. But stories are told in different ways, and this difference is crucial for the kinds of worlds that are currently taking shape. Thus, this work makes sense in two interconnected registers. On the one hand, the story makes sense as a narrative of the struggle in which the Yshiro, experts, governmental agencies, private interests, and social movements are involved to give shape to the different worlds that will characterize the global age. On the other hand, the story makes sense as a performance whose specific purpose is to help shape the global age in a particular way, that is, as a pluriverse in which the *yrmo* can exist and thrive along with other worlds. As the two registers of this story unfold, it will become evident that a critical move to achieve the pluriverse involves doing away with modernist ontological commitments deeply ingrained in our knowledge practices; this book is, above anything else, an attempt to do this.

One part of the story I am about to tell emerged from over seventeen years of interaction, friendships, and collaborative work with the Yshiro communities. Since 1991, I have visited the communities at least once a year (except in 1992, 2001, and 2002), for periods ranging from one to three months, and during 1999–2000 I stayed for eighteen months. Through all these years, the patience, affection, and sense of humor of my Yshiro friends have created in me an everlasting debt of gratitude. First and foremost, and in spite of the ups and downs of our relationship, I am thankful to Bruno Barras, who, when I was a young undergraduate student from Argentina, invited me to work with his community and thus changed my life in ways I would have never expected. His children, especially Alejo and "El Coti," have been my good friends since that time.

Perla Ortiz, the "matriarch of Karcha Bahlut," has always taken good care of me, making sure I was comfortable and well nourished. Her husband, Benito Romero, and their *boshesho terror* (scary children) Camargo, Tusi, and Lederman; my compadre Modesto Martinez, Sonia Ozuna, and their children; and Babi Ozuna and his many girlfriends have been my family in Karcha Bahlut. Estanislao Baez, Fanny Martinez, and their children, as well as Teresa and Gaspar Paya and their children took me into their families when I was in Diana. "Cachique Oso" Candido Martinez and his wife Maria Romero; and Don Pablo, Victor and Graciela Romero have been very generous hosts every time I have visited Ynishta. Zulma Franco and Julio Baez, in Ylhirta, have been always great hosts and much fun. From all of them I have learned the everydayness of a relational world in which one's duty toward others is experienced not as an imposition, but rather as an opportunity to express love and respect.

Although I had to get accustomed to his wild sense of humor, which has scared more than one visitor, Don Veneto Vera has turned out to be a great teacher and guide through the complex landscape of the *yrmo*; and so have been Don Gines Rizo and Don Tito Perez. For their kindness and generosity in sharing a knowledge that has transformed me in many ways, I will be endlessly grateful. My gratitude also goes to the many elders and friends who taught me and who have passed away: Abuelo Sixto (Keiwe), Doña Tama, Abuela Eva, Abuela Elsa Boyani, Abuelo Miranda, Don Vierci, Artigas Rizo, Papito Medina, Ama Ferreira, and Don Bruno Sanchez Vera (Tamusia).

In Asunción, my friend Malu Vazquez Tande helped me to understand the intricacies of the *indigenista* world from the perspective of an insider; that, in addition to providing me housing with *mate a la mañana*. The embryos of many ideas presented in this book emerged from conversations with Ursula Regher, who has been for almost ten years a loyal friend and esteemed colleague. Rodrigo Villagra and Valentina Bonifacio have both been dear friends and colleagues from whom I have learned much about the dynamics of the *indigenista* world. To all of them, a heartfelt thanks.

Another part of the story I am about to tell emerges from the enriching relations I have sustained through the years with colleagues and friends in North America. Early on Harvey Feit helped me to come to terms with the idea that there was much more going on with my Yshiro friends than what a political-economy approach could encompass. But Harvey's influence on my intellectual growth goes beyond this; his combination of sharp political analysis with a real commitment to dialogue is a beacon for me of what an engaged intellectual should be like in a relational world.

In those beginnings I also counted on the invaluable intellectual and emotional support of Amanda White, for which I will forever be grateful, and perhaps forever indebted.

Will Coleman provided me with a unique opportunity to connect my research with the globalization debates by welcoming me to the Major Collaborative Research Initiative on Globalization and Autonomy. My work and exchanges with colleagues in this setting has been key in giving shape to this book. I am particularly thankful to Deborah McGregor, Marcelo Fernandes Osco, and Pablo Mariman Quemenado, who shared their insights and perspectives. Discussions and exchanges with Ravi de Costa and Alex Khasnabish have been also very illuminating.

As many before me, I was lucky to experience the generosity of Arturo Escobar, who without other references than a couple of writing samples accepted to host me as a postdoctoral scholar at the University of North

Carolina, Chapel Hill. In addition to enabling me to learn from Arturo, this afforded me the opportunity to interact with a group of enormously talented graduate students and faculty in the Modernity/Coloniality Working Group and the Social Movements Working Group. I am grateful to all the participants in general for discussions that helped me to sharpen several aspects of this book. I am especially indebted to Juan Ricardo Aparicio, Maribel Casas-Cortes, Jason Cross, Gonzalo Lamana, Walter Mignolo, Michal Osterweil, and Dana Powell for their comments and discussion of the ideas in this manuscript.

In the last couple of years my friends and colleagues Marisol de la Cadena, Justin Kenrick, and Brian Noble have pushed me to take the work presented here in new and unexpected directions. To avoid the risk of delaying an already overdue publication, I have included only hints of these possibilities in the manuscript, but the ground to build on is here.

Finally, I want to thank my wife, Elena Yehia, who provided insightful critiques of earlier versions of the manuscript; this, as a bonus to having made my life much more interesting and relational than it ever was.

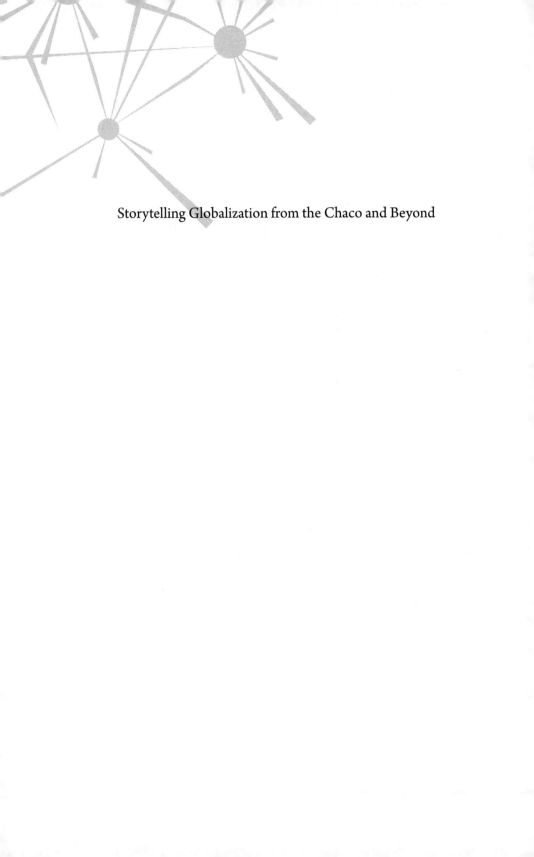

Storytelling Globalization from the Chaco and Beyond

Map 1. The Paraguayan Chaco and the current physical connections to the Yshiro area.

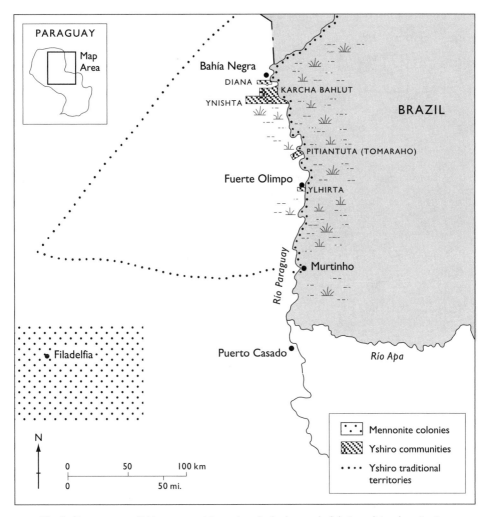

Map 2. Contemporary Yshiro communities against the background of their traditional territories.

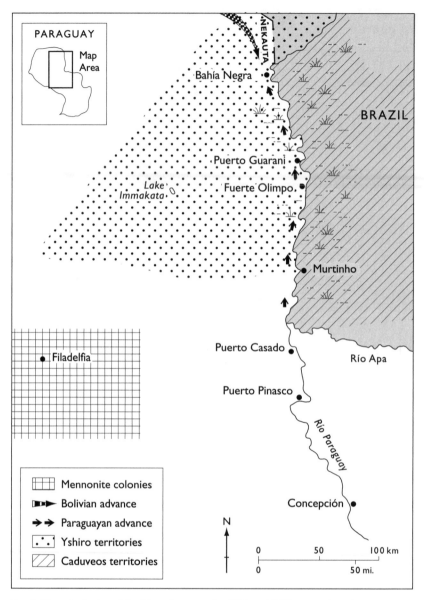

Map 3. The colonization of the Chaco between the 1880s and 1930, approximately.

Introduction Globalization and the Struggle
for Worlds and Knowledges Otherwise

Since about the 1990s, the present moment has been increasingly narrated as one of globalization and, with more intensity in the last few years, also as one of crisis. Beyond the controversies on whether globalization is a new phenomenon or
not, there has been tacit understanding among scholars that the
concept refers to ongoing processes that are bringing about social, economic, cultural, and political orders worldwide, which
in some respects mark a difference from those said to characterize earlier stages of modernity. Although there are some dissent-
ing voices, as we will see later, most scholars involved in these
discussions tend to agree that certain processes are bringing
into being globality, or the global age. In turn, the nature of the
"crisis"—or its very existence—and its relation to globalization
greatly complicates this agreement. Commentators, the media,
and social movements have signaled various environmental, social, economic, and political crises as indicative of great transformations that require adequate response. Of course, what kinds
of responses are advocated greatly depends on one's diagnosis
of the present moment. Is this a moment marked by the crisis of
hegemony of neoliberalism? Is it the crisis of capitalism in its different forms? Is it a crisis of the modern state? Or is it the crisis
of modernity?

The story I tell in this book is offered both as a plausible diagnosis of the present moment and as a response to that diagnosis. The present moment can be most fruitfully understood as
marked by the increasingly visible and generalized ontological
conflicts that are associated with the struggle to shape the global
age as an alternative to, rather than a continuation of, modernity.

Ontological conflicts are central to the times both because they reveal that alternatives to modernity do exist and because they force modernity to re-shape itself in order to deal with radical difference. The mobilization of the Yshiro and other indigenous peoples can be grasped in a conceptually and politically productive way if one situates it within the dynamics generated by ontological conflict. Seen in this light, the Yshiro (and other indigenous peoples') process of political organizing emerge as one aspect in the pursuit of their own life projects. Life projects are based on visions of a good life premised on densely and uniquely woven threads of ontological assump-tions, the materiality of landscapes, memories, practices, expectations, and desires. Among other things, they diverge from the various projects of modernity in their attention to the uniqueness of peoples' experiences of place and self and in their rejection of visions that claim to be universal (see Blaser 2004b). Although the pursuit of life projects by diverse indigenous peoples delineates a series of particular trajectories, these trajectories have increasingly begun to converge and gain visibility at the point of their en-counter with a modern world that denies other worlds any reality.

While the scale and visibility of indigenous mobilization has generated a profuse literature with various approaches and foci, these have largely con-centrated in *la conjuncture* of the twentieth century, thus occluding the on-tological aspects of these processes and, therefore, their most far-reaching implications. In Latin America this is evident in the debates around whether the present conjuncture, to a large extent shaped by indigenous mobiliza-tions, constitutes a "left turn," with the consequent reshuffling of social forces thus implied. Whether this description is accurate or not, modernist assumptions about what is at stake in politics (e.g., recognition of subjects and redistribution of objects) have remained firmly established. It is not that these assumptions are wrong, but rather that they are insufficient, for they cannot grasp those aspects of indigenous mobilization that literally do not fit within modern categories (of subjects and objects for instance) because they express a different ontology (see de la Cadena 2009). More-over, modernity's tendency to forcefully make other ontologies fit into its categories is itself one of the triggers for ontological conflicts.

Three layers of meaning shape my working definition of ontology. The first layer is drawn from the *Dictionary of Sociology*: "Any way of understand-ing the world must make assumptions (which may be implicit or explicit) about what kinds of things do or can exist, and what might be their conditions of existence, relations of dependency, and so on. Such an inventory of kinds of being and their relations is an ontology" (Scott and Marshall 2005). The second layer I borrow from the insights and language of science and technology studies, and in particular from Actor Network Theory: ontologies do not precede mundane practices, but rather are shaped through the practices and interactions of both human and nonhumans (see Latour 1999; Law 2004; Mol 1999). Hence, ontologies perform themselves into worlds—thus, I use the terms *ontologies* and *worlds* as synonyms. The third layer builds on a voluminous ethnographic record that traces the connections between myths and practices: ontologies also manifest as "stories" in which the assumptions of what kinds of things and relations make up a given world are readily graspable. Yet, while myths are a good entry point to an ontology, attending only to their verbalized aspect, and not to the way in which they are embodied and enacted, reveals only half the story. Ontologies must be understood as the total (i.e., including discursive and nondiscursive) enactments of worlds. In this sense, myths are neither true nor false; they just engender different worlds which have their own criteria for defining truth.

Ontological conflicts entail questions about what counts as knowledge and what kinds of worlds different knowledge practices contribute to perform. Thus, knowing ontological conflicts requires following a circuitous route, for rather than directly approaching them as being "out there," one must begin by interrogating and disclosing the conditions of possibility for such an endeavor. For a scholar writing from the entrails of a modern institution such as the academy, the first step is to question and disclose the ontological assumptions implicit in "our" knowledge practices—that is, the first step is to pry open the modern myth.

John Locke's assertion in his *Second Treatise of Government* ([1690] 1980) that "in the beginning all the world was America" is perhaps the most succinct utterance of this myth. Certainly, the categorical distinctions and the temporal dynamics embedded in this sentence had been taking shape for several centuries before Locke's treatise appeared: Christian linear temporality, punctuated by the fall and the promised salvation of humanity, is already entangled with the experiences and effects of European encounters with peoples and places not foreseen in medieval worldviews or in biblical and ancient sources, and with a dualist ontology that had Greek roots but was most fully expressed in its modern shape by Descartes's *cogito* (see Albanese 1996; Blaut 1993; Dussel 1995, 1998; Elliott 1970). Cartesian dualism operates in the modern myth as a generative principle of ever expanding sets of opposing pairs such as mind-world, culture-nature, representation-reality, and the like. This dualism is the product of successive conceptual layers laid prior to (and after) Descartes's *cogito*; however, as Plumwood argues, it is Descartes who articulates a philosophy in which nature (the world "out there") is rendered as "ineluctably alien" and mindless (1993:107–9).[1]

By the late seventeenth century, when Locke wrote the treatises, the relation between the two terms of Cartesian dualism, nature and culture, was firmly framed in a temporal matrix. Implicit in the claim that "in the beginning all the world was America" is the premise that nature is the ground, the starting point of humankind's voyage toward some sort of paradise located somewhere in the future. Progress is thus marked by the increasing dominion of humankind over nature; the more man masters nature, the farther humanity moves along the line of progress. Yet it was in light of their experiences with those humans indigenous to other places (Indians), who had been falling under European domination since the sixteenth century, that the European writing elites could imagine themselves and their societies to be the result of a natural historical progression, an interpretation which then justified further European expansion and the violent imposition of the modern myth as a universal (see Elliott 1970; Dussel 1995, 1998; Fabian 1983).

Modernity can thus be conceived as the state of being that obtains from the enactment of a modern myth composed of three basic threads: the great divide between nature and culture (or society), the colonial difference between moderns and nonmoderns, and a unidirectional linear temporality that flows from past to future.[2] However, I must make two points regarding this particular depiction of the modern myth or ontology. First, although I use the singular term *modernity*, I do not intend to suggest that ontologies more or less different from the one depicted here cannot legitimately be called modern. Indeed, Lawrence Grossberg (n.d.) has made a compelling argument for the necessity and political advantages of keeping open the possibility that modernity can be something other than the ontology that

I depict here and that he qualifies as Euromodernity. I retain the singular to signal both that I am referring to the dominant and most widely recognized form of modernity (i.e., Euromodernity) and that the possibility of other non-Eurocentric modernities in the present conjuncture seems to be closely connected to a different way of engaging radical difference and hence still remains largely in the realm of potentiality rather that actuality (for a more extended discussion of these points see Blaser 2009b). Second, when I speak of modernity in this book I am always making reference to a specific arrangement of the three constitutive threads mentioned before. Thus, remove or change this arrangement and one is speaking of another myth, for the effects of certain shifts and changes pushed by ontological conflicts in these constitutive threads are precisely what ground narratives of the present time as one of passage from modernity to globality.

A change of myth implies a change in how the people that tell themselves these stories live, more centrally because such change implies a transformation in how knowledge and truth are conceived. For example, the modern myth brought with it what Szerszynski calls the "modern problematic," that is, how one might know (in moral and practical or instrumental terms) in a context in which "word and world" are ontologically distinct (1996:106–7). This way of posing the problematic implicitly delineates the contours of a "modern regime of truth" according to which truth (or true knowledge) obtains from establishing the universal equivalence between the world out there (nature) and its representation. This regime of truth has continually reproduced itself through the practices of governmental apparatuses, including expert institutions that cooperate to define certain ways of imagining reality as knowledge while dismissing others as mere belief (see Foucault 1973, 1980:131–33). Of course, knowledge is central to governmental practices, for one governs self and others (human and nonhuman) according to what one takes to be true knowledge about the world (Dean 1999:18). By assuming the dualism between representation and reality, modern governmental practices have deployed and redeployed the modern regime of truth along with the asymmetries inherent in producing "other/objects."[3]

Yet the present moment seems to bring along a questioning of the modern regime of truth and its dualistic assumptions. What does this questioning mean? How far reaching are its consequences? How is this related to ontological conflicts? Throughout this book I address these questions by focusing on how the modern regime of truth has produced, or has tried to produce, objects of government and the institutions and values through which these are governed; and, in turn, how these objects of government have responded and in the process transformed those institutions and values meant to govern them. In this way, I use transformations in knowledge, objects of government, and governmental practices as indexes to the continuities and discontinuities between modernity and globality. Development is the lens through which I will look at this. As a practice and discourse, development is (or has been until very recently) rather explicit with regard to its aim of universalizing modernity and its institutions (Arturo Escobar 1995:156; see also Ferguson 1990; Rist 1996). More importantly, since the nineteenth century, this aim has been pursued with increasing input from expert knowledge, the epitome of true knowledge in the modern regime of truth. Thus, through development one can see how the modern regime of truth has changed along with the expertise that has contributed to producing its objects of government.[4] In this sense, it is important to recall James Ferguson's (1997) discussion of the intimate connections that exist between anthropology and "its evil twin," development. These connections, he argues, imply co-emergence and parallel transformations. Paraguay exemplifies this dynamics. There, anthropology specialized in producing objects of government suitable for incorporation within changing ideas of development while the actual practices of development and their effects provided the conditions that made possible the emergence and ongoing transformation of anthropology. These transformations, in turn, have fueled the production of new "objects" that require other kinds of interventions or treatment, and so on.

Although this dynamics lends credence to the depiction of anthropology, among other disciplines, as "an academic offshoot of a set of universalist technologies of domination" (Pels 1997:165), the relation between academics (or academically trained experts) and domination has not been always and in all cases that clear and straightforward. For instance, in Latin America, anthropologists have often been involved as collaborators in processes of indigenous organizing (see Varese, Delgado, and Meyer 2008). More generally, anthropology, along with other disciplines, has also contributed to a critique of colonialism and development, and even, particularly since the 1960s, of its own implication in these and other forms of domination (see Asad 1973; Hymes 1974; Fabian 1983; Clifford and Marcus 1986). To fully grasp how these disciplines contribute to shape the present moment, it is crucial to recognize the heterogeneity of experts' practices in general and, given the context of this ethnography, of anthropological practices in particular.

In broad strokes, one could distinguish two general tendencies in anthropological practices in the last thirty years. The first has been associated with a critical tradition that has roots in the Enlightenment and is concerned with unearthing "real" processes, structures, or dynamics that are somehow veiled by naïve or unsystematic thinking and methods, appearances, or ideology. The second, more recent, tendency is associated with a critique of the positivistic assumptions implied in the notion of a "reality out there" (or at least in the notion that this reality can be somehow accessed without interferences) and is concerned with the politics of representation and self-reflexivity. Especially in North America, both tendencies became clearly distinguished and to some extent antagonistic, with the publication of *Writing Culture* (Clifford and Marcus 1986) and the debates that followed it (see Fox 1991; Marcus 1994). Those espousing the first tendency responded to the self-reflexive turn by accusing it of being over-concerned with textual and representational issues while disengaging from real and urgent problems, while those espousing the second tendency argued that issues of representation and self-reflexivity were part of real and urgent problems (see Arturo Escobar 1993). In the ensuing years, these tendencies have been incorporated as ingredients of actual anthropological practices, which, while mixing them, often emphasize one more than the other.

In Paraguay the tendency to unearth "real," underlying "truths" has been and continues to be the predominant way by which experts produce knowledge in relation to indigenous peoples. When aimed at countering the subordination of indigenous peoples, these knowledge practices exemplify the murky relationship that "enlightened critique" sustains with modernity. Enlightened critique is that produced from a standpoint which, as Sahlins notes, allows "dogmas of the common average native Western folklore [to stand] as universal understandings of the human condition" (1999: ii).

While enlightened critiques might be aimed at destabilizing the power asymmetries generated by modernity, they also contribute to reinstating them in subtler forms. In Paraguay, for example, there is a long tradition of committed experts who have sought in different ways and at different times to counter the subordinating practices of the state and other actors in relation to indigenous peoples. Yet, when producing academic or policy documents, these experts (among whom I include myself) have themselves tended to reinforce the asymmetries between modern and nonmodern knowledge practices, thus countering the relatively more symmetrical relations they strived to co-construct with their indigenous partners in the field. The knowledge practices of such experts have in this way contributed to the wider subordinating processes of the modern regime of truth. Nevertheless, precisely because they are not fully coherent, these modern knowledge practices reveal cracks that open up the possibility of pursuing transformations based on dialogue.

Precisely a disposition for dialogue is what the self-reflexive turn made pressing in anthropological practices. In effect, a veritable tradition of experimental ethnographies has refused to uncritically reproduce modernist representational tropes in ethnographic texts, and to some extent has sought to conceive the relation between fieldwork and the production of ethnographies, and between ethnographers and "informants" in new and dialogical ways.[5] The dialogical dispositions that this experimental mode produced in anthropology and beyond has contributed to the emergence of academic frameworks that are prone to engage in more symmetrical ways with other knowledge practices. In Latin America, this disposition came to join an existing tradition of dialogical engagement between academics and subordinate groups, best represented by the paradigmatic figures of Paulo Freire and Orlando Fals Borda, although anthropologists have also figured prominently in this tradition (see Varese, Delgado, and Meyer 2008; Hale 2008).

The heterogeneity of knowledge practices is a crucial component of the processes by which the present moment is made "to make sense" in different ways. Indeed, along with social movements and governmental institutions, this heterogeneity has contributed to create the intramodern conditions of possibility for the emergence of new and newly visible stories of the significance of the present moment in terms of globalization.

The different ways in which globalization (i.e., the passage from modernity to globality) is narrated, and how these narrations are embodied in practices, contribute to perform different kinds of globality. Stories of globalization which have acquired high visibility in the last decade or so can be seen as stretching between two poles: the modernist pole and what I call the rupturist pole.

The modernist pole takes modernity as an ontological condition reached by humanity through a long evolutionary process which adopted its form as modernization proper in Western Europe and later expanded to the rest of the world. Globalization is considered to be the unavoidable continuation of this process. Being inscribed in the telos of "society" (in singular), the process of globalization universalizes and radicalizes central features of modernity (see Beck 1992, 1999; Beck, Giddens, and Lash 1994; Giddens 1990, 1998). Thus, to paraphrase Arjun Appadurai (1996), globality is modernity at large. Other versions similar to the modernist story of globalization might contest Eurocentrism, indicating non-European contributions to the making of modernity and highlighting that each society has had a different historical trajectory; together, these stories assert that the experience of "modernity at large" is plural, hence the discourses of multiple modernities, heterogeneity, and hybridity which accompany the process of globalization (see Arce and Long 2000; Einsestadt 2002; Gaonkar 2001). However, this "modernity-cum-globality" version implicitly envisages a homogeneity underlying the heterogeneity in that the whole globe is now modern (see Arturo Escobar 2003, for a similar point). This fundamental homogeneity warrants a vision of globality as a condition of unbounded flows which express themselves in either cultural terms (we are all modern, albeit in different ways), economic terms (capitalism is everywhere, albeit in indigenized forms), political terms (a cosmopolitan global order is taking shape), or terms that combine all of these.

Interestingly, while many proponents of this perspective narrate globalization as a process that will eventually reach every corner of the world by its own dynamics, "some of the most powerful agencies in the world are utterly intent on its production" (Massey 1999:36). This is not a coincidence; such stories are enormously powerful because they are enacted through governmental practices. Indeed, the story of globalization as the universalization and radicalization of modernity nourishes the still dominant neoliberal project, which for many years has performed this universalization and radicalization of modernity. With the Washington Consensus finished, state intervention on the rise across the globe, and Left-leaning candidates reaching office in many Latin American countries, it is not unsurprising that the modernist story now encourages various forms of so-called progressive agendas. As the Bolivian vice-president Alvaro García Linera asserted, in 2007, the agenda of progressive governments in Latin America is to generate a "satisfactory modernity." Given that this modernist narrative redeploys the modern regime of truth, one can say that while modernity has been until recently performing itself as globality mainly through neoliberal globalization, it might now be recasting itself and getting reproduced through "progressive" globalization. In fact, the furthering of modernity through progressive political stances is not new at all.

The rupturist pole or story sees globalization as a contentious process that creates unprecedented conditions in which to challenge and break away from modernity, both as a system of rule and a system of knowledge and representation (Massey 1999:31). Three versions of the rupturist story have profoundly shaped my work, and they are to some degree complementary, as each one focuses on different yet inextricably connected threads of the modern myth. The first version is associated with science studies and more specifically with scholars working within the framework of Actor Network Theory (ANT), which concentrates on theoretically and practically unsettling the system of ever expanding dualism based on the modern ontological great divide between nature and culture, or object and subject (see Latour 1993, 1999, 2004; Law and Hassard 1999; Law and Mol 2002; Mol 2002). The second version is associated with critical theory, cultural, subaltern, and postcolonial studies, and more specifically the consolidating Latin American program of Modernity/Coloniality and Decolonial thinking (MCD), which works to unsettle the epistemological and political asymmetries that span from the colonial difference between modern and non-modern (see Castro-Gómez, Millán, and Rivarola 2001; Arturo Escobar 2003; Lander and Castro-Gómez 2000; Mignolo 2000, 2007; Mignolo, Schiwy, and Ennis 2002; Walsh, Shiwy, and Castro-Gómez 2002). The third version is associated with feminist theorizing at the intersection with the *bios* (both in bio-techno-sciences and ecology), particularly the works of Donna Haraway (1991, 1997, 2003, 2007) and Val Plumwood (1993, 2002), which have sought to unsettle the hierarchical relations with nonhuman "others" (i.e., nature in a modern framework) while at the same time showing how these relations are profoundly entangled with the hierarchical relations between moderns and their human "others."

In conjunction, these versions of the rupturist story contest the modern myth, that is, the story that modernity tells itself about itself as pure(ified), self-generated, and self-contained. This rupturist perspective allows one to see modernity as the product of a particular place (time-space location) and of a particular blindness to both the set of relations and the actual coercive practices that constitute the "reality" of modernity and modernity itself.[6] And precisely by contesting modernity's fundamentals, the rupturist story ruptures the veil of universalism with which the modern myth had covered the pluriverse, that is, the multiple interconnected realities/worlds which make up the cosmos.[7] In doing so, the rupturist story allows for a diagnosis of the present moment that questions the modern categories and understandings of politics through which one usually makes sense of it. Moreover, the rupturist story foregrounds that these categories and understandings are fully implicated in the struggle to shape the present moment.

In the cases of ANT and MCD, the pursuit of their critical inquiries with an almost exclusive focus on either the great divide or the colonial difference generates some blind spots (for a similar point see Yehia 2006). While ANT shakes the modern ontological ground by proposing a flat ontology in which performance precedes entities (objects and subjects, for instance), it seems to have little to say about the role that violence plays as a key performative act in the constitution of (modern) entities.[8] In contrast, by focusing on the modern–nonmodern divide, MCD compensates for this blind spot of ANT and brings forward the notion that modernity strives to establish itself as a universal ontological condition through a relentless process of expansion and colonization, which involves a great deal of violence and coercion (Dussel 1995; Quijano 2000; Mignolo 2000). For this reason, authors associated with this program speak of modernity/coloniality to refer to modernity: once one takes off the modern blinders, modernity appears as genetically constituted by an underside of colonial violence that organizes the differences of the pluriverse into a hierarchical matrix.

But the MCD's almost exclusive concentration on the colonial difference comes at the price of a tenuous assimilation, in practice although not in theory, of the full extent to which a critical examination of the nature-culture divide pushes one to, first, keep in focus nonhuman others as part of how the colonial difference gets established and, second, give precedence to performance over epistemology. While MCD recognizes that the divide between nature and culture is part of the colonial difference, as Arturo Escobar (2003) has pointed out, thus far this research program has produced very little, if any, work on this issue. The contributions of feminists like Haraway and Plumwood are therefore critical, for they raise a danger flag over (and provide some escape routes from) the trap into which a critique of the colonial difference that is focused on the human might be prone to fall, namely, humanism. Haraway puts it thus: "The discursive tie between the colonized, the enslaved, the noncitizen and the animal—all reduced to type, all Others to rational man and essential to his bright constitution—is at the heart of racism and flourishes, lethally, in the entrails of humanism" (2007:18). The trap is that humanism grounds the kinds of "unidirectional relations of use, ruled by practices of calculation and self-sure of hierarchy," with animals that ultimately return to haunt, via the mind-body divide, the relations among humans as well (Haraway 2007:69–75).

In addition to the problem of humanism, MCD's partial assimilation of the consequences of shaking the nature-culture divide leads the program to maintain a central concern with the "locus of enunciation" (that is, standpoint) of knowledge (in geopolitical and epistemological terms) which is not matched by a (self-reflexive) concern with how knowledge is performed. In contrast, ANT moves one step in this direction with its practice of "tracing," whereby it is recognized that "things" or "events" do not exist out there but come into being, at least in part, through the work done by researchers and other "actants" (see Latour 2003; Law 2004).

In general, those who enact the rupturist story seek, as I do, to erode the dominant system of rule and subalternization of others (human and nonhumans) begotten by modernity and to open up spaces for the unfolding of the pluriverse. The multiplicity within this objective is rendered by its diverse labels: "counter-hegemonic globalization" (Arturo Escobar 2008;

Santos 2006), "*mundialización*" (Mignolo 2000), "the common world" (Latour 2004), and "multispecies living on earth" (Haraway 2007), among others. Yet all these terms signal recognition of the need for "worlds and knowledges otherwise," that is, for "worlds that are more just and sustainable and, at the same time, worlds that are defined through principles other than those of Eurocentric modernity" (Arturo Escobar 2004a:220). Latour (1993, 1999, 2004) and Haraway (2007), for instance, coincide in the belief that nonhumans must be recognized as part of the collective in an equally problematic standing as humans, for this is the only way of averting the continuing injustices and destruction being brewed by modernity-cum-globality. Authors associated with MCD, in turn, point out that while modernity/coloniality is transmuting into globality/coloniality under capitalist globalization, this project is encountering strong opposition from social movements (of environmentalists, women, indigenous peoples, peasants, the poor, and so on) all over the world, many of which are not only contesting market dogma but also challenging the very tenets of modernity (Arturo Escobar 2008; see also Dirlik 2001; Massey 1999; Notes from Nowhere 2003; Santos 2006; Sen, Armand, and Waterman 2004). In no small measure these movements enact, in ways other than writing, the rupturist story of globalization and challenge the story of modernity-cum-globality.

The modernist and the rupturist stories are two poles in a continuum of existing narratives and enactments that often mix, in diverse proportion, elements from each of these poles. For example, authors like David Harvey (1996), Michael Hardt and Antonio Negri (2000, 2004), and Immanuel Wallerstein (2004), as well as the movements that they reference, come close to the rupturist story in that they oppose neoliberal globalization, yet they fall back into the modernist story in that they can only conceive alternatives within the terms that modern thinking makes available (see Castro-Gómez 2007). But the most radical voices of the rupturist story face a similar problem, for while from these perspectives it is possible to conceive alternatives to modernity, such alternatives remain mostly in the realm of programs rather than of practices. The crux of the matter is that while the stories I have sketched constitute poles in a continuum, this continuum is fundamentally modern. In effect, as a programmatic statement, the rupturist story is a critique of the universalist pretensions of modernity performed primarily from a modern standpoint. Thus, while this story is powerfully enabling with regard to making alternatives to modernity-cum-globality visible and viable, the way in which it is being "told" (or performed) reveals some problems that need to be addressed.

Other Stories

In an article about the World Social Forum (WSF), arguably one of the most visible expressions of the rupturist story in action, Boaventura de Sousa Santos (2004a) brings forward the extent to which the struggle to define and shape globality is as much about cognitive justice as it is about social justice because neither one is possible without the other. Thus, central to the tasks of the WSF, and of the rupturist story in general, are a sociology of absences and a sociology of emergences. The sociology of absences "aims to explain that what does not exist is, in fact, actively produced as non-existent," while the sociology of emergences "aims to identify and enlarge the signs of possible future experiences . . . that are actively ignored by hegemonic rationality and knowledge" (Santos 2004a:238–41). This is an exceedingly clear and succinct programmatic statement of the rupturist story, yet one that seems to be extremely difficult to enact since in the very process of telling the rupturist story one reenacts some ontological commitments to modernity, thereby reintroducing absences and obstructing emergences.

According to some versions of the rupturist story, the present moment is characterized by the struggle between a hegemonic neoliberal globalization, mainly promoted by markets and governmental institutions, and a counterhegemonic globalization, promoted by a heterogenous "movement of movements" variously connected by the common trait of being against neoliberal globalization (Dirlik 2001; Arturo Escobar 2004a, 2004b; Esteva and Prakash 1998; Santos 2004a). This movement of movements is considered a break with the past because it opposes the hegemonic designs of neoliberal modernity-cum-globality in novel ways: a nonhierarchical logic of self-organization and engagement; a broad conception of power and oppression; its valorizing of equality and difference as equally important; and its privileging of rebellion and nonconformity at the expense of revolution (Santos 2004a:242–43). From this perspective, former modes of struggle were insufficient or inadequate to fulfill the "conceptions and aspirations to a better life and society, *ever present in human history*" (Santos 2004a: 236, emphasis added). But, one may wonder, is not much of "human history" left out of the picture here? For instance, can one say that the ghost dance in the North American plains (see Hittman 1997), the *taki onqoy* in the Andes (Millones 1990), or the Indian revolts in the South American Chaco (Mendoza 2004) were hierarchical movements with narrow conceptions of power and oppression that valorized equality over difference and revolution over rebellion and nonconformity? Or could one say that they were fundamentally defined by their opposition to a hegemonic order? The answer in all these cases would be no.[9] Yet why are these movements not part of the history of the movement of movements that challenge the modernity-cum-globality furthered by neoliberal globalization? The absences begin to become obvious.

If one agrees with David Graeber that the struggles of indigenous peoples have "an extraordinary importance . . . in that planetary uprising usually referred as the 'anti-globalization' movement" (2004:34), then it is telling that their historical trajectories are not accounted for in these versions of the rupturist story. This is because the rupturist story is not theirs. The anti-(neoliberal)globalization movement can be narrated as new without further qualifications only if one assumes modernity as an ontological given. The problem is not so much that the rupturist story is indeed the story of many movements who have in common their attempts to challenge modernity from a standpoint that is itself modern; the problem is that this story is rendered as *the* story when such standpoint is not made explicit. In this way, the modern regime of truth, which makes other stories invisible and subaltern, is redeployed.

But even when the rupturist story consciously tries to make visible those invisibilized and subalternized stories, problems arise. MCD, for example, identifies a site of knowledges otherwise in the exteriority of modernity and assumes (correctly, in my view) that recognizing those knowledges as such and opening the space for them to become visible and fully operative has liberating potentials for everyone. But MCD has only partially engaged those knowledges in their own terms. To a large extent this is due to an asymmetry in how different kinds of "border thinking" and "decolonial thought" (arguably the central political vectors and categories of this academic version of the rupturist story) are performed.

Border and decolonial thinking make reference to the knowledge practices of various "intellectual others" (i.e., non-Westerners) who think from a "double consciousness" or from two different traditions, the dominant modern and the various subalternized others (see Mignolo 2000:67). By melding their own traditions of knowledge with the modern canon, intellectual others generate a new location for themselves, that of border thinking, which is between and betwixt the sides marked by the colonial difference. By engaging dialogically with these intellectual others, MCD scholars formed within the Western canon also generate a new location for themselves, another place of border thinking. What becomes evident is that the various relations between dominant and subalternized knowledges generate different kinds of border thinking. However, these different kinds of border thinking are also differently shaped by power relations. In effect, there are asymmetries between them, which become evident if one considers the issue of visibility.

MCD has been able to engage with intellectual others because they are visible, and they are visible because they are literate in academic languages (i.e., the Western canon). Thus, intellectual others have to labor hard because they do not only bridge, mix, and meld categories from different traditions of knowledge (modern/academic and their own), but also have to overcome the asymmetries by conveying their work in the dominant language.[10] In effect, total illiteracy in the academic language would imply almost complete invisibility. Symptomatic of this is that most "others"— although not all (see Rappaport 2005)—recently recognized as intellectuals in academic circles are in one way or another familiar with the protocols, the language, and the concepts of the academy, or at the very least have been educated or trained in academically informed institutions (see, for instance, the profiles of various "intellectual others" in Kay B. Warren 1998; Mignolo 2000). Indeed, unless they are (re)presented by ethnographers, intellectual others who do not speak the language familiar to academics (or who do not perform border thinking but rather a "thinking" that is further removed from modern categories and also less overdetermined by the dynamics of the colonial difference) seem to be out of the latter's radar screen. This bespeaks the power differentials that confronted me when Don

Veneto "explained" my presence and work in the Yshiro communities in his own terms; these power differentials imply that academic intellectuals do not need to learn the language of others. In this sense, the border thinking of intellectual others is not matched by a similar gesture by MCD; and while the latter's performance is critically important and enabling, it is not sufficient.

The problem is one of translation in a terrain marked by asymmetries, and to the extent that performances of border thinking remain asymmetrical they will not be fully able to contribute toward the kind of translation that, as Santos envisions, would allow "mutual intelligibility among the experiences of the world" (2004b:341). As revealed by the absence of indigenous trajectories and knowledge practices in the making of the rupturist story, the translation that has taken place thus far tends to force some peoples to fit into the story of others.[11] Much is lost in this. If the rupturist story is to open up spaces for "worlds and knowledges otherwise," then one needs to render this story in a way that opens itself up to be contaminated by the full extent of existing worlds and knowledges otherwise. One cannot rely solely on the knowledge that those intellectual others recognized by academics offer; one must perform a gesture similar to theirs and engage with knowledges otherwise that stand further removed from the language of academics.

In no way do I mean to imply that intellectual others who perform border thinking are less "authentic" (and therefore less important for dialogue) than those who, for different reasons, are not compelled to perform such thinking but rather remain within a regime of truth that is less impacted by the colonial difference. The point I am making is that the effects of dialogues between academics formed by the Western canon and these differently positioned intellectual others are bound to be different than those generated by dialogues between those familiar with the Western canon. One central difference is that such dialogue forces us (academics) to perform knowledge otherwise rather than enunciate it as a program of action.

Some directions on how to carry on with this dialogue are provided by Latour in his book *We Have Never Been Modern* (1993). He argues that the end of the socialist utopia and the increasing visibility of the "environmental debacle" in the 1990s punctuated the crisis of modernist assumptions and the consequent opportunity to see our whole past and ourselves "in a different light" (Latour 1993:8–10). Under this new light, one can see that underlying what moderns have neatly allocated to either side of their ontological dualism are the relations that weave the world into a web, or as Latour calls it, a network. The multiple epistemological, political, moral, and ultimately existential challenges that exist today are of a quality that mocks efforts to capture them through the usual modernist distinction between nature and culture—even as we attempt to stitch these separate domains with the "glue" of discourse—and thus impel us to reconceptualize the world or reality as networks that are simultaneously real (like nature), political (like society), and narrated (like discourse) (Latour 1993:1–8).[12] Yet these webs or networks are not new; it is simply that moderns, given their ontological commitments, could not see them. Once these commitments are abandoned one begins to see what many others have been seeing all along, that relations woven into life-giving webs are what constitute the world or reality.[13]

Latour (1993:11–12) has argued that when one begins to notice the networks hidden by modernity's blind spots, one's relations with the others of modernity change, for there is no longer the "great divide." Indeed, the great divide that rendered moderns incapable of seeing networks at the same time converted those who could see those networks into "traditional societies." In the past, the great divide allowed ethnographers to write the classical monographs whose interest lay in showing how traditional societies, "trapped in their beliefs," kept on mixing what for moderns was obviously separate: subject and object.[14] Precisely for this reason, analytic continuity was not possible; ethnography could not produce the same kind of study about modern society. But now that one can appreciate that the pluriverse is a continuous network of networks, simultaneously real, political, and discursive, Latour (1993:1–12) argues that there is no longer any reason for analytical discontinuity in how one looks at one's own world and those of others.[15] One can now proceed with a symmetrical anthropology and produce ethnographies that show how particular worlds/networks weave themselves into being and with what consequences.

The idea of a symmetrical anthropology is excellent, for it proposes to put modernity on the level terrain with other ontologies. The challenge, though, is how to carry out the ethnographic endeavor envisioned by Latour without rehearsing the standpoint of modernity. In other words, those who are at least partially located in academia face a central challenge, which is to find ways to tell stories of the present in a politically meaningful way, that is, to tell them in ways that avoid reproducing the modern regime of power/knowledge and system of rule that many peoples around the world, like the Yshiro, are directly or indirectly undermining. Deep commitments to the modern regime of truth serve as the back door through which modernity reproduces dominance and subalternization in spite of the best critical efforts to dismantle them. Thus, if one wants to avoid complicity with the contemporary configurations of power produced by modernity (in any of its forms), one must avoid producing stories of the present that implicitly perform the ontological commitments that ground the modern regime of truth. The difficulties one encounters when attempting to perform the rupturist narrative in such a way only make more salient the challenge that this urgent task poses for those who have been raised and trained to live by the modern myth.

In a sense, part of the problem is that while a relatively clear program of actions exists, they have yet to be performed in full. Performances of knowledge otherwise have thus far been shouldered mostly by those marked as the "other" of modernity. While the works by indigenous scholars and intellectuals that perform border thinking and signal knowledge otherwise deserve their own annotated bibliography, a few relevant examples most clearly connect with the "narrative threads" of the rupturist story, including those that run parallel to and partially connect with (intramodern) MCD's critiques of Euro- and logocentrism (Smith 1999; Youngblood Henderson 2000; Waters 2004a; Patzi 2004; Fernandez Osco forthcoming), and those that reveal how ANT's "new understanding" of reality as networks is old news for indigenous traditions of knowledge (Cajete 2000; McGregor 2004). These performances of border thinking, along with the everyday practices and social mobilization of many indigenous peoples, have started to become visible for what they are: ongoing cosmopolitical struggles aimed at sustaining and furthering the diverse worlds that make up the pluriverse.

The idea of a cosmopolitical struggle builds on the term *cosmopolitics*, coined by Isabelle Stengers to speak of a politics that both recognizes and engages the unruly radical diversity of the "cosmos" we inhabit. Cosmopolitics asks us to "slow down" and question the assumption that there exists a common world (a universe), and to recognize the diversity and contingency of the pluriversal cosmos. In this way, the notion of cosmopolitics opens up the possibility for "risky" coexistence or, in other words, for an always emerging coexistence that might be achieved through the hard work of a politics without the guarantees of a preexisting common ground such as "reality out there" (see Stengers and Zournazi 2003; Stengers 2005). Taken together through their "partial connections" (Strathern 2004), the work of intellectual others, the rupturist story, and the various social mobilizations of which they are both part implicitly signal parallel processes of internal and external critiques of modernity that give hope for the risky coexistence between different knowledge practices.[16] Yet, while those of us who experience the present moment as a rupture may recognize the possibilities presented by these parallel critiques, we still have to fully join this cosmopolitical struggle by finding different ways of telling our stories of the present moment, or, what is the same, performing knowledge otherwise. This book is an experiment in doing so.

From Program to Performance I: Border Dialogue

The rupturist story traces a genealogy of the present moment from an explicit moral stance in order to open up the possibilities for more symmetrical translations and relations between diverse worlds. Yet in its current form the rupturist story falls short of fully performing what it enunciates as a program of action, for it is still produced from an eminently modern standpoint which cannot but reinstate absences. The question is how can one join forces with those social movements that are directly or indirectly struggling with the impositions of the modern regime of truth when one is situated within expert institutions and traditions of knowledge production that tend to reproduce that very same regime of truth? The challenge is how to tell stories of the present that explicitly assume a moral stance; disclose their own enunciative position; and do not foreclose open-endedness and symmetrical engagements with other stories as the myth of modernity does.

A necessary step in this direction involves evening out the epistemological ground, which implies that in telling a rupturist story one does not take the modern myth as the ultimate ontological condition. In this way, and as it has been shown by ANT, one can begin to perceive the diverse webs or networks that weave the pluriverse. However, while seeing networks is a necessary condition to do away with modernist commitments, it is not sufficient. One must find ways to address the question of how to produce knowledge when one is part of the network one intends to know. The form in which one performs this knowledge is critical. Why? Because webs/networks, including those that shape the pluriverse nowadays submerged under the universalist claims of modernity, enact themselves through content *and* form. Thus, in order to avoid reproducing the pluriverse in the terms dictated by modernity (i.e., forcing it to fit into a universe), one must be able not only to see networks but, in Annelise Riles's (2000) words, to turn the network inside out.

In her ethnography of the networks of nongovernmental organizations (NGOs) and institutions involved in the United Nations Fourth World Conference on Women, Riles addresses the epistemological challenge implied by what, paraphrasing Latour, one may call absolute "analytical continuity," that is, by the absence of distance between the knowing subject and the object of knowledge. In effect, the "object" of Riles's ethnography is the practices of knowledge through which networks generate the effects of their own reality. Yet, given that the practices being "ethnographied" turn out to be very much like the ethnographic practices of Riles, there is no outside from which she can write about them. In this sense, Riles and I face a similar challenge: how to do an ethnography of something in which one is unavoidably implicated (the struggle of the Yshiro people, in my case). Her answer is to collapse the distinction between the content and the form of her ethnography by bringing to light that her ethnography is itself an enactment of the knowledge practices being ethnographied. Through this recursiveness—what she calls turning the network inside out—Riles produces the effect of a critical distance that brings into sharp focus those modern knowledge practices that are almost invisible because they are so familiar.

While sharing the challenge of doing ethnography from within that which is being "ethnographied," my project differs from Riles's on a crucial point: I want to avoid reproducing modern knowledge practices altogether. Because the networks analyzed by Riles produce the effect of their own reality through modern knowledge practices, and because these practices

are in turn mimicked by her own ethnography, Riles's ethnography ultimately contributes to bringing those networks of modern knowledge practices into reality. As she puts it, "In turning [the network] inside out, the
very modern knowledge practices that are the subject of [the] analysis are
confirmed by their enactment even as a critical distance of those practices
is achieved" (Riles 2000:19, emphasis added). The challenge that remains
is to find a way of turning the network inside out—or, what is the same,
producing through recursiveness a distance that will make visible the net-
work/reality in which I am immersed—while enacting nonmodern knowledge practices. In what I call "border dialogue" lies the possibility of achieving this balance.

The notion of border dialogue builds on two sets of works: first, the elab-
orations of MCD (and of Walter Mignolo, in particular) on border thinking;
second, the tradition of "experimental ethnographies" that have engaged
in dialogical fashion knowledge practices that are radically different from
modern ones. Border dialogue owes to the MCD notion of "border thinking" as an epistemological principle that might allow the articulation of different networks or worlds under the assumption that the totality is pluriversal rather than universal. Articulation under this supposition "means that
people and communities have the right to be different precisely because
'we' are all equals" (Mignolo 2000:311). Border dialogue differs from border thinking, however, in that the latter emerges from a locus of enunciation that is already *in the border*. In contrast, border dialogue signals the
necessary displacement from the modern locus of enunciation that must
occur in order for border thinking to flourish among those who are still
situated on "this side" (modern) of the border.

Once dialogues commence, various borders emerge, as is evident in existing interactions between MCD scholars and other intellectuals who perform border thinking. The border to which I refer is necessarily "internal"
to the continuous web or network that makes up the pluriverse in which
we are all immersed and for which there is no outside. In general, this is the
border that emerges from the encounter of worlds/realities that in performing themselves differently constitute turning points and stoppages for each
other. In particular, I am speaking of the border that modernity performs
in bringing itself into being as different and superior from other worlds,
the border that articulates the "colonial difference" at its rawest, that is, as a

hierarchical relation with radical difference that is unmitigated by the border thinking of intellectual others cognizant of academic language. Here is where experimental ethnographies nurture my own.

There is a long tradition of ethnographies that have sought to engage intellectual others operating with categories not overly determined by the colonial difference in a dialogue that helps to denaturalize modern ontological assumptions.[17] Some of these ethnographies have been criticized for overstressing ontological coherence at the expense of a full recognition of the impact that colonial dynamics have in those ontologies. However, another set of ethnographies in several ways influenced by the first set not only have taken these critiques into account but have approached colonial dynamics (in the widest sense of a conflictive ontological encounter) as a key issue to be explored in novel ways through the frameworks emerging from the dialogues with indigenous intellectuals.[18] Elsewhere I have labeled this emerging approach "political ontology" (Blaser 2009b). The term has two connected meanings: On the one hand, it refers to the power-laden negotiations involved in bringing into being the entities that make up a particular world or ontology. On the other hand, it refers to a field of study that focuses on these negotiations, but also on the conflicts that ensue as different worlds or ontologies strive to sustain their own existence as they interact and mingle. Building on the tradition of dialogical ethnographies and contributing to the emerging political ontology framework, the border dialogue I envision aims to engage the radically different knowledge practices of those worlds/realities deemed inferior by modernity, and to be willing to allow modern ways of knowing be "contaminated" by them. This does not mean that one ends up located where one's interlocutors are; rather, it means that through dialogue with them one becomes dislocated from the modern enunciative position. Ultimately, this border dialogue aspires to produce a standpoint that performs itself as a mediation articulating in symmetrical terms the worlds/realities that the colonial difference articulates hierarchically.

The story I am about to tell comes out of an enunciative locus that has emerged from dialogues I have sustained for over a decade with Yshiro intellectuals who struggle to maintain and further their life projects and the *yrmo* (the Yshiro reality/world) in which these projects might unfold. The Yshiro indigenous people, better known in Paraguay as Chamacoco, consist of around 2,000 individuals who live in a region known as Alto Paraguay, the northeastern corner of the Paraguayan Chaco that borders Bolivia and Brazil. More precisely, the Yshiro communities are located along the banks of the Paraguay River between the towns of Bahia Negra and Fuerte Olimpo (see maps 1 and 2). The area, which remains marginal with regard to decision-making and economic activities in Paraguay, is without permanent roads, and only a weekly boat physically connects it to the rest of the country.

Paraguayans differentiate themselves from the Yshiro by calling themselves "whites." The Yshiro also use this label to identify non-indigenous peoples, but, depending on the contexts, they also divide this wide category into two subgroups: *maro* (Paraguayans) and *dihip'kunaho* (white foreigners). The contemporary Yshiro are subdivided into two groups, the Yshiro-Ebitoso and the Yshiro-Tomaraho.

The Yshiro intellectuals I have worked with form a heterogeneous group of people composed mostly of male elders and leaders. Although there are female intellectuals, only in the last few years have I begun to develop deeper relations with them, and thus the influence of male intellectuals in my work has been more pronounced. Furthermore, the majority of the intellectuals with whom I have had close relationships are Ebitoso, as my interaction with Tomaraho intellectuals was interrupted between 1995 and 1999. In contrast to the indigenous intellectuals who appear in most recent scholarship (see Kay B. Warren 1998; Gutiérrez 1999; Rappaport 2005; Boccara 2006), the ones I refer to here have had little or no familiarity with modern educational institutions. The majority are illiterate, a few read and write with difficulty, and only four or five do so in a relatively quotidian manner. Also, for historical reasons that will become visible as I proceed, the spectrum of relations that these intellectuals (and in general the Yshiro) sustain with the state and other modern institutions is less diverse than the ones presented in the aforementioned studies. What foregrounds these individuals as intellectuals is that they ponder and question more systematically than most Yshiro the meaning and consequences of the contemporary order existing in the Chaco region. Hence, they have become referents to which loosely connected groups in the Yshiro communities resort for advice or for opinions in private consultation or during community meetings.

The authority and expertise granted to these intellectuals emerge from a different regime of truth than the modern one.

Through the years, and attempting to find my place and purpose in the world, I became involved in the struggles these intellectuals endured to further their life projects. With some of them I have spent so much time in conversation that I would be unable to specify who articulated first the interpretations that I and they hold today about Paraguayan politics pertaining to indigenous peoples. I note this not for the purpose of investing my "storytelling" with special authority, but to emphasize that I do not stand in a neutral position with regard to these intellectuals' goals.[19] In fact, I have become thoroughly involved in these struggles, although not for exactly the same reasons and not with the same stakes as my Yshiro friends and acquaintances. My aim is thus not to explain and re-present these intellectuals' views of the world, as traditional ethnography would, but to narrate/enact the present moment from a standpoint that has emerged from the relation with their embodied views of the world. Trying to re-present these intellectuals' views and practices would betray the purpose of this border dialogue: to contribute to performing the pluriverse by enacting a nonmodern knowledge practice.

The majority of the Yshiro individuals with whom I have had an opportunity to talk about the topic agree that, in one way or another, their practices and visions of a good life are connected to Yshiro myth-history. However, how different groups and individuals actually relate (to) this myth-history varies in significant ways. The diversity of perspectives does not escape many Yshiro's self-awareness, yet there is also widespread agreement that the arrival of Christian missionaries marked the beginning of these differences. Indeed, there is a tacit understanding that, until that point, the Yshiro did have a relatively homogeneous and widely shared version of their myth-history, which is said to be more closely maintained by the Tomaraho, by some male and female Ebitoso elders, and by a few mature males who went through the initiation ritual in the 1950s. For expediency, I will refer to this version of the Yshiro myth-history as the elders' version, although at a closer look this version is not as homogeneous as the use of the singular conveys. Even among elders there are differences and debates about the meanings of stories and rituals, as well as about the colonization of the area by the whites. Despite these differences and de-bates, there are also many commonalities. In my discussion, I will mostly remain at the level of commonalities, but I will indicate where important divergences exist among the elders. Although there are several published works about myth-history, I rely on what I learned from Yshiro intellectuals through stories, conversations, and conduct.[20]

Several reasons warrant that I engage the elders' myth-history as a ful-crum from which to force myself out of the modern enunciative position. First, in the last decade "traditions" have increasingly become a focal point for discussions about the present situation of the Yshiro communities and their prospects. In this context, the views held by or attributed to the el-ders, and to past generations of Yshiro in general, have special weight. Sec-ond, from the perspective of most Yshiro, their own divergent positions historically emerged from a formerly "common version" of their myth-history. Third, besides being central in the making of the place from which some Yshiro intellectuals see and enact the world and themselves, the el-ders' myth-history also plays a central role in my own sense of place, which has been affected by an ongoing border dialogue with these Yshiro. Finally, a border dialogue with the perspective afforded by the elders' myth-history generates an enunciative position from which it is possible to enact an on-tology which operates according to different principles than those of the modern myth. This difference might contain the promise of another, per-haps less oppressive, regime of truth which is conducive to perform the pluriverse without constraints. In order to realize this promise, storytelling rather than "accurate representation" is needed.

From Program to Performance 2: Storytelling

In order to grasp what storytelling entails as a nonmodern knowledge prac-tice, one must take a cursory look into the myth with which such practice is associated. First, though, it is important to note that the most basic assump-tion of Yshiro myth-history, that reality emerges out of a primordial state of fluidity and indistinction, is remarkably similar to Actor Network Theory's methodological assumption that everything is symmetrical in principle. Much of Yshiro myth-history resonates with the insights that ANT's authors argue become evident once Cartesian dualism is abandoned, a resonance that illuminates "storytelling" as an Yshiro knowledge practice. When I found the explanations, metaphors, and allegories of my Yshiro mentors obscure, ANT helped bridge the gap, and vice versa. Thus, to most clearly convey the idea of storytelling as a knowledge practice, I draw from both sources.[21]

Yshiro myth-history has three stages, which a few of the most knowledgeable elders equate to a sequence of generations that goes from bygone ancestors, to grandparents and parents, and to ego and his or her progeny (see also Cordeu 1990:153–60). This sequence transposed to myth-history locates the first stage, of the Yshiro *puruhle*, in times beyond memory and only fully accessible through dreams; the second stage, of the Yshiro *porowo*, in past times that are accessible through memory; and the third stage, of the Yshiro *azle*, in contemporary times, the site where forthcoming times are produced through renewal or *eisheraho*. However, the logical connections and the practices associated with these "stages" make clear that their character as a temporal sequence is just superficial. For many Yshiro, the three stages are above anything else dimensions of what constitutes the *yrmo* (reality/world).

Underlying these dimensions there is a generative principle of the yrmo which can be conceived as the dynamics taking place on a continuum between two poles: *sherwo* (roughly translated as indistinction) and *om* (distinction/being). Because the continuum between indistinction and distinction is tilted toward the former, entities sustain their being or distinctiveness only through a permanent struggle against their tendency to fall back into indistinction. The same idea can be conveyed by saying that the tendency is for relations to fluctuate and thus that, to sustain their distinctiveness, entities continually fight to control the effects of those fluctuations. In this struggle the management of *wozosh* is critical. Wozosh is a kind of potency immanent to the generative principle of the yrmo and can be visualized as the tilt in the continuum between distinction and indistinction. For this reason, wozosh tends to manifest itself as a force leading to death and indistinction, which in turn implies that it must be treated very carefully in order to manifest the positive pole of the continuum.[22]

Many times, the elders who were telling me a story of the Yshiro puruhle would append a puzzling commentary: "One says dead, but it is not dead, there is no death yet. One says the *ylipiot* [jaguar], but it is not the ylipiot, there is no ylipiot yet." These apparently paradoxical statements were meant to underline two characteristics of this stage/dimension: first, that the bedrock of myth-history is a state of indistinction or absolute symmetry; and second, that given this primordial indistinction, the events taking place in the puruhle stage/dimension can only be narrated by referring to entities that become distinguishable from one another through the events being narrated. Thus, the stories corresponding to the Yshiro puruhle convey the idea that the distinguishable entities that inhabit the yrmo co-emerged from an originally fluid and indistinguishable situation.[23] The basic fluidity and indistinction of the cosmos is usually emphasized in Yshiro puruhle narratives by the introductory comment "Oa pehrtit je elehert pe" (At its beginning it was not like now) (see also Cordeu 1990:155–56). This comment indicates a change of state rather than an absolute beginning.

The stories that compose this first "stage" of myth-history do not have a pre-established sequence. As an elder once told me, when stories from the puruhle are used, storytelling resembles the work of making necklaces with beads and seeds. The beads and seeds come in different sizes and colors that the artisan arranges along a string according to her or his own intent. Thus, the sequence in which stories within this stage are arranged depends on the intentions of the storyteller, and the context in which the story is being told. This characteristic allows for a high degree of flexibility regarding the incorporation of new stories which address the beginning of some feature of the cosmos. This is particularly visible in the case of origin stories from the Bible, which, with a few exceptions, most people locate alongside other stories of the Yshiro puruhle.

The flexibility of the puruhle narratives allows the narrator to arrange stories in order to convey specific messages. Through these messages one can intervene in the unfolding of ongoing events according to particular contexts and intentions. Several Yshiro point out that puruhle narratives can be used for transmitting morals, for healing purposes, to attract good luck, to produce sexual arousal, and so on. It is known that stories have wozosh and that, depending on the circumstances of the telling, this can express itself as a lively or deadly force (see also Cordeu 1988:80–81). Very few people can clearly articulate why stories have this power. Most Yshiro, when asked, said that this is "what people say." Others deny that stories have any power at all. Those who know—typically male or female elders with various degrees of expertise as *konsaha* (shaman)—explain that when the events by which certain entities came into being are narrated, the wozosh of those circumstances is reactualized. The connection between the original events and the event of their telling is predicated on storytelling being itself a distinction-making event and thus charged with wozosh (see also Susnik 1957a:12). In other words, storytelling can bring entities out of indistinction or can plunge them back into it.

In addition to storytelling, ecstatic journeys and dreaming are also procedures the *konsaho* (pl. of *konsaha*) use to manage wozosh. By these means they enter into contact with the realm of the Yshiro puruhle, the very source of wozosh, and try to draw its potencies into a given ongoing effort. The three "stages" of myth-history constitute contemporaneous dimensions of the yrmo precisely because through ritual action (which includes storytelling) and konsaho interventions, wozosh can be taken care of at its source (the puruhle dimension) and, in this way, the very shape of the yrmo can be influenced.

As all entities that compose the yrmo co-emerge from indistinction, there is no conception of a knower and a known that are not implicated with each other. Thus, knowledge here never implies a statement about a world "out there." Rather, knowledge is the careful shaping through storytelling (in its widest sense as enactment) of a world in which the negative tendencies of wozosh are forestalled. In effect, while puruhle narratives describe the events that brought into existence entities that are necessary for life (see also Cordeu 1991c), they also describe how careless actions brought into being other entities such as death and disease (see also Wilbert and Simoneau 1987:131–47). Implicit in this is both that humans can do something to forestall the "negative tilt" of wozosh and transform it into a life-sustaining force, but also that their actions are always dangerous and ambivalent. *Eiwo*, the capacity to distinguish the positive from the negative, is a key instrument to navigate through this ambivalence. This capacity came into being in the porowo stage.

The flexibility of the Yshiro puruhle narratives stands in stark contrast to the inflexibility of the Yshiro porowo narratives. While different versions of the stories that compose porowo narratives certainly exist, the differences are consistently attributed to mistakes, misunderstandings, or the feeble knowledge of the narrator. In other words, there is a clear consensus that there is only one correct version of the porowo stories, although there are disagreements over which one is correct. The insistence on the immutability of the porowo narratives arises from the fact that they lay down the ethical and moral foundations of society and, by extension, the yrmo—fertile terrain for controversy and dispute.

The core of the Yshiro porowo narratives is contained in the *Esnwherta au'oso* (lit. "the word of Esnwherta"), a story narrating the encounter between the Yshiro and the Anabsero beings and how the former acquired, through their relation with the latter, social orderings (e.g., clans, age ranks, and gender distinctions), moral precepts to regulate their conduct, and eiwo.[24] The intricate connections between the *Esnwherta au'oso* and the ways the ancient Yshiro came to conceive and live their lives are practically innumerable (for details on some of these connections, see Susnik 1957b and Cordeu 1991a). However, the most visible and institutionalized connection between one and the other is *debylylta*, the male initiation ritual that actualizes the events narrated by the *Esnwherta au'oso*. Through this enactment, *weterak* (young males going through the initiation) are endowed with new dimensions of eiwo, thus making them Yshiro (lit. "human persons"). Yet debylylta is not exclusively meant to "make" Yshiro, but rather to make Yshiro is part of a permanent process of remaking the yrmo in a way that the positive aspects of wozosh are maximized and the negative forestalled. This is because to make Yshiro means to endow beings with a richer eiwo, a capacity which contributes to bring being (distinction) out of the primordial indistinction.

Several elders with whom I had a chance to discuss the meanings of the term *eiwo* pointed out that it refers to the human capacities, shared in different degrees with other beings, of discerning the meaning of situations, of value making, of thoughtful naming, of envisioning what is now and what might be later, and of learning (see also Cordeu 1991a:125–26). Through their contact with the Anabsero, the Yshiro acquired the capacity to discern those relations that expressed the positive aspects of wozosh. This capacity is clearly associated with language, since it is through language that myth-history is made intelligible and the values implicit in the *Esnwherta au'oso* can be transmitted. In this way, generation after generation, humans can tell/enact the distinctions between the positive and the negative out of what initially presents itself as an indistinguishable state. Eiwo thus must not be interpreted as an acquired capacity that allows humans to discern what is already distinct; rather, eiwo collaborates to bring distinction out of indistinction. Deployed through storytelling, ritual performances, and conduct, eiwo contributes to the distinction-making processes that bring Being out of the indistinction of the puruhle dimension. The association of eiwo with the porowo dimension indicates that the worlds that obtain from storytelling, ritual performance, and conduct are always moral. Therefore, stories must always be evaluated by the kind of worlds they produce. Precisely, the connection between the puruhle and the porowo dimensions underlines the idea that in storytelling as knowledge practice the knower and his or her values are always implicated in the known and vice versa.

A key concept for telling the story of the present, or turning the present network inside out, without reproducing modernist commitments is that of "imagination." Imaginations are the entities that emerge (or might be at different stages of emergence) from the power-laden interconnections that exist within the ever-changing continuous network that weaves the pluriverse. The concept borrows from Yshiro myth-history and from ANT the notion that all that exists is in a permanent process of co-emergence, and that human intervention (in the form of storytelling for the Yshiro) is a critical component in this process. Thus, one can envision the different versions of globality being struggled over as imaginations.

According to the *Oxford English Dictionary*, the most common meaning of the word *imagination* is "the mental faculty of forming images or concepts of external objects not present to the senses." I use the term to emphasize the idea that entities do not preexist the process of imagining them (i.e., of forming images of them); rather, they become "present to the senses" or come into existence in this process. However, as I use it, imagination must not be understood in terms of external objects or reality. In my use, the real is an imagination that, through struggles and negotiations (i.e., the process of imagining), has become relatively more (corpo)real than other imaginations.[25] Thus, for example, I do not speak about the "imagination of modernity," which equates imagination to the representation of the "thing" modernity; instead, I speak of the "imagination-Modernity," which assumes that between the imagination and the thing modernity, there is no difference.

Contrasting the concept of imagination with that of representation helps clarify the former. Representation assumes an ontological divide between an extradiscursive reality (the world) and its discursive or symbolic signifier (the word). When one deems a representation to be accurate, one in essence asserts that the gap between these two disparate things (world and word) has been bridged by an equivalence; in other words, the real thing and its representation are considered equivalent. An imagination can be seen as the way in which the relation between representation and reality appears when one does not assume such an ontological divide. Thus, what from a modern perspective is called an accurate representation (a representation closely equivalent to an external reality) I will call an "authorized imagination," that is, one that has become relatively more (corpo)real than others. In effect, while a representation is deemed to be more or less accurate in representing an independent reality, an imagination only can become more or less real.

The degree of (corpo)reality that an imagination may acquire depends on the number and stability of the relations that constitute it and on how "the vital energy" that those relations generate circulate in the network thus formed. Latour (1999:69–70) has coined the term "circulating reference" to account for what I am calling "vital energy." According to Latour, meaning is not the product of a relation of reference understood as the equivalence between world and word. Rather, reference is the collective attribute of a chain of several entities that produce meaning/being through a circulation (hence, circulating reference) that flows by short jumps and small transformations from one link (i.e., entity) of the chain to another. In a sense, circulating reference can be equated to the Yshiro notion of wozosh in both its positive (distinguishing) and negative (de-distinguishing) potential. Depending on how wozosh is circulating through the relations that weave a reality/world, the entities that emerge from those relations will remain more or less real (that is, more or less distinctive against a background of indistinction).

Imaginations are both constituted by the chains of connections of which they are part and constitutive of those chains insofar as they operate as links in them as well. An authorized imagination is an entity whose links to other entities have been occluded and that thus appears to the "modern eye" as an independent and self-contained entity, that is, as reality out there. Yet at

INTRODUCTION

all times I take to heart the Yshiro's and ANT's tacit understanding that the backbone of reality is constituted by relations in a permanent state of flux. Thus, I do not conceive that imaginations achieve the status of "authorized imaginations" once and for all. Continued successful storytellings/performances are needed to produce and sustain authorized imaginations such as modernity or different versions of globality, because the stability of the circulations which might give life to them are always frail and reversible in the face of intended or unintended contestations, or to use Yshiro terms, in the face of wozosh. Throughout this volume I narrate the transformation of modernity and the struggle to bring into being different versions of globality in terms of these authorizing and deauthorizing operations.[26]

Overview

Most contemporary Yshiro take the arrival of Christian missionaries, and not the arrival of the whites in general, as the turning point that in Yshiro myth-history marks the threshold where the azle stage/dimension (i.e., contemporaneity) begins.[27] Before the missionaries appeared, and continuing for about half a century, the whites coerced the Yshiro into a subordinated position and exploited them in several ways, but they did not make concerted, sustained, and systematic efforts to suppress or transform the ways in which the Yshiro had learnt to perform the yrmo. By attacking the initiation ritual, the most visible performance associated with the porowo dimension, missionaries struck a serious (but not definitive) blow to the ability of future generations of Yshiro to work collectively through the connections between the porowo and the puruhle dimensions in the way their ancestors had done. Some Yshiro intellectuals see the increasingly antagonistic moral perspectives that began to appear after the arrival of the missionaries as the most dangerous situation the Yshiro communities currently face, for this translates into a further degraded yrmo. Indeed, many express that the challenge is to (story)tell or "perform" the Yshiro people in a way which would transform the current state of the yrmo. A growing consensus has emerged among several Yshiro intellectuals around the idea that this new storytelling of the Yshiro involves relating with each other and with others (human and nonhumans) in ways that heed the ontology underlining the elders' myth-history. I believe that this project of Yshiro intellectuals contributes to bringing into being globality as an alternative to modernity, primarily in that, by seeking to sustain and further another world, it challenges the universal pretensions of modernity-cum-globality. While similar challenges have been posed since the very inception of the modern myth, that myth is currently unraveling and transmuting into a myth of globality that is not yet clearly shaped. This opens a window of opportunity for storytelling globalization in a way that resonates and amplifies other projects, such as the Yshiro's, seeking to make the global age something other than a reiteration of modernity by other means.

In relation to this, I pursue two parallel and intrinsically connected tasks. On the one hand, while highlighting some of the dangers and some of the promises embodied in different stories of globalization, I provide my own richly textured and ethnographically informed story about how the passage from modernity to globality is being contested. On the other hand, I seek to exemplify, by enacting it, how an ethnography reconfigured by a border dialogue might be part of these struggles and can contribute to bringing globality into being as an alternative to modernity. To accomplish these tasks I focus on the struggles around an eminently modern practice, development, exactly at the point where it tries to tame and discipline nonmodern practices. Following the deployment of changing conceptions of development among the Yshiro since the late nineteenth century, I first trace how competing versions of the story of globalization took shape, then address how these different versions are currently embodied by development projects and social movements that struggle with them. The two parallel tasks correspond to what I have referred to as content and form, respectively, and are reflected in the double titles I have given each of the three parts that make up the main body of this ethnography. With this tripartition, I mimic the structure of Yshiro myth-history as a way to convey the notion borrowed from Yshiro intellectuals that this storytelling is purposeful performance geared to sustain and foster pluriversality.

In Part 1: *Puruhle*/Genealogies, I provide an overview of how the modern world and the yrmo became entangled asymmetrically. Following the transformations undergone by three imaginations that are central to modernity (Indians, Nature, Progress) as they were deployed through development practices among the Yshiro people, I trace the "symptoms" of the passage from modernity to globality. In chapter 1 I draw a general sketch of how the yrmo was violently subalternized and invisibilized under the universalist claims of modernity through practices promoted by a policy of laissez-faire progress. In chapter 2 I discuss how state-driven development stabilized these universalist claims, and its underlying asymmetry, through the expansion of a patronage network which displaced open violence by subtler forms of coercion. Finally, in chapter 3, I show how new Paraguayan legislation on indigenous peoples as well as new blueprints "for their *sustainable* development" signal the emergence of new imaginations (Indigenous Peoples, Environment, Risk) that mark the ongoing shift from modernity to globality.

In Part 2: *Porowo*/Moralities, I follow moralities as a guiding thread to understand what the performance of different knowledge practices entails for the project of fostering the pluriverse. In chapter 4 I focus on how, since the mid-1980s, a renewed performance of the yrmo began to emerge among the Yshiro-Ebitoso at the intersection of various developments: the moral conundrums they had to face when development projects pressed on them modern values that were at cross-purposes with their own; the increasing disagreements between sectors of the non-indigenous society that defined policy for indigenous peoples; and the renewed contact between some Yshiro and powerful nonhumans. In chapter 5 I address how these kinds of developments have been translated by experts in Paraguay who are part of the transnational human-rights and environmental movements that, to some extent, enact the rupturist story. With concrete examples, I demonstrate the limitations of the rupturist story and advocate for a knowledge practice inspired by my Yshiro interlocutors.

In Part 3: *Azle*/Translations, I come to the Yshiro's ongoing efforts to perform the yrmo amid the deployment of modernity-cum-globality through development projects informed by neoliberal prescriptions. My central aim here is to bring forward the liberating potential of Yshiro ways of struggling while showing how one-way translations, unavoidable when modernist assumptions are operative, impede the kind of dialogue necessary to perform globality as an alternative to modernity. In chapter 6 I describe how Prodechaco, a development project that targeted the Yshiro, took shape as neoliberal principles were translated into and articulated in the Paraguayan context. In chapter 7 I look at how, through the logic of framing typical of neoliberal governmental practices, Prodechaco intended to convert indigenous communities into "links" in a chain through which the modernist story of globalization could be further circulated and thus authorized. In chapter 8 I show how the Yshiro leaders translated and subverted Prodechaco's attempts to turn their communities into links for neoliberal globalization and, further, how they used this very same impulse for their own purposes, rallying their internally divided communities to create Unión de las Comunidades Indígenas de la Nación Yshir (UCINY), a pan-Yshiro organization that could allow the Yshiro to perform the yrmo more in accordance with their life projects and, by extension, to further the pluriverse. In chapter 9 I focus on the events surrounding the planning, implementation, and demise of a "sustainable hunting program" jointly operated by Prodechaco and UCINY, demonstrating that, under neoliberal globalization, violence continues to play a central role in the process of authorizing imaginations because modernist assumptions, while slightly modified, are still fully operative. In effect, by appealing to notions of objective reality, one-way translations make reasonable the use of violence to check the "unreasonable" demands of the Yshiro, which are so deemed in part because their roots in a different ontology are never recognized or are rendered "absent."

I warn the reader against taking this ethnography as an exercise of ventriloquism. Although the ideas of some Yshiro intellectuals have been very influential in my thinking and writing, my aim is neither to represent Yshiro subjectivities, nor to describe how the world might look from their perspective. Thus, if Yshiro voices at moments appear tamed, it is because I do not pretend to claim that this is the story of "the Yshiro," or even of some of them. The story I am about to tell must be understood as a puruhle narrative in which bits and bites of information are arranged (as "beads and seeds in a necklace") into a storyline that has a purpose: contributing to performing globality as an alternative to modernity. How this purpose has taken shape will become clear as I tell my story, but in the meantime I must stress that this is a story told from my own perspective and purpose as these have been affected by my interaction with some, and only some (mostly male), Yshiro intellectuals. Yet the partiality of the story does not invalidate it; on the contrary, the story's value resides in that it thoroughly assumes partiality as an opportunity to open up to readers the dialogue that I have had with some Yshiro intellectuals and that has proven very useful in forcing me out of the modern enunciative locus. In this sense, this work is an example of how to take some steps (perhaps clumsy) toward unlearning the modern myth; but it is also, and above all, an exploration of the possibilities offered by storytelling as a fruitful epistemological and ethical principle to foster worlds and knowledges otherwise.

1   *Puruhle*/Genealogies

> These Genealogies are a combination of erudite knowledge and
> what people know. They would not have been possible—they
> could not even been attempted—were it not for one thing: the
> removal of the tyranny of overall discourses, with their hierar-
> chies and all the privileges enjoyed by theoretical vanguards.
> —Michel Foucault, *Lecture of 7 January 1976*

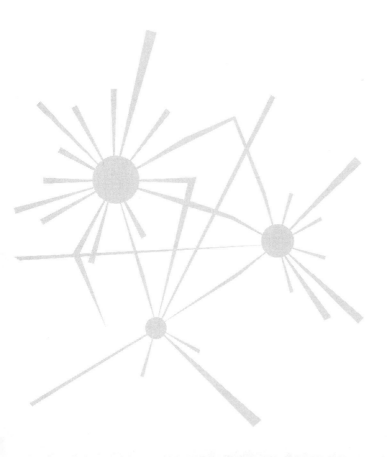

One   Laissez-Faire Progress
INVISIBILIZING THE YRMO

The standard storyline of the European encounter with indigenous peoples in the Americas begins with a shallow pre-
lude, a snapshot at best, of what was supposed to be here before
the wheels of history were put into motion by the arrival of the
settlers. In lieu of written records are archaeological, linguistic,
and ethnohistorical hypotheses (compare Wolf 1997:52), rather
than indigenous (hi)stories; after all, we moderns use those hypotheses when the written record falters for our own (hi)story.
Precisely the inescapable gap between the written record and the
"beginning" of our (hi)story is a key point at which the modern myth does its work. All those hypotheses that retrieve our
remote past are neither more nor less than a translation of the
modern myth expressed through the science it enables. The written record then just fills in with content a genealogy whose structure has already been traced by the myth. Considering this, the
implicit claim that the encounter with modern Europeans sets
history in movement for "others" is actually an index of another
kind of movement, that through which the myth of modernity
makes invisible other stories, other myths, and the worlds emerging from them.[1] Tracing a genealogy that makes visible that which
the modern myth effaces thus requires a different beginning, one
that refers to a different myth and a different world. In this case,
the genealogy begins with the *Esnwherta au'oso*, the core narrative of the porowo stage, for it informed in the most immediate
ways how the Yshiro imagined the early contact.

The Yrmo: Reciprocity and the Possibility of Coexistence

The *Esnwherta au'oso* narrates the encounter of the proto-Yshiro and the Anabsero, and how from this encounter emerged the actual Yshiro and their social orderings. After an initial encounter with the women, the Anabsero decide to meet the men in a secluded place in the forest, the *tobich* (lit. "place of the dead"). There, they transmit to the proto-Yshiro eiwo, a fine-tuned discerning capacity, thus making them fully Yshiro. The relation between the Anabsero and Yshiro is nevertheless ambivalent since many Anabsero are unpredictable in their behavior, at times showing great consideration and at others displaying reckless anger toward humans. Eventually, in response to an Anabsero's excessive display of anger, the Yshiro indiscriminately massacre the Anabsero. Only one Anabsero, Nemur, survives, and he creates the Paraguay River, which he puts between himself and his Yshiro persecutors. Nemur curses the Yshiro, and together with Esnwherta, the *lata* (mother) of the Anabsero, he commands them to replace each clan of the Anabsero, generation after generation, by initiating young males into the society of the tobich exactly as the Anabsero had done with the proto-Yshiro.[2] Failing to perform the ritual, or performing it in an inappropriate manner, would spell the extinction of the Yshiro.

The *Esnwherta au'oso* simultaneously depicts these events, works as a template for the male initiation ritual (debylylta), and structures the male secret society instituted by the Anabsero. According to the recollections of the Yshiro elders, in addition to the initiation ritual, food-sharing rules were one of the most visible ways in which the *Esnwherta au'oso* was embodied in everyday life. Food sharing, based on the complementarities of taboos corresponding to different age ranks, genders, and clans, indexed a person's place in a web of social relations encompassing humans and nonhumans. The strict observation of food taboos and their associated rules for sharing was among the key strategies for managing the negative element of wozosh (the dynamic or energy which results in Being or indistinction). Although by all accounts these rules were extremely detailed and extensive, food taboos were only one of the more visible expressions of the social labor the Yshiro porowo invested in the management of wozosh; according to many contemporary Yshiro, the social arrangements originated after the encounter with the Anabsero were characterized by the severe vigilance—some would call it tyranny—of the elders over males and females of younger generations. Keiwe, an Ebitoso elder who passed away in 1996, at the age of at least eighty, once told me,

> The Yshiro porowo have many *agalio* [advice, rules] for their youth, they don't want them to eat this or that, they don't want them to fuck with old people, they don't want them to talk nonsense, they don't want them to walk at night, they don't want them to go alone into the bush . . . those elders were very strict. If the youth do not follow their advice they warn them once, twice, three times, then they kill them. (14 June 1995, field notes)

Asked why the ancient elders were so strict, most contemporary elders answered that if they did not kill the offender, disgrace would fall not only over the offender but over the entire residential group. While the elders' strict vigilance assured the proper management of wozosh, it also created tensions between generations. Food and other restrictions were progressively lifted as an individual aged, yet indirect evidence (in stories as well as in the ways in which contemporary Yshiro narrate how their ancestors lived) suggests that some younger people experienced the restrictions imposed on them by the elders as unjust. These tensions, especially in critical circumstances such as a scarcity of food, produced schisms. Indeed, a quarrel between elders and youths over food consumption is one of the reasons Yshiro commentators give to explain why the Tomaraho and the Ebitoso splintered from each other and became enemies (see also Cordeu 1989a:72).

The sharing of food is central in both Tomaraho and Ebitoso versions of the story about contact with the whites. "This is the way our elders tell us our history. It is not like that of the whites, because we do not write it on paper. My father's father told it to him and he told it to me and me to my children. In that way we know our history."[3] Thus began Tamusia (Don Bruno Sanchez Vera), a Tomaraho elder, in telling the version of the story about the Yshiro's first encounters with the whites with which he was familiar. While there are different versions of this story, the core of the narrative remains the same across them. Few elders know this core well, and bits and bites of it have become part of other stories about the early interactions with the whites. As this story speaks of something new (i.e., the whites) that came up in the yrmo, it has a *puruhle* tone, punctuated by the "anomaly," in relation to the contemporary reality, that no diseases were supposed to have existed at the moment where the events narrated begin. I have chosen Tamusia's version because it most clearly conveys this *puruhle* tone.

After his introductory remark about the difference in how whites and Yshiro pass on their history, Tamusia said,

> At the beginning it was not like now. In the old times we did not have diseases. People died because of snake bites or because they were too old. When one was too old, you asked your children to make a hole and to put you inside. "I am too old, I cannot see or chew, leave me to die now," said the old people. An old man decided to die but his children were not around, so another man dug the hole to bury him. But later the son of the dead man did not share his food with his *agalo* [lit. "they eat together"], the gravedigger.[4] The gravedigger then said, "It seems that I buried an animal. His son does not remember that I buried his father." The son of the elder was very angry at being criticized and decided to kill the gravedigger. When everybody moved to another village, the son remained hidden in the forest and ambushed the gravedigger, killing him. Then he was afraid of that man's family and escaped with his friends and family toward the river. (June 1994, tape recording)

Knowledgeable Tomaraho and Ebitoso elders tell this story in remarkably similar terms up to this point in the narrative, but then they diverge. According to the Tomaraho version, the runaway group encounters a soldier who is shooting birds. Faced with this strange entity, the group forgets its fears and decides to go back and tell the elders of the main group about what they have seen. The elders send a scouting group of four warriors to the soldiers' camp, where they are given food, blankets, and mosquito nets, which they like very much. The commander of the soldiers tells the warriors to bring the rest of their people to the camp to receive more gifts. The whole residential group comes and stays with the soldiers, trying their food and other goods. But after two months the Tomaraho begin to die of an unknown disease and thus return to the bush, avoiding permanent contact with the whites until the late 1930s.

In 1993, Bruno Barras, then a forty-five-year-old Ebitoso leader of the Karcha Bahlut community, related the Ebitoso version of these events in the context of explaining the relevance of the place where his community was settled. In this place, the Anabsero beings established the original tobich. But, interestingly, Karcha Bahlut is also where the Ebitoso and the whites met for the first time. According to Bruno, after the runaway group met the soldier shooting birds, and then informed the main group that something strange was taking place, a party of warriors was sent to investigate.

> [The Ebitoso warriors] came to Karcha Bahlut and found these white men living there. The Ebitoso attacked them. However, one of the whites made it to a garrison they had established in [what is now] Bahia Negra. The soldiers from the garrison followed the Ebitoso and began to shoot to scare them. But the Ebitoso were not scared—rather they decided to attack because they thought that otherwise the soldiers would follow them to their settlement and would take over their territory. They prepared their arrows. In the afternoon the cavalry came and surrounded them. The Ebitoso killed some soldiers, and the soldiers wounded several Ebitoso. The Ebitoso took one of the dead soldiers and, following the advice of the elders, split him apart and put the body in a barbecue. When the soldiers found the body they said, "We better stop following these people, they are cannibals and they are probably going to eat us." From that time on there were no longer persecutions. When things cooled off, some elders met the commander of the garrison, and they agreed not to fight and to befriend each other. They made a pact and the commander gave them food. . . . That's how the relationship with the white men began. The Yshiro would work and the whites would share their food. . . . The elders were who first came near the white men. Then the younger people stayed working with them while the elders went back to the "bush." This is a story told to me by my grandmother Yilipe. (15 July 1993, field notes)

The similarities and the differences between the two versions are illuminating. That a breach of reciprocity is the immediate antecedent of the encounter with the whites signals that this event is very dangerous. Yet it is also an ambivalent event insofar as it introduces the Yshiro to new things that they quickly come to appreciate. What follows in the story after the emergence of the whites in the yrmo is, in both the Ebitoso and Tomaraho versions, an attempt to grapple with this ambivalent entity. For the

Tomaraho, the ambivalence of the situation quickly resolved when they began to die and thus decided that the best way to deal with the new entity was to avoid it entirely. For the Ebitoso, the situation was less straightforward. Informed as they were by their experience of laborious but nevertheless successful coexistence with the Mbya-Caduveo, the Ebitoso were not easily discouraged by the initial violence of their encounter with the whites. From the early nineteenth century, the Mbya-Caduveo, who were from the (now) Brazilian side of the Paraguay River, obtained horses and firearms from the Portuguese (see map 3). Using the advantage conferred by these technologies, they began to raid the indigenous groups in the Chaco, taking captives to be traded with the Portuguese. The Ebitoso fought the Mbya-Caduveo with mixed results, and eventually a working arrangement emerged: the Ebitoso would take captives from other communities and exchange them for manufactured goods to which the Mbya-Caduveo had access. The Tomaraho, being among the groups targeted by the Ebitoso's raids, retreated into the Chaco and returned to the Paraguay River only sporadically.

Many Ebitoso stories tell of betrayals and ambushes while the Ebitoso were trading with the Mbya-Caduveo, and thus show that the agreement between these two groups was not always honored. Yet the stories also suggest that while their relationship was at times antagonistic and at other times cooperative, they consistently renewed efforts to establish some sort of reciprocity. The experience of coexistence with the Mbya-Caduveo played an important role in shaping the imaginations that mediated the Ebitoso's relation to the whites. Indeed, the Ebitoso initially dealt with the whites much as they had with the Mbya-Caduveo; that is, they fought them until they could establish a working arrangement for coexistence. The stories that portray this scenario illuminate why contemporary Ebitoso intellectuals reject portrayals that suggest that the ancient Yshiro responded with simple resistance and were defeated during the whites' drive to integrate the Chaco into the nation-state. On the contrary, many of the intellectuals with whom I spoke insisted that the Ebitoso were cheated, rather than militarily subjugated into the subordinated position that they feel they occupy in contemporary Paraguayan society. As Bruno Barras argued, "Our people helped the whites in their works, but in their thoughts there was never the suspicion that the whites would take all the land for themselves and leave us with nothing. They [the ancient Yshiro] did not know that words on a paper were the only ones with value" (15 July 1993, field notes).

The Ebitoso's persistent reference to working *with* rather than working *for* the whites indicates that they perceive work to be a more equalitarian bond that implies reciprocal duties (see also Susnik 1995:83–85). Thus, from the stories told by the elders, one can infer that working with the whites was, for many Ebitoso, an appealing way to obtain goods, which were quickly incorporated into their daily life (see also Susnik 1995:52–112). However, this does not mean that the Ebitoso graciously incorporated working with the whites as just another subsistence activity. On the contrary, the terms of this form of engagement with the whites were matters of contention and conflict.

To begin with, working with the whites had an impact on the intergenerational tensions that already existed among the Ebitoso. The prescriptions regarding food consumption contained in the *Esnwherta au'oso* had no provisions for the whites' food, the consumption of which was therefore, in principle, unregulated. This opened up a space of uncertainty regarding the reciprocal duties and rights related to sharing the whites' food. Many stories, like Bruno's, that describe the early times of contact with whites suggest that the younger Ebitoso preferred to remain near the whites rather than return to the "bush." For both male and female youth, these stories emphasize, working with the whites created a space of freedom from the heavy impositions of the elders. Other stories and recollections recount that the elders tried to regulate the consumption of the whites' food without success. Thus, gradually, working with the whites became integral to the younger generations' daily tasks for subsistence. Yet, working with the whites was not free from conflicts.

From most stories about the early contacts, one can conclude that the Ebitoso imagined the whites as strangers with whom they could coexist on the basis of reciprocity. Perhaps the relationship would not always work harmoniously, but, at least from the Ebitoso perspective, it would be based on the equal status of all parties. It is clear also that the Ebitoso had their own ideas of how to respond when this assumption was challenged. Don Vaso, one of the oldest Ebitoso men at the time of my research, said that in his childhood he heard his elders narrating how they had killed a *patron*. Noticing my interest in the story, he continued in a matter-of-fact way,

The Yshiro killed many *patrones*. Yes, they killed them because the *patrones* were stingy. At night they [the Yshiro] would go where the *patron* was sleeping and with an old musket, pum!! Down like a bird. . . . Once there was this *patron*, the Yshiro gave him many wood logs. The *patron* gave them a little piece of material. Just a little piece for each one. One of the Yshiro came and said, "You have to give me more." "No, that's enough," said the *patron*. That Yshiro man refused to accept anything at all. He was angry. That very same night they killed the *patron*. (15 August 1999, tape recording)

Don Vaso is one of the few aged elders who describes himself as a convinced Christian, and he told me this story in the context of relating incidents in which the ancient Ebitoso had behaved as *avá* ("savages" in Guarani, the other official language of Paraguay). He finished by telling me, with a big smile, "We [the Ebitoso] do not do that any longer. We learned in the Bible that it is not good to kill your fellow human beings, we are civilized now." Yet if one attends to other sources, and even other stories told by Don Vaso, it is clear that the Ebitoso learned to refrain from using violence against the *patrones* through means other than the Bible alone. Indeed, the whites did not tolerate for long the Ebitoso's use of violence to protect their imaginations of the contact and the yrmo. According to the whites' own imaginations, violence was legitimate only in their hands.

Laissez-Faire Liberalism and the Annexation of the Chaco

"At the beginning all the world was America," wrote John Locke to build his argument for a "civil government." In this sentence are implicit the three imaginations—Indians, Nature, and Progress—that, closely knit together, constitute the kernel of the story with which "moderns" came to make sense of themselves and the world they lived in. America, and implicitly the Indians that inhabited it, stand for the past of humanity, a past in which the laws of Nature ruled supreme: that is, it was a state of nature prior to the emergence of society proper. Having this state of nature as a background, liberal theory postulated that some humans (propertied men) had progressed (i.e., moved further along the arrow of time) toward a civil government, the true expression of society. A legitimate (i.e., authentic) civil government was one that respected the "natural rights" of those men who constituted society, particularly their right to autonomy, which was intrinsically linked to property ownership (see Macpherson 1980). Liberalism thus emerged as a doctrine of "limitation and wise restraint" to be exercised by the government in the face of men's natural rights, as these rights were intrinsic to society.

The argument for restraint eventually came to be based on the assertion that the government has a limited capacity to know and intervene beneficially in the self-ordered and autonomous domain of the market, the space where propertied men interacted (see Gordon 1991:14–22). The government should therefore take a laissez-faire approach. Yet, from the beginning, liberalism was restrictive and exclusive insofar as "society," the opposite of Nature, was equated to elite bourgeois males, the enunciating self, and the governing modern subject. Thus, the specific domain in which the government was expected to restrain itself from intervening was the autonomy of the elite. In contrast, and drawing on the physiocratic tradition, which deemed governmental interventions appropriate as long as they followed the "natural" dispositions of the governed object (Drayton 2000:70; Herlitz 1997), liberalism considered legitimate a wide range of interventions in the domain of Nature. This philosophical perspective was premised on two ideas: that Nature was an incomplete, inert, volitionless resource to be used and molded to its full potential according to the designs of the acting subject (see Latour 1999:145–73, 216–57; Merchant 1983; Phelan 1993:45; Plumwood 1993); and that the government should, and could, know this "object" so as to design proper interventions.

In the pursuit of Progress, almost any kind of intervention in Nature was considered legitimate. Of course, by legitimizing such intercessions, liberalism implicitly sanctioned intervening in the lives of humans who in modern man's view were closely associated to Nature.[5] Thus, the "active principle" of Progress—"according to which new and higher stages of human society might emerge out of old and more simple ones: the driving motive in human history" (Ferguson 1997:153)—has been critical in mediating the projection of nature's properties onto "other" humans, and vice versa. Just as the imagination Progress facilitates the idea that "others" are closer to nature, it also allows the domination of colonized human others to become "natural." In effect, as long as the temporal dynamics of Progress have located Indians (among other Others) closer to nature, Western modern "man" has been justified in treating them as objects to be used according to "his" designs.

Based on these key modern imaginations, liberalism generated a sort of "restricted governance," that is, a form of governance in which concerns about the autonomy of, and therefore the legitimacy of rule over, Nature and Indians were minimal or nonexistent. The idea that it is the right of man to almost unrestrictedly reign over Nature remained largely operative, until very recently. How to address the question of man's rule over Indians, in contrast, presented a more complicated negotiation, given that Progress implied the possibility that Indians would eventually "catch up," thus becoming modern and therefore autonomous. To be sure, as long as this catching-up process remained incomplete, Indians could be considered a legitimate object of intervention, but insofar as they were also construed as humans, there was a ground from which to partially contest their status as objects.

I have taken this detour through some core tenets of liberal thought because it was under the aegis of liberalism that the yrmo would be articulated with the modern world. Although the Spanish and the *criollos* (people of Spanish descent who were born in the colonies) had explored the Chaco region since the sixteenth century, neither succeeded in establishing strongholds within this area until the late nineteenth century. Thus, in contrast to what happened in earlier times and in other parts of the Americas, the modern myth had already congealed into highly stabilized political and epistemological institutions when it came into contact with the yrmo.

Criollos obtained independence from the Spanish Crown during the first two decades of the nineteenth century, but the republics they formed were beset by internal turmoil until the end of the century. Paraguay was an exception: Spanish rule was terminated without extended military campaigns and was quickly replaced by the autocratic government of Gaspar Rodriguez de Francia (1814–1840), which was followed by the autocratic government of the Lopez family (1841–1870) (see Williams 1979). In spite of this internal stability, Paraguay's rulers had to devote much energy to keep the country safe from the tendencies of its two larger neighbors, Argentina and Brazil, which were inclined to co-opt Paraguay into their sphere of influence and geostrategic maneuvering. Eventually, between 1865 and 1870,

Paraguay fought a catastrophic war against Argentina, Brazil, and Uruguay, which left the country in ruins and its population decimated (Harris G. Warren 1978; Whigham and Potthast 1999). Bolivia, the other country besides Paraguay and Argentina laying claim to the Chaco, was recovering from a war it had fought, in 1883, against Chile, which not only weakened its military capacity, but also turned it into a landlocked country. Thus, at the end of the nineteenth century, when states in the Southern Cone began forcefully integrating territories that had been in the control of indigenous peoples, Argentina was the only one of the three republics laying claim to the Chaco region with the capacity to do so by military means.

Although clearly in control of indigenous peoples, both the Paraguayan and Bolivian states perceived the Chaco as the key for national progress. Successive Bolivian governments saw in the region a coveted passage to the Atlantic, via the Paraguay River, whereas Paraguayan governments saw landholdings that could be sold in order to pay war debts and rebuild the nation, which was in ruins. In contrast to Argentina, which started a military campaign to take control of the portion of the Chaco region on which it laid claims, Paraguay and Bolivia relied on private entrepreneurship. Taking advantage of the growing international demand for raw materials and the consequent expansion of extractive economies into so-called marginal areas (Weaver 2000; Bartolomé 1998), both governments designed policies that were attractive for adventurous entrepreneurs who would pursue progress in a laissez-faire manner.

The loss of population as a consequence of the war, conjoined with racist ideas dominant among the Latin American governing elites of the time (see Weaver 2000:68; Schelling 2000:11), compelled the Paraguayan government to promote European immigration and colonization as a means to achieving "progress" in the country. As a result, the first leading agents of progress in the Paraguayan Chaco were foreign companies (from Argentina, the United Kingdom, Germany, and the United States) and independent entrepreneurs variously related to them, who in a short period of time came to own almost all the land in the Paraguayan Chaco (Pastore 1972:237–44; Abente 1989; Borrini 1997:19–40). These foreign companies and entrepreneurs, mostly interested in extracting timber and tannin from the Chaco forest, established their factories and logging camps along the western margin of the Paraguay River (see Luis A. Romero 1977;

Kleinpenning 1992:251–81; Borrini 1997:31–54). As they rapidly expanded north, they encountered another "spearhead" of "progress," this one coming from Bolivia. The Bolivian governments had established contracts with private explorers and entrepreneurs who proposed to build a road and a railway that would connect the Bolivian city of Santa Cruz de La Sierra with the Paraguay River (see Bravo 1879; Suarez Arana 1919). The point where these spearheads of progress met was in Ebitoso territory, around the area of *nekauta* (see map 3). There, entrepreneurs from Bolivia founded the settlement of Puerto Pacheco, around 1885 (Suarez Arana 1919). In 1888, the Paraguayan government took over the settlement, renamed it Bahía Negra, and installed a small garrison that retained control until the dispute between Paraguay and Bolivia over the Chaco was settled, in the mid-1930s (see Ayala 1929:84–85; Ibarra 1930).

The overwhelming majority of entrepreneurs and explorers who formed these two spearheads of progress were Europeans (from Spain, Italy, England, Germany, and the Austro-Hungarian empire). Among them was Guido Boggiani, a young Italian who had made a name for himself among the intellectual and artistic circles of his country (Puccini 1999:225–72). Because of his triple role as entrepreneur, artist, and ethnographer, Boggiani serves as a good model for understanding the complex and ambivalent ways in which the Chaco and the Indians were imagined by the early nonindigenous settlers.

Imagining the Paraguayan Chaco and the Chaco's Indians

Boggiani arrived in Argentina in 1887 and later moved to Paraguay, where the "exotic natural surroundings" provided bountiful resources for his aesthetic, intellectual, and economic aspirations. Soon after arriving in Paraguay, Boggiani made acquaintance with European entrepreneurs who had already begun to exploit the advantageous economic prospects offered by the Chaco and who advised him of existing opportunities (Leigheb 1986; see Majavacca and Perez Acosta 1951:63–65). In 1892, Boggiani established logging camps in the places known to the Yshiro as Ynishta and Karcha Bahlut, which he named Puerto Esperanza and Puerto 14 de Mayo, respectively (see map 2).

While living with the "Chamacoco Indians" (Yshiro) who worked in his logging camps, Boggiani developed an interest in ethnography, and during a visit to Italy, in 1894, he held a series of conferences about the Chamacoco and their land at the Italian Geographical Society and the Anthropological Association of Florence. In these conferences, he described the Chaco in ambivalent terms.

> Mystery surrounds these flat, extended lands covered with a marvelous mantle of greenery. . . . The bad luck that has befallen those audacious travelers who . . . found their death at the hands of the Indians or who were overwhelmed by hardships . . . has left these immense forests in the most primitive state, comparable only to the most remote of prehistoric times. . . . Numerous tribes of savages inhabit the Chaco's immense forests, and they are another obstacle added to the natural difficulties that a green desert poses to exploration, making this region resistant to civilization. . . . While Argentina, by deed of love or by deed of force, has been subjecting the savage hordes to the new system of life, Paraguay and Bolivia, due to idleness, lack of means, or because they have other more important businesses at hand, have remained indifferent or inoperative in this region. (Boggiani 1894:9–12)

These harsh images were countered by others in which he described the Chaco as a place of "silence, grandiose solitude, freedom without limits, and endless peace" and the Chamacoco as people who developed great affection for him and who readily joined his logging camp to help him with his endeavor (Boggiani 1894:27–31).

Boggiani's contradictory portrayals of the Chaco and its inhabitants reveal the modern subject's ambivalent perception of Nature, of which the Chaco was a metonym, as both an incomplete object and a source of uncontaminated truth and authenticity (for this ambivalence, see Arnold 1996, 2000). Often, as in the case of Boggiani, European colonizers deployed these contrasting tropes side by side, grounding what Rosaldo calls "imperial nostalgia" (1989:68), a longing for those imagined spaces (natural or cultural) which are pure and untouched by Progress. Thus, the colonist could at the same time lament and contribute to the passing away of other worlds without feeling fully responsible for it. Boggiani's contradictory images reflect the very process by which the Chaco and its inhabitants were starting to become "known" in the modern sense of the word. That is, they reflect an ongoing process, which Boggiani embodied, by which Nature and Indians were being made to surrender their "otherness" to become malleable material for "modern man." In effect, for Boggiani, the Chaco represented a natural order "comparable to the most remote of prehistoric times" from which modern man had succeeded in lifting himself up (Boggiani 1894:10). Yet, as Europeans were taking control of the Chaco, its threatening otherness was being translated, tamed, and assigned its proper place within the "story of modernity." In this regard, an epigraph that introduces one of Boggiani's ethnographic works is telling: "Classifying the Indians of South America within a natural order is one of the most challenging problems of ethnography." As dominant evolutionist ideas of the time had it, the "manly" effort required to civilize the "virgin lands" of the Chaco implied classifying this natural order, mastering its laws, and ruling over it.[6]

As effective control over the territories occupied by indigenous peoples was being secured, European entrepreneurs began to imagine the Chaco not as a green desert, but as the "salvation for the forty million Europeans that [were] called to contribute to its progress with intelligence, capital and work" (Cominges, cited in Velasco del Real 1892:177). This change in the perception of the Chaco ran parallel to a new way of imagining the Indians. According to the Spanish entrepreneur Juan de Cominges, Indians were often misunderstood and misrepresented; they were not an obstacle to progress, but "the indispensable and economical assistance needed to set the basis of civilization" (cited in Velasco del Real 1892:177). Cominges's view of the Indians reflects not a change from "misrepresentation" to accurate representation, but rather a change in the conditions that gave (corpo)reality to the imagination Indians.

Stabilizing the Imagination Indians

The imagination Indians, as malleable material which could be used in the pursuit of progress, was easily adaptable to diverse European agendas. For example, while European entrepreneurs imagined Indians as the "indispensable and economical assistance" for their capitalist enterprises in the Chaco, European missionaries imagined Indians as a "material" susceptible to Christian uplift.[7] When, in the 1920s, the Catholic Church attempted to establish a mission to "serve" the Yshiro, the undertaking was likened to the exploitation of natural resources by capitalist enterprises: "Adjacent to the tannin industries, implanted by capitalist entrepreneurs . . . to exploit the . . . virgin forest, emerges at last an *enterprise of souls* ready to save so many ignorant savages from the Devil's claws, and bring them to faith, civilization and Christendom" (Alarcón y Cañedo and Pittini 1924:85–86).[8]

In these imaginations, Indians were nature-like entities characterized by a lack of volition, and as such, their actions could not be more than the expression of their nature. Accompanying these imaginations was the presumption that the "nature" of the Indians was knowable for Europeans. For example, in a letter from a priest, Father Turricia, to his superiors, Boggiani is quoted as saying in a conference that "the Chamacoco, as all Indians, have a great defect: they are absolutely ignorant of everything that lies beyond the circumscribed circle of their primitive customs" and that "the Indian recognizes the superiority of the civilized man; but he is able to distinguish one kind of [white] man from another and does not submit to just anyone because of the [whites'] higher civilization. . . . [T]he Indian recognizes and respects the authority of those who, as he knows, given their position, have the right to command" (cited in Heyn 1996:88). It is in this context that one can understand why Boggiani wrote that after he had demonstrated his interest in logging, "*naturally* the Chamacoco, who had already developed much affection for [him], followed suit . . . taking care of the clear-cutting work" for his logging camp (Boggiani 1894:28, emphasis added). Taken together, these statements make clear that Boggiani interpreted the Indians' ignorance of other customs and their tacit knowledge of social ranks as a "natural" inclination to follow the white man.

Boggiani's reference to the Indians' capacity to distinguish "one kind of [white] man from another" also contains an implicit reference to Paraguayans and the racial hierarchy that, to his eyes, positioned them beneath Europeans and to some extent even beneath the Indians. While these (other) whites were necessary participants in the process of annexation of the Chaco, it is striking how all the European chronicles of this early period of settlement only fleetingly mention Paraguayans as protagonists in the events described. But such omissions do make sense because, as Cominges expressed, it was Indians, not Paraguayans, who in European visions of the

Chaco were the indispensable "material" for building civilization. Europeans not only disregarded Paraguayans as central protagonists in the process of "building civilization" in the Chaco, but in fact regarded them as obstacles to this goal. When Indians proved reluctant to be either "economical assistants" or to be rescued from the "devils' claws," for example, Europeans blamed this behavior on the example set by "lower Paraguayan people," who allegedly not only distracted Indians from their education, but also corrupted them (Boggiani 1900:114–18; Sosa Gaona 1996:41–42).

Blaming the Paraguayans for the difficulties that besieged the perfect relation that Europeans had envisioned with the Indians facilitated the stabilization of the imagination Indians as nature-like entities. If Indians were naturally disposed to be raw material in the hands of the Europeans, and the Europeans were doing their work (i.e., civilizing), what could possibly explain the problems that arose? By blaming the Paraguayans, Europeans were able to avoid questioning the ways in which entrepreneurs, missionaries, ethnographers, and the like imagined Indians and their own relations to them.

As non-indigenous peoples began to take control of the Chaco, dominant imaginations of the region and its inhabitants as obstacles to progress began to be superseded by others in which both Indians and Nature constituted building blocks in the hands of the European architects of civilization. Europeans imagined the Yshiro as Indians who naturally loved the whites and who recognized their superiority, feelings the Yshiro purportedly expressed by joining the Europeans in their endeavors. In turn, Europeans imagined themselves to reciprocate those feelings by contributing to the Yshiro's uplift toward civilization (see Boggiani [1896] 1975:71; Alarcón y Cañedo and Pittini 1924:85–87). In this interplay of imaginations of the other and the self, the Yshiro's love of and natural submissiveness to the Europeans were simply mirror images of the latter's superiority. So convincing were these imaginations that, in a public talk, Boggiani claimed never to concern himself with his possessions or his life, in spite of the fact that their preservation was "entirely at the Indians' discretion" (cited in Heyn 1996:90). Shortly thereafter, the Yshiro killed him.

Since that time and into the late twentieth century, many musings that attempt to explain what might have led some Yshiro to kill Boggiani have appeared in print (see Leigheb 1986:141–62; Cordeu 1991a:87n129). But not one of these discussions has considered Boggiani's role as a *patron* (boss, employer) as a possible factor, an omission that may be due to how Europeans settlers imagined the Indians and their behavior. Europeans understood actions such as the killing of Boggiani as anomalies or irregularities, ultimately anecdotal to the necessary unfolding of history as the coming of civilization. For example, the missionary Barbrooke Grubb noted that as the Europeans helped the Indians to achieve a superior stage of civilization, many Indians wound up in worse situations, as exemplified by their lack of discipline and their moral dissolution. However, he surmised that "without doubt, no reasonable man would ever assert that keeping those people in ignorance and slavery is better than allowing them to attempt reaching a superior and more dignified life, just because in the transition some irregularities and disorders occur" (Grubb [1925] 1993:187). Grubb's statement makes clear that behaviors displayed by indigenous peoples that did not correspond to European expectations were nothing but "irregularities and disorders." Alternatively, as in Fric's hypothesis (see Fric and Fricova 1997), that Boggiani was killed because the Yshiro suspected him to be a witch, such behaviors could be explained as resulting from "primitive beliefs," that is, mistaken knowledge. In any case, for the Europeans, these acts were anomalous or irregular in relation to an ineluctable historical process.

That the Indians' responses to colonization were understood by Europeans as anomalies signals how the yrmo was being evacuated from the "radar screen" of the settlers. For the Europeans, the "anomalies" justified violent pedagogic actions aimed at correction (Dussel 1995:66). However, the actual effect of this violent pedagogy was to further stabilize the imagination Indians by pushing into the "hidden transcript" (James Scott 1990) the most visible and destabilizing traces of the yrmo. In other words, pedagogic violence came to provide the "brutal epistemological guarantee" (Lange 1998:135) that the imagination Indians would remain stable. Keeping this imagination unchallenged was essential to the European ability to articulate, on a general level, the whole web of interrelated imaginations that contributed to (corpo)realize modernity and, on a more circumscribed level, the diverse interests and visions that drove the incorporation of the Chaco. Indeed, the imagination Indians was central to sustaining a "hegemonic coincidence" that shaped in conceptual and practical terms the terrain within which white–Indian relations unfolded in the Chaco and elsewhere (for a similar point about the Chaco, see Thorndahl 1997:76–84). I refer to a hegemonic coincidence because the imagination Indians, along with the other, more stable imaginations, Nature and Progress, articulated a varied group of otherwise antagonistic interests and perspectives, such as those of state agents, missionaries, entrepreneurs, philanthropists, and the general public. Of course, points of articulation among dominant groups are, in colonial situations, imposed on subordinated groups by violent means (see Ranajit Guha 1997). Thus, one must see the imagination Indians and pedagogic violence as two mutually reinforcing moments of the hegemonic coincidence through which modernity has been performed: Europeans would have not been able to sustain their imagination Indians without pedagogic violence; yet pedagogic violence would have not been possible without the imagination Indians helping to justify it.

The operation of pedagogic violence is clear in the aftermath of Boggiani's death. As his friends in Asunción began to worry about his absence, they sent an expedition to search for him. The diary kept by the expedition's leader, Jose Cancio, is rather explicit about how the Ebitoso were "taught" that they could not use violence in their relations with the whites. In the diary, he writes of women and children running and crying as soon as they see the armed white men coming, of "tough" warriors shivering in panic when questioned by the leader of the expedition, and of the use of torture to make people confess to the crime (see Comitato Pro-Boggiani 1903).[9]

Many elders (Ebitoso and Tomaraho) remember or have heard about similar expeditions, organized or condoned by the Paraguayan authorities, to punish the Yshiro for having attacked *patrones* or for having defended themselves from the abuses of settlers. For example, Don Vaso described how, in the late 1920s or early 1930s, his grandfather had suffered the consequences of resisting the theft of his only cow by a Paraguayan settler.

> He [my grandfather] had a cow called Bonita. He put me and all his stuff on her to go from one place to another looking for *changa* [casual labor]. Then this Paraguayan came and tried to take the cow with him. My grandfather told him to leave our cow and go away. . . . They fought and my grandfather cut him with his machete. The Paraguayan went away. Then my grandfather took our stuff, the cow, me and my grandmother, and we all went hiding into the bush. We stayed there several

weeks hiding from the soldiers. . . . An uncle told my grandfather that the commander said we could go back to the logging camps if he [my grandfather] gave the cow to the Paraguayan who had tried to take her away. . . . At the end my grandfather gave Bonita away but had to keep avoiding that thief and his friends because he knew they would take revenge and the commander would do nothing about it. (17 September 1999, tape recording)

I have heard and recorded many stories in which the Paraguayan authorities are depicted as doing nothing to defend the Yshiro from abuses perpetrated by the settlers, while giving carte blanche to or even supporting the settlers' repressive measures against the Yshiro when they took matters into their own hands. Through these sorts of experiences the Yshiro learned that violent means could not be used to stabilize their imaginations of coexistence and reciprocity. Indeed, there is evidence that by the 1920s the Ebitoso attempts at authorizing their own imagination of *patrones* as partners with whom they could share bonds of reciprocity had become unsuccessful. Moreover, it seems that the Ebitoso had already "learned" that they could not use violence against the whites. For example, when the ethnographer Herbert Baldus visited Bahía Negra in 1923, he saw a drunken Paraguayan man brutally assault an Ebitoso man, while the latter only tried to avoid his attacker's blows, without even attempting to reciprocate. Baldus observed that in spite of the bad treatment and the conditions of exploitation, the Ebitoso's movements within their territory had become dependent on the availability of work in logging camps (see Baldus 1927:30–31). Thus, one can argue that although the new order of things was not accepted by the Ebitoso without a critical eye, they found themselves with few alternatives to escape this situation of increasing exploitation and abuse.

Although the tannin companies owned their own lands, they also bought wood from individual entrepreneurs, who, like Boggiani, obtained concessions to open logging camps on "government lands" (see Borrini 1997: 30–54). Most of these logging camps were in Yshiro territory, and it was through the camps, rather than through direct work in the tannin factories, that the Ebitoso, and later the Tomaraho, became integrated into the emerging economic system (see Carlos Romero 1913:50–51; Baldus 1927). The logging camps (*obrajes* in Spanish) were relatively stable settlements where wood from the surrounding areas was processed. Some of the first logging camps that were settled on the margin of the Paraguay River eventually became ports for the shipment of wood and also small towns where Paraguayan overseers and European *patrones* had their families. These incipient towns grew into centers of economic activity, exchange, and trade, and from the perspective of the Ebitoso, they were good places to find work. Thus, entire residential groups of the Ebitoso began to move from one logging camp to another, depending on the opportunities they found for work.

During the first decades of the contact, working conditions for males were arranged by the *polotak* (war leaders), but emerging *cabezantes* (headmen) of small groups of workers, who were more familiar with the white's language and ways of doing things, quickly became the main brokers. The polotak also arranged the working conditions for females. Initially the women who worked with whites were mostly Yshiro-Tomaraho captives who provided domestic and sexual services to whites.[10] Soon these women saw that they could avoid the control of their "adoptive parents/captors" by remaining with their employers. Also, as the Ebitoso began to restrict their movements according to the work opportunities they found in the logging camps and Paraguayan settlements, women began to develop their own, more constant connections with Paraguayan *patronas* (female *patrones*), who hired them for domestic chores.

Cohabitation with whites in logging camps and permanent settlements and the progressive abandonment of food prescriptions let loose the negative manifestation of wozosh in the form of diseases that decimated the Ebitoso groups (see Baldus 1927:10). As the konsaho (shamans) were unable to cope with the magnitude of the disruption, dependence on medicines provided by the whites further reinforced the Yshiro's tendency to stay near white settlements. Bush subsistence was still an option but limited by the fact that to move away from white settlements meant to enter territory controlled by other indigenous groups, like the Tomaraho and the Ayoreode, or, more importantly, to render oneself susceptible to random attacks by white settlers. In effect, besides pedagogic violence, piecemeal and relatively random violence operated in tandem with other forms of engagement that were shaping the complex interconnections being established between the modern world and the yrmo. For example, as the tannin companies attracted Paraguayan workers from the eastern part of Paraguay, groups of discontented, unemployed, or disenfranchised whites began to loot the area. The authorities seldom punished these looters for their attacks on and robberies in Yshiro settlements. Yet when other whites were the victims, the authorities' reprisals often extended to the indigenous camps outside the immediate vicinity of white settlements (see Olmedo 1946:21–24). Thus, remaining in the proximity of logging camps, as well as of the more permanent white settlements, not only provided opportunities to obtain food and other goods, but also offered some protection from looters and the punitive expeditions of the authorities. Thus, open pedagogic violence was slowly displaced, although it never disappeared, by more subtle forms of pedagogic violence effected through white control of the means of subsistence.

Coda and Prelude

At least four generations of Yshiro were born and raised in an yrmo whose entanglement with the modern world was, through laissez-faire progress, increasingly asymmetrical. The specificity of the practical circumstances in which this process of interconnection occurred often involved the collision between the tendencies of both Europeans and Yshiro to act according to their conventional wisdom. Thus, points of overlap between these worlds often constituted areas charged by tensions where, seen against the background of the expectations raised from within either world, entities appeared to behave in anomalous ways. At the beginning, both Yshiro and settlers tried to contain these anomalies through stabilizing operations that included violence. However, the whites were soon able to monopolize the tool of violence and to frame the interconnection of worlds in ways that reinforced their own imagination-world, a world in which Indians were by definition subordinate to "modern man."

A series of conditions, which operated in tandem, characterized the process by which the yrmo became asymmetrically entangled with the modern world. Central among these conditions was the hegemonic coincidence which, on the one hand, made it acceptable for the whites to use pedagogical violence to correct the "anomalous" behaviors of the Indians (i.e., behaviors that contradicted the whites' imaginations) and, on the other hand, made unacceptable under any circumstance for the Yshiro to use violence to stabilize their own imaginations. Certainly, the hegemonic coincidence was aided by the existence of tensions specific to the yrmo, which acted simultaneously and in concert with white pedagogic violence to frame the interconnection between worlds in asymmetrical ways. For example, in their desire to escape the control exercised by elders and polotak, and by joining the whites in their economic endeavors, the younger generations of Ebitoso and the Tomaraho captives acted in ways that reinforced European imaginations of Indians as building blocks of progress. The impossibility of asserting their own imaginations of how this relation should work meant that, in the long run, those younger generations saw their imaginations and the yrmo becoming invisible and irrelevant to the settlers. In short, by the late 1920s, the hegemonic coincidence reined supreme, making it possible for the Indians and the Chaco to be firmly imagined, for all practical purposes, as objects in need of progress and, by extension, for the myth of modernity to become further stabilized.

Two State-Driven Development
STABILIZING MODERNITY

In 1926, Mennonites from Canada obtained important concessions from the Paraguayan government and began to settle
lands that the tannin companies had already clear-cut in the Central Chaco (see Hack 1978, 1979, 1980; Plett 1979; Redekop 1980;
Ratzlaff 1993; Borrini 1997:55–105; and map 3). Both Bolivia and
Paraguay had been using private companies and private schemes
of settlement, such as that of the Mennonites, as their surrogates
for the integration of the territories they claimed in the Chaco.
With the arrival of the Mennonites in the Central Chaco, and
rumors that oil deposits had been found, tensions mounted,
troops were brought to the area, fortifications and roads were
constructed, and finally war broke out. Among the consequences
of the Chaco War—which spanned three years (1932–35) and
led to numerous casualties and deaths—one had great importance for the Yshiro: the Paraguayan victory linked Indians, the
Paraguayan people's identity, and nationalism into an emerging
vision of "progress" in the Chaco that depended on more direct
intervention by the state with the assistance of experts.

By the 1930s, the idea that progress would be achieved in
Paraguay by entrepreneurs harnessing the bounties of the virgin
lands was being displaced by one in which the state appeared as
the privileged agent of progress. This change was fueled by three
mutually reinforcing processes: the emergence of a nationalist
rhetoric with indigenista undertones; the decline of the tannin
industry's profits, coupled with their increased exploitation of
workers; and the adoption by Paraguay's governing elites of an
integrationist approach to development.

At the beginning of the twentieth century, and as happened in other Latin American countries, Paraguayan intellectuals began to reconsider the role of the Guarani "Indians" in the formation of the "Paraguayan people." They came up with a national origin myth according to which the Paraguayan people were descendants of a Guarani Indian mother and a Spanish father (see Susnik and Chase-Sardi 1995:282–98; Robbins 1999:112–15; Horst 1998:64). The value of the Guarani heritage was further intermingled with nationalist sentiments when, during the Chaco war, Guarani-speaking groups from the Chaco (Guarayu and Guarani-ñandeva) joined the advancing Paraguayan army (Susnik and Chase-Sardi 1995:256–57). Emerging nationalist movements coupled these ideas with Paraguay's hard-won victory over Bolivia in their rhetoric to assert that the Paraguayan nation-state, rather than foreign companies, should control the Chaco's resources.

Although after the war, in 1936, a nationalist revolution took over the government (see Lewis 1980:22–25), the nationalist rhetoric did not translate into action. That is, the new government did not take measures to radically change the overwhelming control that foreign companies had over the Chaco's resources. Nevertheless, this rhetoric introduced a new element to the way in which the Chaco was imagined: the blood shed by Paraguayans during the war, which according to nationalist discourses, made the Chaco more Paraguayan than ever. Consistent with this idea, nationalists claimed that Paraguayans were the only ones with a right to decide the future of the Chaco.[1] This rhetoric was further fueled by the increasingly intense exploitation of workers that ensued as synthetic tannin was invented and the tannin industry began to see a steady decline in its profits.

The nationalism spawned by the Chaco War, growing discontent with foreign exploitation of Paraguayans living in the Chaco (including Indians), and the decline of the tannin industry provided the specifically Paraguayan imprimatur to the adoption by Paraguayan governing elites of emerging European and U.S. models of government. After the Great Depression, state interventionism became increasingly accepted, in different guises, in most Western countries (see Arturo Escobar 1995:38). The state had not only the right but the duty to intervene in order to ensure that every element of the nation was fully integrated into the movement toward development. But in order to intervene the state had to "know" and therefore had to enroll the aid of experts. In the case of Indians expertise came from the "indigenista field" that took shape after the Chaco War.[2] To contextualize the particulars of how the indigenista field informed development interventions, one must first understand how development was generally conceived in Paraguay after the Second World War, as well as the nature of the situation in the Chaco when this conception was initially deployed.

The Decline of the Tannin Economy and Developing Patronage

The tannin industry was the major supplier of foreign currency and fiscal revenues for the Paraguayan state into the 1940s (Kleinpenning 1992:280). Thus, when the industry declined and foreign aid began to flow in, it was welcomed with open arms by Paraguayan governments. As early as 1937, and as part of a strategy to entice Paraguay away from Nazi Germany, the United States provided economic aid to Paraguayan governments (Mora 1998:453–55; see also Horst 1998:70). When, at the end of the Second World War and the beginning of the Cold War, Truman launched the "development era" (Esteva 1992:6), Paraguayan internal and external politics were already heavily entangled with foreign aid (Mora 1998:455–58), and this only intensified when General Alfredo Stroessner took power, in 1954.

In the eight years preceding Stroessner's ascension to power, seven presidents had come and gone. Stroessner, however, accomplished the dubious feat of keeping himself in power for more than thirty-four years. The power and endurance of the regime rested on a tripartite structure formed by the government bureaucracy, the armed forces, and the Colorado Party.[3] In his triple role as president of the republic, honorary president of the Colorado Party, and commander-in-chief of the armed forces, Stroessner was at the apex of this structure. Membership in the Colorado Party was mandatory for all state employees, as well as for all members of the armed forces, except conscripted soldiers. A network of *seccionales* (party offices or cells), which extended nationwide, operated as a parallel structure to the state, and at times the distinction between them was blurred. Loyal party cadres were rewarded with government positions. Within the armed forces and security forces, positions were allocated with the implicit recognition that they were to produce profits for the person who received the position and for the *patron* who had provided it.

In addition to direct coercion, Stroessner's regime had nearly the whole country bounded through a patronage system as a way to obtain acquiescence and loyalty. This system extended to the rural poor, to blue-collar workers, to state employees, to cadres of the regime, and to private businessmen. For the regime, external economic support was critical since it contributed substantially to the "resources" which circulated within the nationwide patronage network. Stroessner fashioned himself as a committed anticommunist who faithfully supported the United States and its foreign policy. In turn, he received support from the United States in the form of military supplies, and direct or indirect financial assistance through loans from the World Bank and the Inter-American Development Bank (income that at times approached the Paraguayan state's total annual expenditures). Those who occupied the higher echelons of the regime were given the administration and execution of development projects (from big civil-engineering projects to rural-development schemes) as recognition for their loyalty to the regime. During the thirty-four years of the regime, these "officials" amassed considerable fortunes from embezzlement, bribes, and "commissions" paid by contractors.

The "development scheme" of the regime was based on infrastructure building that would allow the integration of unexploited natural resources into the economy of the nation (see Lewis 1980:151–67; Kleinpenning 1988; Kleinpenning and Zoomers 1991). This scheme was carried out primarily in the eastern part of the country, where hydroelectric dams and roads were built (Ferradás 1998). In the Chaco the only important infrastructure project executed was the Trans-Chaco Highway, which connected the Mennonite colonies in Central Chaco to Asunción. Yet, in spite of this highway, the environmental conditions of the Chaco continued to discourage the settlement of small peasants (Kleinpenning and Zoomers 1991:47). For this reason, the Chaco did not suffer as intense and fast an expansion of the "agricultural frontier" and exploitation of its natural resources as the eastern region did. Nevertheless, the highway project had enormous impact in the region, as it underwrote the Mennonite's agroindustrial boom, which reshaped the demographics of the area and shifted the center of market-related economic activity away from the Paraguay River to the Central

Chaco (Renshaw 1996:36–37; Borrini 1997:87–88). Indeed, as the require-
ments for a labor force increased in the Mennonite colonies, indigenous
peoples from all over the Paraguayan Chaco, except the Yshiro, were attracted to the Central Chaco (Stunnenberg 1993:221; Borrini 1997:101–2).

As the effects of the decline of the tannin industry became more evident,
in the late 1950s (see Luis A. Romero 1977; Kleinpenning 1992:251–81), and
as the Mennonite colonies became the center of economic activity in the
Chaco, the region of Alto Paraguay was slowly marginalized.[4] Logging
camps closed, and the lands were converted into cattle ranches (Stunnenberg 1993:46–50). These ranches, called *estancias*, were owned by former
logging-camp overseers, military officers, and a few successful local storekeepers. Other lands were acquired by real-estate speculators or remained
in the hands of the state. In the estancias, only a few Yshiro obtained *changa*
(casual labor); the rest had to search for alternative means of subsistence.

The end of the tannin boom did not effect great changes in the kind of
economic activities in which Ebitoso women engaged, since they continued
to have access to market goods by offering domestic services to Paraguayans
and by selling handicrafts to the people who navigated the Paraguay River.[5]
For men, however, the labor outlook changed substantially, as changas
in estancias were insufficient to keep everybody fed. Consequently, men
turned to hunting, an activity that throughout the tannin boom had been
performed primarily within a frame of values connected with the *Esnwherta
au'oso* and the Yshiro puruhle narratives. Although trade in wild species had
existed before, in the new circumstances hunting was intimately linked to
market demands, which created another point of convergence between the
yrmo and the modern world. Thus, since the 1950s, when the demand for
wood decreased, intensive exploitation of animal species highly valued in
the market has been a key source of Yshiro subsistence.[6]

Given the economic marginality of Alto Paraguay, the Ebitoso became
more independent from the market than other indigenous peoples of the
Chaco. However, to the extent that certain needs and desires could only be
fulfilled through the market, the market still had an enormous influence
on the way the Ebitoso pursued subsistence. And under the new socioeconomic circumstances, continuous access to market goods was dependent
on an individual's capacity to secure and maintain a responsive *patron*.
Patrones were male Paraguayans, usually store- or estancia-owners, active

members in Colorado Party local offices, and associated with military authorities. *Patrones* would choose their "personnel" and give them credit in the form of food and other items so they could feed themselves and their families during the hunting season of a given species. By the time the hunting season was over because of seasonal conditions or because the animals had become scarce, a hunter would probably owe the *patron* almost exactly or more than what he had earned. Between seasons, the *patron* would give goods on credit in exchange for the next season's catches to those hunters who had proved "more productive" and who had not accumulated large debts. In any case, *patrones* made sure their hunters were always indebted to them, so that the chain of debt was very difficult to break (Renshaw 1996:131–32). Since local authorities were involved in this business, there was no way to escape one's debts without risking, if not violence, at the very least the loss of patronage and the relative security it offered. State-driven development did not challenge this patronage system but actually complemented and expanded it with the assistance of the indigenistas.

Indigenismo and Development

While indigenous and non-indigenous peoples in Alto Paraguay were adjusting to the changes brought about by the decline of the tannin industry, the Paraguayan state was expanding its intervention through its particular version of development. Ideas of state-driven development of the Chaco were, as with laissez-faire progress, charged by images of "total conquest" and the conversion of the "green desert" into an oasis of work, production, and welfare (see Olmedo 1966:11–12). In relation to indigenous peoples, state-driven development was more clearly articulated as a process of integration into "society," whose explicit corollary was the disappearance of Indians as such (see Horst 1998:82–157). The state's Departmento de Asuntos Indígenas (Department of Indigenous Affairs, or DAI) was created, in 1958, specifically to carry out this vision. For instance, the director of this institution wrote in a contribution to an edited book on the prospects for the development of the Chaco,

> The Chamacoco [Yshiro] have always been recognized as skillful workers in ranches, as cart drivers, and as woodcutters. In this indigenous

environment, far away from the centers of cultural influence, the habit of working has produced in them the first rudimentary signs of evolution. This phenomenon . . . had its complement twelve years ago when two self-sacrificing New Tribes missionaries started their evangelizing work. They . . . also taught children, youth, and adults how to read and write. . . . [I]t would not be audacious to assert that, [by] speeding up this task [i.e., development], only memories will be left of the fact that this region was once inhabited by Chamacoco Indians. (Borgognon 1966:38–39)

For this integrationist objective to be accomplished, DAI's director understood, indigenous peoples would need lands for agriculture, credits, education, health, and employment. All of this was to be delivered through indigenistas, a set of institutions and individuals who since the late 1930s had been shaping a field of expertise on the "Indian problem" (Borgognon 1968:349–50; see also Horst 1998:126–55).

The Chaco War put Paraguay's army officers in contact with indigenous peoples. Paramount among these officers was Juan Belaieff, a Russian émigré. Commissioned during the prewar years to explore and prepare defenses in the area of Bahía Negra, Belaieff proposed to form a cavalry regiment with the Chamacoco (Belaieff 1928). At the end of the war Belaieff was given the directorship of the new Patronato Nacional de Indígenas (Indigenous Peoples' National Trust), the first state institution created to further the well-being of Indians (see Asociación Indigenista del Paraguay 1945:4; Prieto and Bragayrac 1995:29–30). Belaieff understood his duties toward the Indians within an emerging Latin American indigenista agenda that had been taking shape for some years before it became public policy in Congreso Indigenista Inter-Americano, convened, in 1940, at Pazcuaro, Mexico, and the subsequent creation of the Instituto Indigenista Inter-Americano (see Belaieff 1941:1–3). In Paraguay, Belaieff and a group of philanthropists who self-defined as "friends and defenders of the Indians" enthusiastically embraced the goals of this institution, and in 1942, when the state failed to economically sustain the Patronato Nacional de Indígenas, they created Asociación Indigenista del Paraguay (AIP). The association's aim was to integrate the "national Indians" into "civilized life" and to convert them to Christianity (see Asociación Indigenista del Paraguay 1945; Horst 1998: 70–71).

While AIP was constituted as a philanthropic nongovernmental association, its members' liaisons with or direct participation in the government
positioned it, alongside the religious missions, as a privileged interlocutor in
the shaping of state policy related to indigenous peoples. With the creation
of AIP, a specialized field which had the Indians as its "object" of expertise
reached maturity. As laissez-faire progress was displaced by state intervention and the Departmento de Asuntos Indígenas was created, religious and
secular indigenistas claimed, and were granted by the state, special jurisdictions over development policies pertaining to Indians on the basis of the indigenistas higher moral standing or scientific authority (see Asociación Indigenista del Paraguay 1945:32–50; Bejarano 1976; Horst 1998). Questions
of what was best for the Indians often caused tensions and disagreements
among the indigenistas, but never to a degree that might have challenged
the hegemonic coincidence that Indians, and the Chaco, had to be "developed" and that the use of coercion (mostly in its euphemized forms) was
legitimate in this pursuit.

The form of engagement that initially emerged from the hegemonic
coincidence contributed to the subordination and invisibilization of the
yrmo. However, until the 1950s the Ebitoso were still in a situation in which
they could more or less reproduce the yrmo through ritual practices and
the forms of conduct promoted by the *Esnwherta au'oso*. For example, as
described by the Ebitoso elder Don Tito Perez, the system of relations
which emerged during the first decades of white settlement of Yshiro territories generated its own sets of expectations and regularities, including the
availability of resources and the freedom to perform debylylta (the initiation ritual). These expectations and regularities started to be disturbed by
the late 1950s.

> Before, we did not stay long in any place. It is only now, since we have
> got the legal ownership of some land, that we stay put. I have seen the
> times of my grandparents. They moved from here to there, from there to
> here . . . always looking for *changa* [casual labor] . . . those *patrones*, they
> respected our culture [i.e., rituals]. When the time comes, the *patrones*
> stop all the work, they give food, clothes, tobacco, *caña* [alcohol] and
> gave the people five days free for the Yshiro to have their "party." There
> are no *patrones* like this any longer. Before the *patrones* were responsive,

they gave work and food, even those military men, they gave work so that the poor people have something to eat. But then the *patrones'* children just took the money and never returned to give us work. (23 January 2000, tape recording)

As the logging camps' *patrones* started to withdraw, missionaries started to arrive. In effect, although the Catholic Church had attempted to establish a mission in Fuerte Olimpo in the early 1920s, it was not until the 1950s that the Ebitoso came into permanent contact with missionaries. At that time, two female missionaries of the New Tribes Mission (NTM), Ms. Jones and Ms. Nelson, arrived at a logging camp which eventually became the Yshiro community of Diana.[7] Most elders comment that the missionaries came to their territory at a moment when the Ebitoso had started to feel that they were likely to be exterminated by diseases. Given the critical circumstances, it is not surprising that the Ebitoso experienced this event as a turning point in their history. Indeed, the missionaries brought "aid" (medicines and food) which helped to forestall the grim destiny that most elders say awaited the Ebitoso. With this aid, the NTM missionaries slowly convinced most Ebitoso to settle in Puerto Diana where they would have the missionaries' protection, in addition to access to *patrones* from the nearby Paraguayan town of Bahía Negra. The rest of the Ebitoso settled in Ylhirta, near the Paraguayan town of Fuerte Olimpo, where the Catholic Church had reserved 200 hectares of land to set up a new mission, although this was not operational until the 1960s.

The Tomaraho avoided contact with the whites until around the 1940s. According to the elders I spoke with, the Tomaraho generally stayed deep in the bush and away from the Paraguay River, which they would visit sporadically and barter with the whites, sometimes cutting trees for them and staying around the logging camps for short periods of time. Often the Tomaraho were attacked by settlers and soldiers who encountered them unexpectedly. These kinds of attacks increased significantly during the Chaco War (for Tomaraho stories of the contact, see Cordeu 1999:337–52). According to the elders, it was also during the Chaco War that the Tomaraho became acquainted with Paraguayans, who allowed them to pass behind their lines in order to avoid being trapped by enemy fire. Some of these Paraguayans later served as overseers in Carlos Casado Company and after the war convinced the Tomaraho to settle in San Carlos, one of the company logging camps. These *patrones* promised to give the Tomaraho protection from abuses and work as tree-cutters. By this time, the Tomaraho had lost so many people that they formed a single residential group.

The logging camp where the Tomaraho settled was in the interior of the Chaco, away from the Paraguay River. The Tomaraho men cut wood, and the women provided sexual and domestic services to the Paraguayan overseers and workers. The Tomaraho remained in this camp for almost fifty years, until 1986. During this time, they had little or no contact with missionaries or other indigenistas. The Paraguayan overseers and workers allowed the Tomaraho to perform debylylta and did not try to transform them, aside from expecting them to be obedient and productive workers. Thus, although the living conditions in the camp were such that their numbers kept decreasing year after year, the Tomaraho were able to transmit their ritual knowledge and associated values to the younger generations without much direct interference. This was not the case with the Ebitoso.

According to some Ebitoso, the Catholic priests and nuns at Ylhirta did not attack the Yshiro's beliefs as ferociously as the NTM missionaries did in Puerto Diana. The Yshiro leader Bruno Barras told me that he thought Catholic missionaries were more tolerant because they saw Yshiro's beliefs as simple superstition. In contrast, the first New Tribes missionaries understood those beliefs to be an expression of the devil. Barras based his assessment on his experiences with both sets of missionaries. When he was ten years old, he was taken into a Catholic boarding school, where he remained for two or three years. Later, in his early twenties, he was trained by, and worked with, the New Tribes missionaries as a teacher. When I asked him to narrate how some Ebitoso had become Christians, he responded,

> They [New Tribes missionaries] first befriended Cleto [a mature Ebitoso man] and made him a teacher. They gave him gifts. That's how they prepared their teachers. They visited people, giving gifts or some aid [food, clothing, and medicines] in order to gain their friendship. . . . Eventually these women [the missionaries] came with their [Ebitoso] friends to the sacred place, the *tobich*, and discussions and disagreements began to spread among the men. The Ebitoso almost fought each

other because some were on the side of the missionaries and others were on the side of the culture. Little by little, more people sided with the missionaries and the others have to ask for permission to do debylylta. This minority group got smaller and smaller until they asked permission for one last ritual. My grandfather says that many cried because they saw that their culture was going to disappear. It was 1956 when the ritual was abandoned and many embraced evangelism. . . . They [missionaries] did not understand that [the ritual] was our belief and they said, "If you keep on doing this you are all going to die little by little because you are doing something improper, but if you join the mission you will see things differently because this is a diabolic ceremony and it is not good for you." Many things they said. And this is how the Ebitoso abandoned their rituals . . . the joy of our own games, the healthy foods, the extraordinary happiness, all of that faded away as the Yshiro became Christians. (16 July 1996, tape recording)

Although different commentators have different interpretations about the arrival of the missionaries, it is clear that for most Yshiro the abandonment of debylylta epitomizes the changes that had been operating since the arrival of the whites. Don Vaso, who was very fond of the missionaries, had a perspective on their arrival that differed from Bruno's.

Before, there were lots of Yshiro, but then too many of them died. There was no cure when they got sick. The people cleared a circle . . . and performed their ritual. . . . Then two young women [the New Tribes missionaries] arrived and they made friends with Cleto, they gave him gifts. Then they came where the ritual was being performed. It was prohibited for a woman to enter there, in the *tobich*. The elders rushed over to kill those women, but Cleto stopped them. He said that it would be better to befriend them. So the two women stayed. . . . Before, the Yshiro had no religion, they only knew the Anabsero. They dressed up and sang all day. Then the missionaries told us about the Bible. They told us that in the Bible it is said that we should not do debylylta anymore because we were all going to die. They said we have to recognize the Lord Jesus, to save ourselves. . . . They preached and gave medicine to the people, and taught the Yshiro to read the Bible. So, these missionary ladies stayed here for a while but there was a *patron* here. He used to give work to the

Yshiro. He expelled the ladies. He did not want the missionaries to teach the Yshiro to read and to know how to keep their accounts. Because he was a mean man and he expelled the missionaries, he later fell in the river and the piranha ate him. Then the ladies stayed and gave us medicines. They took care of us. You see my children, they are all alive because they saved them. (15 September 1999, tape recording)

Regardless of how people now value the arrival of the missionaries, it is clear in their stories that, due to a series of circumstances, the Ebitoso who wanted to practice the initiation ritual became increasingly powerless to stop the missionaries from interfering and convincing people not to participate in them. The evangelizing of the missionaries certainly produced frictions with some Ebitoso, yet these frictions were mollified by the missionaries' offerings of aid in the form of food, medicines, tools, and clothing. In a context of growing insecurity created by diseases as well as the withdrawal of old *patrones* and the arrival of new ones, this aid provided some relief for the predicaments the Ebitoso faced. For example, many elders say that by the time the missionaries came, the ancient powerful konsaho had almost disappeared and that those who remained were unable to cope with the new diseases. The medicines brought by the missionaries were of much help (see Susnik 1995: 217–35); and, as Don Vaso hinted, literacy provided a partial defense against the most blatant stratagems that the whites deployed with regard to the Yshiro. Aid in the form of food also became a critical resource for the Yshiro when there was no work available. In addition to all this was the always present dissuasive force of the army, as well as the ways in which the Yshiro's own subsistence had become intertwined with the whites' economic activities and implicit values. Whether due to conviction or to coercion, depending on who tells the story, the Ebitoso performed the last initiation ritual in 1956.

The process unfolded in a different way for the Tomaraho. The company that owned the logging camp where the Tomaraho settled was the last to close down. Yet, once it stopped producing tannin, it continued to exploit other wood products and ventured into cattle raising. The Tomaraho therefore continued to subsist through a mix of labor for the company and of noncommercial hunting. As the years passed and the logging company became increasingly diffident in relation to the Tomaraho, the latter grew more reliant on subsistence hunting to survive. However, as cattle ranches proliferated and wire fences were raised, hunting became less and less reliable, leading to an accelerating decline of the Tomaraho population, which by the 1980s was near final collapse. Unlike the Ebitoso, the Tomaraho received no aid from missionaries or the government, and so were not subject to the processes that the Ebitoso experienced.

Aid, Patronage, and Leadership

The aid that the missionaries provided, in the form of food, clothes, tools, and medicines, became critical for the survival of Ebitoso families when for any reason *patrones* were not offering work or credit was insufficient. When aid came directly from the state, either through the military or the Colorado Party, it usually became part of the "business" circuit, since it would be used at the discretion of the military authorities, state employees, or party officials who acted as *patrones* in hunting activities to reinforce the bonds between themselves and the hunters.

The complementarity between established patron-client relations and the state-driven development promoted by missionaries had profound repercussions in how resources (food, market goods, tools, and the like) circulated within the Ebitoso communities. Until the arrival of the missionaries, the circulation of resources among the Ebitoso was still shaped by a combination of clan and gender ascription, by age ranks, and by the composition of residential groups, which were mostly formed by uxorilocal extended families.[8] The abandonment of the initiation ritual due to missionary pressures deepened the process that had started with the incorporation of the whites' foods, which had no regulations regarding consumption (Susnik 1995:97–98). That is, the abandonment of the initiation ritual intensified the Ebitoso's progressive disregard for age, clan, and gender considerations in the distribution and consumption of food. Along the way, the nuclear family displaced the uxorilocal extended family as the basic unit of distribution and consumption (see Susnik 1995:169–71; Renshaw 1996:174).

New values, of course, played an important role throughout this displacement. Susnik (1995:92–93), for example, mentions that, by 1968, younger couples were emphasizing the possession of market goods as a symbol of prestige, a notion most strongly embraced by those who had developed close rapport with the missionaries and their ideas of work and progress. Susnik argues that the new values, which centered on the nuclear family, conspired against the maintenance of reciprocal ties beyond the closest relatives. The intensification of debt-bondage relations also contributed to changing family patterns, especially since the "hunting *patrones*" allowed only the hunter's nuclear family to acquire food through credit while the hunter was away (see Susnik 1995:88–95). All this ultimately reshaped networks of sharing within the communities. Today, although sharing usually extends beyond the nuclear family, and ideally should involve the whole residential group, the tendency is to restrict sharing to the closest kin (see Renshaw 1996:149).

The combined effect of patronage and development through aid also prompted the emergence of new forms of leadership. When the ethnographer Branislava Susnik visited Diana for the first time, in 1955, people told her that Cleto, the "friend of the missionaries," had displaced the old polo-tak Curbit as the "person in charge" of the community (Susnik 1957b:6). This may be an indication of shifts in what criteria were used to determine the authority of Ebitoso leadership. A polotak's authority was, during the laissez-faire period, predicated on their age, their prestige among peers of the tobich, their skills at negotiating with the *patrones* of the logging camps, and their capacity to mobilize groups of laborers, either through persuasion or by activating bonds of reciprocity established through the initiation rituals (see Susnik 1957b:119–26, 1995:43–45, 90–97; Cordeu 1989c:568). Polotaks progressively lost authority and influence along with the elders in general. As many contemporary elders say, "[When we were younger] we did not want to hear the *agalio* [advice] of the elders. Those were old words and each one wanted to do things in his or her own way" (14 June 1995, field notes).

In the late 1950s, Ebitoso individuals would become leaders (of a sort) based on their relations with particular *patrones*, who would provide them with reliable access to credit and aid, which they would in turn distribute among their followers. These individuals were leaders "of a sort" because they wielded influence, rather than authority. Indeed, these influential individuals were able to maintain a leadership role only as long as they could position themselves at nodal points in the network through which market goods circulated into the Ebitoso communities. In this sense, patronage networks and networks of circulation and distribution were in many senses intertwined with each other. Since networks of circulation and distribution were shaped also by kinship, the latter also became intertwined with patronage networks.

Given the importance that market goods acquired for the Ebitoso's subsistence between the late 1950s and the mid-1980s, networks of circulation and distribution, and kinship alliances became centered around the relations between certain Ebitoso individuals and the *patrones* who provided market goods on credit. Since there were several *patrones*, many loosely bounded groups or networks extended from the relation between specific "influential" Ebitoso individuals and specific *patrones* (see Renshaw 1996:234–38). In these networks, circulation and distribution had a centripetal character: the farther in terms of kinship any individual or family was from the influential individual at the center of the network, the less access they had to the circulating goods. While those Ebitoso closer to the center of the network had more secure access to credit from *patrones*, this security came at a price, for they were under greater pressure to respond to their *patrones'* demands than were those in the outskirts of the network. Moreover, the latter obtained some degree of economic security by being situated at the intersection of several circulation networks. Although less reliable, this arrangement provided a greater margin of independence from particular *patrones*. In any case, the networks of circulation and distribution were by no means straightforward, as those individuals who were closer to the center in a given network could be on the outskirts of another. However, those who were at the center of a network through which market goods circulated were under great pressure to be responsive to the demands of their *patrones*. These demands varied depending on whether the *patrones* were involved in the trade of animal hides or in missionary work (for the latter ended up acting as *patrones*, too).

In the patronage network connected to commercial hunting, an individual could position himself (the role of women in hunting activities was irrelevant for *patrones*) at the center of a circulation or distribution network by possessing good hunting skills and by maintaining a good balance in his account. Paraguayan *patrones* economically enticed these "trustworthy employees" to take responsibility for large credits for groups of hunters. In this way, the *patron* handed down to a few influential individuals or *encargados* (person in charge) the task of discerning those who were trustworthy and deserved credit from those who did not deserve it. This implied that encargados had to be especially careful and selective with regard to whom they would extend the benefit of credit, and they usual restricted it to their closer kin. This form of restricted circulation and distribution was resented by those relatives of influential individuals who were located beyond its reach and mistrusted by those who were at its borders. As a consequence, the influence of these encargados was always on shaky ground. The more successful they were in securing the trust of their *patrones* by carefully selecting who deserved credit, the more they became the target of gossip and resentment among those community members who were less close to them.

In the patronage network that extended from the missionaries (Catholic in Fuerte Olimpo, New Tribes Mission in Diana), an individual could position himself or herself at the center of a circulation or distribution network by responding to the missionaries' demands to abandon the "old ways." By refraining from practices such as the initiation ritual, ritual chanting, fasting, storytelling, retelling of visionary dreams, and the like, an individual would receive aid and in many cases administer the distribution of aid in the community. According to several Ebitoso, the NTM missionaries also demanded that the Ebitoso convert to Christianity, send their children to school, show work discipline, and participate in biblical studies.[9] In the community of Diana, as a consequence of these demands, those families who were closer to the missionaries ended up being among the most literate and shared to a greater extent than others the missionaries' discourses about progress. Moreover, the missionaries handed down responsibilities to those individuals and families who, in their views, had made more "progress," that is, those who had moved away from everything that the missionaries considered Indian. For example, Cleto, the man who initially befriended the missionaries, and who Susnik described as being "very acculturated," became the first teacher, the first Yshiro pastor, and the first Yshiro to administer the store opened by the missionaries.[10]

If, as Ferguson (1990) argued, development's instrument-effect is the extension of the state's bureaucratic power, then in the Paraguayan context development extended a form of power which was expressed through an all-pervasive patronage system that reached deep into the Ebitoso communities. The extension of patronage networks was not a deviant form of development; it was, rather, the specific way in which "development" materialized in this particular setting (see Barreto 1996). Concrete development projects for indigenous peoples of the Chaco amounted to little more than the granting of aid. This form of development directly or indirectly (by complementing the system of debt-bondage common in the area) contributed to the displacement of earlier forms of Ebitoso authority and the emergence of new ones that were compatible with, and further contributed to, the process of asymmetrical entanglement between the yrmo and the modern world. Thus, the (corpo)realization of modernity and the invisibilization of the yrmo, concurrently achieved through openly violent coercion at the beginning of the twentieth century, were stabilized and expanded through euphemized forms of coercion embodied by state-driven development. In this sense, although with a language that varied from that of laissez-faire progress, the hegemonic coincidence continued to play a central role in the way the whites related to the Ebitoso. Consequently, while the Ebitoso's life could not be totally engineered, as development rhetoric claimed, the hegemonic coincidence effectively narrowed the space within which those lives could unfold. Enacting the yrmo became thus restricted to its less conspicuous (from the settlers' point of view) forms. However, by the beginning of the 1970s, the "hegemonic coincidence" and the imaginations that sustained it began to unravel.

Three Sustainable Development

From the 1940s onward, in Paraguay and elsewhere in Latin America, concerns for the fate of Indians was increasingly framed in terms of the "rights of man" (see Belaieff 1941:1–3), which were closely associated with notions of progress or, in its latest incarnation, state-driven integrationist development. Indeed, the precursors of both international legislation and institutions concerned with indigenous peoples, such as the International Labor Organization's Convention 107, the Anti-Slavery Society, and the Inter-American Indigenist Institute, were concerned with racism and discrimination against indigenous peoples insofar as these attitudes were understood to constrain indigenous peoples' rights to be fully incorporated into modern society or, what is the same, to enjoy the benefits of development. In this sense, the hegemonic coincidence articulated through the imagination Indians remained highly stable for several decades.

In 1968, a potential point of rupture started to become visible when participants at the Thirty-eighth International Conference of Americanists, in Stuttgart, passed a resolution criticizing nation-states which violated the Universal Declaration of Human Rights in the process of integrating indigenous peoples into their national societies. The International Work Group for Indigenous Affairs (IWGIA), which was founded at this meeting, promoted a resolution of the same kind at the Eighth Congress of Anthropological and Ethnological Sciences, in September of the same year (Wilmer 1993:141). In the next meeting of Americanists, held in Lima, Peru, in 1970, a resolution was passed calling for a "guarantee of the indigenes' rights to be themselves and express their own culture, without being subjected to duress in the form of assimilationist programmes or catechetical programmes of a sectarian or intolerant nature" (Martinez Cobo 1986:209). The emergence of this anti-integrationist agenda, and of the international indigenous advocacy network that promoted it, was to a large extent a product of the complex ferment instigated by anticolonial and nonaligned struggles in the Third World, the formation of an international network of human-rights advocates, and social mobilizations fueled by environmental concerns. These developments have had a profound impact on the core imaginations of the modern myth.

Mutating Imaginations

Increasingly since the mid-1960s and peaking in the early 1970s, the Catholic Church changed its "traditionally" uncritical attitude toward the Paraguayan state and entered into direct confrontation with the Stroessner regime over social and political issues (Carter 1992:63–88). The theology of liberation, influenced by the revolutionary environment of the 1960s, changed the way in which many members of the clergy saw the Catholic Church's role in society and thus contributed an important institutional space for "progressive projects" targeting Paraguay's indigenous peoples (Vysokolan 1983: 32; Susnik and Chase-Sardi 1995:325–27). Among these projects, Marandú ("information," in Guarani) stands out for its objectives and for its effects on the Paraguayan indigenista field. The project—inspired by the Barbados Declaration (International Work Group for Indigenous Affairs 1971), which, among other things, demanded that the state respect indigenous peoples' right to be different—was part of the widespread process of organization building that, throughout the 1970s, shaped the transnational indigenous-rights movement, composed of both indigenous organizations and non-indigenous support organizations (see Sanders 1977; Bodley 1982; Van Cott 1994; Wilmer 1993; Ramos 1998; Kay B. Warren 1998; Albó 1999; Brysk 2000).

The Paraguayan indigenista Miguel Chase-Sardi, a signatory of the Barbados Declaration, enlisted the support of IWGIA for Marandú. Later, Survival International (London) and the Inter-American Foundation also became sponsors of the project. Among the objectives of Marandú were to inform indigenous peoples of their rights; to train leaders in organizational skills, with the aim of creating an indigenous organization of national scope; to connect this organization with international support groups; and to promote a national campaign of education in order to fight the racism against indigenous peoples that was rampant in Paraguay (Chase-Sardi and Colombres 1975; Bodley 1982:207–9; Susnik and Chase-Sardi 1995:326–27; Horst 1998:257).

In 1974, members of Marandú joined the anthropologist Mark Munzel and IWGIA in publicly blaming the Paraguayan government and some Paraguayan indigenistas for their complicity in genocidal practices against the Ache-Guayaki in the eastern region of Paraguay (see Münzel 1973, 1974). Formal complaints were filed before the Organization of American States and the UN Sub-Commission for Prevention of Discrimination and Protection of Minorities under the auspices of the Anti-Slavery Society of London and the International League for the Rights of Man of New York. In October 1975, to counter the increasingly successful lobbying efforts of the human-rights network on the Carter administration in the United States, the Stroessner regime reorganized the Department of Indigenous Affairs and renamed it Instituto Nacional del Indígena (INDI). According to Decree no. 18,365, while INDI remained under the jurisdiction of the military, its new task was "to plan and execute development programs for Indigenous peoples *while respecting their cultures*" (cited in Horst 1998:246, emphasis added; also see Bejarano 1976:238).

The regime did not forget that Marandú's members had supported Munzel's public complaint against the genocidal practices of the Paraguayan government. As with any critic of the status quo in Paraguay, the government and some indigenistas depicted Marandú as a communist threat to "National Security" (see Bejarano 1976:109; Horst 1998:219–38; Yore 1992). In December 1975, during a wave of repression, several members of Marandú were imprisoned and tortured, and the project was terminated (Susnik and Chase-Sardi 1995:328–29; Horst 1998:248–49). However, international pressures forced the Paraguayan government to release the prisoners and to allow indigenous leaders who had worked with Marandú to create the Asociación de Parcialidades Indígenas (API), an indigenous organization of national scope (see Sanders 1977:26). While the regime ceded to international pressures, it also tried to capitalize on this move, by depicting itself as tolerant of dissidents, without losing control over the indigenista field. Due to the existence of INDI, which had been authorized to oversee all activities related to indigenous peoples' affairs, the government trusted that conditions were such that it could retain for itself the role of gatekeeper in the indigenista field.

The events of the first half of the 1970s showed that in Paraguay the hegemonic coincidence had come to an end. The indigenista field now formed an arch which had at its ends two opposing stances. On one end were those who not only questioned the legitimacy of the use of coercion to integrate indigenous peoples into national society, but contested the foundations of the integrationist agenda altogether. In effect, they argued that indigenous cultures were valuable on their own terms and were not just the remnants of a universal evolutionary path, marking with this argument a rupture with the modernist storyline that had dominated until then. This stance or agenda, which I will call critical indigenismo, echoed the positions sustained by the then emerging transnational indigenous-rights movement. Since its inception in the Paraguayan context, critical indigenismo largely depended on the international network associated with the indigenous-rights movement for funding and other forms of support. On the other end of the arch stood those who, although rejecting coercive means, continued to favor a model of development that implied the integration and eventual disappearance of Indians as distinct societies. This stance or agenda, which I will call integrationist indigenismo, was more clearly represented by the state's INDI and a group of dependent institutions.[1]

Few indigenistas clearly and explicitly adopted either stance; most located themselves somewhere between these poles. Many individual indigenistas circulated as staff from institutions aligned with one stance to institutions aligned with the other. In general, regardless of their inclinations, indigenistas maintained some degree of collaboration on specific projects, especially during API's first years. Yet the association of critical indigenismo with a transnational network produced a fundamental shift in the whole dynamics of the indigenista field. In effect, critical indigenismo had brought into these dynamics a transnational human-rights network with the capacity to influence a transnational public of decision-makers and the flow of development aid toward the Stroessner regime. This public became an ever-present interlocutor, which played both audience and arbiter of the struggles waged by Paraguayan indigenistas (see Susnik and Chase-Sardi 1995:330; Robbins 1999:116–17; Horst 1998:150–250).

With their mobilization on behalf of the imprisoned staff from Marandú, this human-rights network proved its capacity to effectively pressure the regime, which quickly moved to appease it by convoking several indige-nista institutions and the API in order to discuss the situation of Paraguay's indigenous peoples. The meeting, convened in 1978, was aimed at drafting the Estatuto de las Comunidades Indígenas (Statutes of Indigenous Com-munities), which, in 1981, was passed as Law 904/81 (Robbins 1999:116–22; Kidd 1997a:116; Horst 1998:253–348). The law refuted two "corollaries" of the hegemonic coincidence, that is, that Indians had to be transformed in the name of progress and development, and that pedagogic violence could be used when needed to enforce this transformation. In effect, article 1 of Law 904/81 declared that the law's aim was "the social and cultural preser-vation of the Indigenous communities [and] the defense of their patrimony and traditions." Article 4, in turn, said that "under no circumstance will the use of force or coercion be accepted as a means to promote the integration of Indigenous communities into the national society" (Instituto Nacional del Indígena 1998).

Considering these articles, one could say that Law 904/81 embodied the end of the hegemonic coincidence. Moreover, insofar as the law embodied the notion that indigenous peoples are subjects with the specific right to be themselves, it is legitimate to infer that one is starting to deal with an imagination Indian that has mutated to the point of being something else: the imagination Indigenous Peoples.[2] The imagination Indigenous Peoples thus emerges as something related but distinguishable from the imagina-tion Indians. One aspect of this distinctiveness is that indigenous peoples are subjects with rights as indigenous peoples and, therefore, that their dif-ference and their autonomy as subjects must be respected. However, ac-ceptance by nation-states and development institutions of the "right" to be different has been slow, when not merely rhetorical or superficial.

The international human-rights network played a fundamental role in denouncing gross human-rights violations perpetrated by Latin American governments against indigenous peoples. As exemplified by the Ache-Guayaki case, international human-rights activists were able to lobby donor countries and multilateral organizations in order to make development aid conditional on a recipient country's record of human rights (Sanders 1977:25–26; Tomasevski 1993:84–85; Keck and Sikkink 1998:102–3). However, the international human-rights network lacked the capacity to transform the integrationist development policies of national states. Once the worst violations of human rights were addressed, it remained difficult for indigenous peoples and their advocates to convey the idea that integrationist development agendas could constitute violations of (indigenous) human rights per se (see Bodley 1982; Brysk 2000:202–3; Davis 1977:166–68; Wright 1988:368–71). Not until the late 1980s and early 1990s did international development institutions recognize (at least rhetorically) the need to move beyond mitigating the impacts produced by integrationist development toward actively promoting indigenous visions of development (see Burger 1998; Davis 1993; Deruyttere 1997; Kreimer 1998; Sanders 1998; Swepston 1998; Tomasevski 1993:67–68).

In the Chaco, only in the mid-1980s did critical indigenistas and anthropologists begin to express doubts about the wisdom of promoting development projects that were based on outsiders' objectives and values. They began to ponder whether the neglect of indigenous peoples' objectives and values could explain the repeated failures of development projects based on agricultural schemes (see Regehr 1984; Robbins 1984; Seelwische 1984; Stunnenberg 1991:34–39). Building on these ideas, other anthropologists, such as Volker Von Bremen (1987, 2000) and John Renshaw (1988, 1996), argued that development projects failed in the Chaco because they were based on an agriculturalist mentality or ethic that was antithetical to the mentality or ethic of the indigenous peoples who inhabited the region. The mentality or ethic to which Von Bremen and Renshaw made reference was assumed to be determined by the indigenous peoples' hunter-gatherer way of life.

Von Bremen (1987, 2000), who elaborated the most popular version of this idea, argued that indigenous peoples of the Chaco are hunter-gatherers who live in harmony with nature and thus do not transform it. Rather, they adapt to it and gather whatever nature has already produced. According to Von Bremen, this way of life underscores a "philosophy of passivity" through which indigenous peoples of the Chaco interpret the new circumstances produced by the contact. This philosophy induces indigenous peoples to learn the details of their environment in order to recognize when and where there would be an abundance of resources necessary for their survival. This is a philosophy of passivity in the sense that indigenous peoples' knowledge is oriented not around transforming the environment to make it productive but to anticipating where the fruits of its natural productivity will be available. Looked at through the lens of this philosophy, and to the extent that they offer freely available goods, development projects would appear to indigenous peoples as (modern) hunting and gathering grounds where resources abound. Von Bremen concludes that development projects fail because they try to convert people whose mentality is averse to transforming nature (i.e., hunter-gatherers) into people who do transform it (i.e., agriculturalists), thus missing the actual way in which indigenous peoples engage with development.[3]

The impact of these ideas in the Paraguayan indigenista field was enormous.[4] Every indigenista or anthropologist working in the Paraguayan Chaco, at one time or another, criticized integrationist development or explained the dynamics between indigenous peoples and the whites by reference to the hunting-gathering mentality (see Asociación Rural del Paraguay 1994; Delport 1998; Fritz 1993; Kidd 1995a, 1995b; Miller 1989; Prieto and Bragayrac 1995; Rojas 1996). In other words, this new imagination, in which the Chaco Indians were characterized as hunter-gatherers, became an "authorized imagination" with the status of a paradigm. For those opposed to integrationist development, the hunter-gatherer paradigm suggested a form of development which would not only be culturally appropriate for indigenous peoples of the Chaco, but would also be beneficial for the environment (see Von Bremen 1994; Kidd 1995a; Serafina Alvarez 1995; Grunberg 1997). In the midst of heightened "environmental awareness" (Lanthier and Olivier 1999), the trope of the environmentally attuned Indian proved to be somehow useful for indigenous peoples and their advocates in Paraguay and elsewhere, as it provided a platform to build the argument that indigenous peoples' ways of life were, if not models to adopt, at least models to preserve alongside the environment. In addition to embracing already circulating romanticized visions of indigenous peoples living in idyllic harmony with nature, anthropologists and other development professionals, seeking to make indigenous ways of life agreeable to technocratic consumers, found this argument very compelling (Ellen and

Harris 2000:12–14; see also Conklin and Graham 1995; Conklin 1997). Allison Brysk (1994) has argued that indigenous movements and their supporters shifted the focus of their actions toward "environmental regimes" because of the limitations of "human-rights regimes." However, this shift of focus also indicates that indigenous movements and their supporters recognized the opportunity presented by the impact of and the value changes that accompanied the mutation of the imagination Nature into the imagination Environment.

In the late 1960s a combination of factors, including some widely publicized environmental crises (such as acid rain and oil spills) and the cultural criticism of advanced industrial societies' insatiable materialism, pushed a reconsideration of the environmental costs of development to the doorsteps of industrialized countries' decision-makers (Dalton 1993:50–53; Keck and Sikkink 1998:122–23). Although the history of environmental concerns, movements, organizations, and policies goes back well beyond the twentieth century (Bramwell 1989; Worster 1977; Grove 1995), in the late 1960s a new perception of the relation between Nature and Culture began to gain influence in key decision-making bodies in North America and Western Europe, further contributing to the mutation of the imagination Nature into the imagination Environment.

When, in the mid- to late 1980s, environmental activism became a full-fledged transnational movement, it became clear that the "needs" of Nature could no longer be dismissed in the pursuit of Progress but required some manner of accommodation. Various positions, ranging from deep ecology to the pricing of nature and everything in between, clashed, mixed, and modified each other as they were promoted, attacked, and defended by social movements, political and interest groups, governments, NGOs, and all kinds of institutions and organizations (see Conca and Dabelko 2004; Ramachandra Guha 2000; Hajer 1995; Keck and Sikkink 1998). From this ferment, further complicated by the enmeshment of technology and biology, has emerged the imagination Environment. While retaining traces of its ancestor (Nature), this imagination has some important new characteristics, two of which bear mention here. The first is that the distinction between Environment and Culture is not as stark as that between Nature and Culture; the boundaries are blurred. The second and related characteristic is that Environment is endowed with an autonomy that must be reckoned with.[5] In contrast to Nature, Environment is not simply an object, and thus only certain types of interventions on it are legitimate. This point is further substantiated if one considers how the mutation of Nature into Environment, as well as the mutation of Indians into Indigenous Peoples, unfolded along with the mutation of the imagination Progress into the imagination Risk.

Risk and the (Corpo)realization of the Global Condition

Recent sociological works have interpreted the increasing salience of risk as indicative of a profound transformation of modernity (see Beck 1992, 1994, 1999; Beck, Giddens, and Lash 1994; Giddens 1990; Giddens and Pierson 1998; Lash, Szerszynski, and Wynne 1996). Beck, for example, argues that not only "actually existing environmental risks," but also the very perception that risks of all kinds are pervasive changes the orientation of modern society from being concerned with the distribution of the fruits of "progress" to managing its unexpected, and often harmful, consequences. In addition, the role that experts play in (inadvertently) producing risks and their mutually contradictory claims about the nature of those risks erode their credibility and authority. The combination of risks and the loss of authority by experts sweeps away the certainties that sustained modernization (simple modernity, in Beck's terms), especially the belief in progress. Thus, in contrast to modernization, whose main ontological dynamic (i.e., progress) was represented in the mastery of nature, the salient feature of globalization (reflexive modernity, in Beck's terms) is society's concern with managing itself and its main product, risk; hence Beck's labeling of this new reality as "risk society."

According to Beck, the concept of risk society "combines *what once was mutually exclusive*—society and nature, social sciences and material sciences, the discursive construction of risk and the materiality of threats" (1999:4, emphasis added). The current situation, Beck argues, has superseded the separate concepts of nature and society (or culture). For example, using nature (or "the world out there") as a reference for correct action rests on "a naturalistic misunderstanding" because "the nature invoked is *no longer* there. . . . What is there, and what creates such political stir, are different forms of socialization and different symbolic mediations of nature (and the destruction of nature)" (Beck 1999:21, emphasis added). These different "cultural concepts of nature" are behind experts and lay-people's disputes about risk (Beck 1999:21). Thus, for Beck, risks are not strictly problems of "the world out there," but a deep institutional crisis of (simple) modernity (Beck 1999:33).

The crisis described by Beck is fundamentally one of knowing in a context in which both the ontological dualism nature-culture and the ontological dynamic of progress on which modern knowledge and certainties were based have been radically transformed (Beck 1992:166, 223, 1994:33). The incapacity of (simple) modernity's institutions to address this crisis promotes the emergence of subpolitics, that is, "politics outside and beyond the representative institutions of the political system of nation-states" (Beck 1999:39). Subpolitics imply individual and collective participation (through social movements and NGOs) in political decisions, including those decisions that before were the exclusive concern of experts, for example, development projects. And, indeed, the transformation of development into sustainable development constitutes a good example of the kinds of symptoms that signal the mutation of the imagination Progress into the imagination Risk.

It is useful to compare passages from two documents that are emblematic of two moments in the history of development. The first passage comes from President Harry Truman's inaugural discourse, in what has been regarded as the launching of the "development era": "For the first time in history humanity possesses the knowledge and the skill to relieve the suffering of [the poor of the world]. . . . Greater production is the key to prosperity and peace. And the key to greater production is a wider and more vigorous application of modern scientific and technical knowledge" (Truman [1949], cited in Arturo Escobar 1995:3). The second passage comes from the World Commission on Environment and Development's (WCED) report, *Our Common Future*, which is considered to be a ground-setting statement for sustainable development (see Conca and Dabelko 2004): "Humanity's inability to fit its doings into [the natural cycles of the globe] is changing planetary systems, fundamentally. Many such changes are accompanied by life-threatening hazards. This new reality, from which there is no escape, must be recognized—and managed" (World Commission on Environment and Development 1987:1). From the first passage to the second is a clear shift of attitude. Truman's statement is full of certainty and trust in human capacities, fundamentally in science and technology; it is an aggressive and self-confident stance against the maladies afflicting humanity. The WCED's statement, in contrast, is ominous, hopeful yet uncertain about and assuming a defensive posture against the effects of human action. The first statement is imbued by the spirit of Progress, the second by the presence of Risk.

The passage from *Our Common Future* clearly reflects how sustainable development emerged first and foremost from the same ferment in which the imagination Environment started to take shape. In this sense, Risk was charged with overtones of environmental doom. However, by the early 1990s, the notion of sustainable development, and by extension the imagination Risk, had become much more complex and comprehensive. For example, issues not obviously related to the environment are woven into the Rio Declaration and Agenda 21, the general guidelines for sustainable development agreed on by several governments during the UN Earth Summit in 1992. The preamble of Agenda 21 declares,

> Humanity stands at a defining moment in history. We are confronted with a perpetuation of disparities between and within nations, a worsening of poverty, hunger, ill health and illiteracy, and the continuing deterioration of the ecosystems on which we depend for our well-being. However, integration of environment and development concerns and greater attention to them will lead to the fulfilment of basic needs, improved living standards for all, better protected and managed ecosystems and a safer, more prosperous future.[6]

Environmental *and* social risks are thus established as the background and rationale for a series of principles and practical procedures that delineate the specific economic and political formation needed to achieve the goal of integrating environmental and development concerns.[7] The implicit assumption that risks can only be confronted by specific political and economic formations has two important corollaries that would not surprise Mary Douglas: first, the legitimacy of these formations becomes a function of whether or not they address risk; and second, illegitimate political and economic formations and practices are not only morally wrong, but also risky. As a reading of the principles and procedures proposed by the

Rio Declaration and Agenda 21 makes clear, in the early 1990s most governments considered neoliberal political and economic formations as those most appropriate for confronting risks. Certainly, risks could be and have been construed in such a way as to require political and economic formations that are the antithesis of those propounded by neoliberalism. Precisely because of its ambiguities, "sustainable development" has lent itself to the embrace of organizations and movements with radically different views about what political and economic formations are necessary to avert the risk of environmental doom (see Ekins 1993; Worster 1993; Adams 1995). This is what happened in Paraguay when notions of sustainable development became part of the indigenista field, a development best understood in light of the significance that the emergence of new imaginations have had for the modern myth.

Doubtless, the emerging imaginations Indigenous Peoples, Environment, and Risk are so much shaped by traces of their ancestors Indians, Nature, and Progress that the distinctions between terms may seem immaterial. However, the use of different terms does help to highlight that the central imaginations of the modern myth have undergone fundamental transformations. I have intentionally provided an incomplete and superficial account of the extent of these transformations and the processes by which they took place, in order to create a puruhle narrative; that is, I have arranged bits and bites of other narrations (the cited works) to tell a story whose purpose is not to provide a detailed account of how the imaginations Indigenous Peoples, Environment, and Risk came into being, but rather to draw attention to the features that distinguish them from their "ancestors." It also would be futile to try establishing simple relations of causality between the mutation of one imagination and the mutation of another; coemergence through mutual resonance offers a better way to understand the shaping of new imaginations. In this sense, one can recognize in the multiple challenges to state-driven integrationist development traces of those resonances.

One of the features that distinguishes Indigenous Peoples and Environment from Indians and Nature, respectively, is that the former are endowed with autonomy—they are ends in themselves and not mere objects in the hands of a modern subject. Thus, the so-called environmental crisis and the Indigenous peoples' demands to shape their own destinies can be seen as the reassertion of the agency of that which the modern myth had relegated to the role of object without agency.[8] The resurgence of these invisibilized "agents" throws into disarray the assumptions grounding the modern problematic of how to know in moral and practical or instrumental ways, as well as that problematic's existing answers. In effect, the resulting questions have to be addressed in a context in which "objects" do not stay in their places, but rather cross the great divide and become subjects. In other words, these questions must be addressed in conditions where the assumed grounds for objective knowledge and certainty have become shaky and where the unruly behavior of objects casts doubt on the whole idea of Progress as the teleological story of the "modern subject's" ever increasing mastery over "his" "objects and others" (i.e., Nature and Indians). Thus, in the process of authorization, or emergence, of the imaginations Indigenous Peoples, Environment, and Risk, one can glimpse the (corpo)realization of a global condition which carries with it a specific problematic.

Constitutive, in part, of the global condition and its problematic are the blurring of the modern distinction between object and subject (and all related dualisms), a reconsideration of the meaning of temporal succession, and the consequent repositioning of modern politics, morality, and epistemology in a context of uncertainty and risk. Unlike Beck and others who interpret this condition as resulting from modernization's alteration of the very fabric of reality tout court, one could be more circumspect and argue that modernization eroded its own conditions of possibility as a myth.[9] The process of (corpo)realizing modernity (i.e., modernization) has stirred the increasingly visible resistance of those entities that modernity intended to make into objects. In this sense, the global condition can be understood as the increasing difficulty the modern project has in keeping the pluriverse invisible and subjugated. The imaginations Indigenous Peoples, Environment, and Risk are the outgrowth of this dynamics "inside" the modern myth. That is, they emerge from an unequal relation of power where agentive but invisibilized entities are able through their resistance to change the "terminology" used in what is largely a monologue (the myth of modernity), but do not quite succeed in transforming that monologue into a dialogue. To paraphrase Lins Ribeiro (2001), the new imaginations can be (and are) indigenized, but that does not mean they are indigenous. The Yshiro instead use the new imaginations (and, by extension, the global condition) as a platform from which they seek to force modernity into a dialogue that so far it has refused to engage in.

While the global condition manifests itself as the reassertion of the autonomy and agency of the others and objects of modernity, putting thus into question notions of progress and associated ideas of certainty in modern knowledge, it also manifests in governmental responses (in the widest sense of government as the conduct of conduct) to these challenges. The shift from development to sustainable development can be understood in these terms. Arguably, sustainable development is itself a program of government that claims to be attentive to the regained autonomy of Indigenous Peoples and the Environment by, for example, enrolling their "free" participation.[10] Under these conditions, notions of governance were transformed. The imaginations Indians, Nature, and Progress grounded a restricted liberal governance where concerns about the autonomy of the former two were minimal or nonexistent, and therefore the legitimacy of governing them was assumed. When the environmental and indigenous-rights movements pushed their critique of the anthropocentrism and Eurocentrism of development to center stage, neither the autonomy of the Environment and Indigenous Peoples nor questions of the conditions under which governing them is legitimate could be sidelined as easily (see Hajer 1995:74–94; MacKenzie 1997:7).[11]

Sustainable Development, Surrogated Controversies, and the Politics of Authenticity

In the early days of February 1989, General Stroessner was ousted by a military putsch after thirty-four years in power. General Rodriguez, the leading officer of the rebellion, acted on the perception, held by a sector of the armed forces and the ruling Colorado Party, that a change was necessary to ensure their privileges and benefits in a rapidly changing national and international context. By the late 1970s, U.S. military and economic aid to Paraguay had become tightly constrained. Later, disagreements on drug trafficking and the unwillingness of the Stroessner regime to follow the Southern Cone region's path toward neoliberal structural reforms and democratization caused U.S. cooperation with Paraguay to largely evaporate (Carothers 1991:163–66; Hanratty and Meditz 1990:155, 196–99; Lambert

1996:102–3; Roett and Sacks 1991:67, 148). By 1989, privatization schemes and state structural reforms had become almost automatic conditions that "developing countries" had to meet in order to receive loans from multilateral lending institutions such as the World Bank and the International Monetary Fund. To accept these conditions would have jeopardized the Stroessner regime, since it depended on the state's discretionary use of economic resources to remain in power. In addition, Brazil and Argentina had entered into a process of economic integration that threatened to nullify the significant revenues the regime obtained by smuggling between these two countries.[12] And, by the time of the coup, all of Paraguay's neighboring countries had adopted democratic systems, which contributed to a general repudiation of authoritarian regimes and thus ultimately increased Paraguay's isolation in international arenas.

All of these factors acted in synergy with internal processes such as the economic stagnation that followed the cessation of international funding for development projects; the increasing demands for democratization from civil-society organizations with transnational support; and the fights within the power structure formed by the armed forces, the Colorado Party, and the government to determine the succession of an aging dictator. The leaders of the coup presented it as a step into a "transition" that would make Paraguay a modern democratic society, fully inserted into the world economy and patterned after the model of "advanced democracies." Free elections were promised soon, a national assembly was called to draft a new constitution, and, in 1991, Paraguay joined Argentina, Brazil, and Uruguay in the creation of a regional economic bloc, Mercosur.

The Paraguayan transition has constituted a bewildering and volatile process that, since the democratic election of a civilian president, in 1993, has been marked by two attempted coups, the assassination of a vice-president, the impeachment of one president, a massacre of protesters, virtually uncountable scandals of governmental corruption, and lack of juridical stability.[13] Several ingredients have combined to produce this panorama. First, the transition has been haunted by the fact that it was engineered primarily by the same powerful groups that sustained the Stroessner regime, and the factionalism that besieged the regime in its final years has therefore continued into the so-called democratic period. Second, the

Paraguayan state that emerged from the Stroessner regime was in a certain way already privatized, as its operations were mostly geared to enrich particular individuals in positions of power; thus while external pressures for neoliberal structural reforms have been rhetorically supported by certain sectors, such reform has taken place in the context of strategic maneuvering by dominant groups competing for control of the state and its assets. Third, in these struggles, public resistance to neoliberal economic reforms as well as public support for political reform (i.e., decentralization, fighting corruption, and the like) have been shamelessly manipulated by these powerful groups. Fourth, established parties, rather than expressing wider political projects, mostly reflect the infighting that occurs within the dominant groups, and thus they continuously shift positions, discourses, and alliances. In short, as most common citizens in Paraguay maintain, the terrain of formal politics resembles more a (slightly civil) battleground on which criminal gangs compete than a field of struggle over societal projects. To some extent, the societal struggles have taken place in more circumscribed issue-fields, where progressive forces tend to operate through NGOs and other civil organizations, but without cohering into a common front or agenda. Following from this is the fact that the recently elected progressive president, Fernando Lugo, a former Catholic bishop influenced by the theology of liberation, emerged from the space of social movements, rather than of political parties.

It was in the formative years of this political terrain that a new national constitution, drafted and approved in 1992, incorporated concerns about the Environment into its chapter 1 and about Indigenous Peoples into its chapter 5. The way in which these and other concerns were integrated into the constitutional debates reflected the existing power relations in three kinds of fields: the specific field of a given issue (gender, environment, indigenous peoples, and the like); the national (formal) political field, where dominant groups struggled for the control of state resources; and the international field, where financial institutions exerted strong pressures for neoliberal reforms on the Paraguayan political class. Thus, the inclusion of these chapters in the Paraguayan constitution must not be seen as the design of top-down neoliberal structural reform; rather, top-down structural-reform agendas promoted by international financial institutions resonated and were transformed by the specific conditions of each country, including the relations of force between local dominant groups and between these and diverse social movements that were pushing for democratization.[14]

The promotion of indigenous rights to the rank of constitutional rights, especially the idea that indigenous communities have the right to lands in quantity and quality enough to ensure the conservation and development of their own ways of life (see Constitución Nacional de Paraguay 1992: art. 64), acted as a catalyst that further opposed different visions of development of the Chaco that had been taking shape since the early 1980s, when Law 904/81 was passed.

The passing of Law 904/81, in addition to experiences with development projects during the 1960s and 1970s, modified the critical indigenistas' strategies regarding land and development for indigenous peoples. Until the 1980s, indigenistas had either purchased lands to settle and promote agricultural development projects for indigenous peoples or convinced governments to donate hectares of state land for those purposes. Afterward, critical indigenistas started instead to support indigenous peoples' land claims by pressuring the Stroessner government to abide by Law 904/81 (see Stunnenberg 1993:179–81; Vysokolan 1992:176–78). According to the law (specifically articles 18, 21, and 24), each indigenous community in the Chaco had the right to obtain from the government a minimum of 100 hectares per family composing the community. Whether an indigenous community could receive more than the minimum was determined by the state-run Instituto de Bienestar Rural (Institute of Rural Welfare), which had to guarantee that the amount of land actually granted to an indigenous community would be enough to ensure its economic *and* cultural survival. For example, the calculation of the actual minimum of land necessary for an indigenous community with "agricultural traditions" had to factor in the quantity and quality of land in relation to agricultural practices. This calculation would be different for a community with a "hunting and gathering tradition." By consistently granting the minimum amount of land, the state adopted the implicit integrationist position that small holdings, properly worked (i.e., agriculture), should be sufficient to address the development needs of indigenous peoples. In contrast, critical indigenistas, who were increasingly embracing the hunter-gatherer paradigm, maintained that only large tracts of land could ensure the maintenance of this indigenous way of life and, in addition, ensure the protection of the environment.

With the new constitution, the different indigenista approaches to development differentiated further. In part, this was connected to the (timid) introduction of neoliberal agendas in state policy and wider debates about the development of the country. The downsizing of the state meant that INDI, the governmental institution in charge of indigenous affairs, had even fewer resources with which to actively intervene in the indigenista field, and it therefore became more susceptible to supporting the idea of market-based sustainable development being promoted by the powerful landowners association of Paraguay, Asociación Rural del Paraguay (ARP). ARP entered the indigenista field in the context of a strong campaign, led by critical indigenista NGOs, to force the state to expropriate lands for indigenous peoples. In response, ARP produced its own version of sustainable development for indigenous peoples, which was based on the neoliberal mantra that the market can solve all problems. Thus, it argued that sustainable development would ensue from purchasing lands freely offered in the market (rather than from expropriating those lands), from fully incorporating indigenous peoples into the market economy as laborers and producers, and from ensuring private property as the best form of environmental protection. With the support of some indigenous leaders, ARP claimed that its version of sustainable development, rather than that proposed by the critical indigenistas—which, the ARP claimed, amounted to a projection of their own romanticized view of sustainable development onto the indigenous peoples—was what indigenous peoples really wanted (Asociación Rural del Paraguay 1994). Thus, ironically, ARP joined other indigenistas in attributing their own development agenda to indigenous peoples with the support of client leaders—a practice that had become commonplace in the indigenista field after Law 904/81 had enshrined the idea of respecting the autonomy of indigenous peoples.

Although Law 904/81 incorporated the most basic demands that critical indigenistas and indigenous leaders had pursued (i.e., lands and respect for indigenous cultures), it also gave INDI an important point of leverage with which to manipulate indigenous communities. According to the law, an indigenous community could claim lands only through leaders who had been legally recognized by the state-run INDI. Without such recognition, a leader could not start the process of claiming lands. As a result, indigenous leaders were pressured to maintain good relations with INDI's bureaucrats. The full dimensions of the problem becomes clear if one considers article 3 of the law, which left open a window for integrationist agendas: "Respect for traditional forms of organization does not preclude that, in use of their right for self-determination, Indigenous communities can adopt other forms of organization . . . allowing their integration into the national society" (Instituto Nacional del Indígena 1998:2).

Some critical indigenistas thought that the state had in this way retained its capacity to promote leaders who, in order to obtain land, would comply with the state's goal of integration. Thus, with Law 904/81, the position of indigenous leaders as community representatives became a focal point of controversies between the different sectors of indigenismo. Critical in these debates was "owning" the voice of indigenous leaders, whereby indigenistas supported those leaders who, in more or less subtle ways, would claim that the development agenda of a given sector of Paraguayan indigenismo was coincident with their own communities' visions. As a result, the controversies between indigenistas regarding what sustainable development meant appeared instead to be controversies between different indigenous visions of development at which those communities had arrived autonomously.

Diverse indigenistas promoted to the status of leaders those indigenous individuals who would better echo their own positions by channeling aid for a community through those individuals and by attacking as "inauthentic" those leaders that they perceived to be aligned with "the enemy" (i.e., the other sector of indigenismo) (see Chase-Sardi 1987:126). Leaders, in turn, used the language of their indigenista *patrones* to frame their own claims over legal leadership. However, as the leaders became familiar with the indigenista field, they were able to achieve some independence from specific *patrones* by strategically switching alliances (see Cordeu 1999: 25–27; Kidd 1995b:63–64; Horst 1998:311–45).

Among the Ebitoso, as well as among other indigenous peoples, the antagonism between different agendas of Paraguayan indigenismo further intensified the centrifugal forces which contributed to subordinate the yrmo to the modern world. The anthropologist John Renshaw, who visited the community of Diana in the late 1970s and early 1980s, observed that several factions had already formed. Each faction and their leaders were associated with different *patrones*: the military, the missionaries, and the ranchers (see Renshaw 1996:234–37). With the passing of Law 904/81, factionalism and the struggle for leadership intensified, since *legal* leadership conferred more influence.[15] An "influential individual" who had the legal representation of a community was in a position to obtain more benefits from the hub of the indigenista patronage network located in Asunción. But in order to do this, leaders had to lend their voices, as "representatives" of indigenous groups, to their *patrones*. This arrangement made it possible and advantageous for an influential individual to create a new faction, claim to represent it, and "exchange" his representation for an indigenista's aid. When "democratic rule" commenced, in 1993, the situation grew even more complicated, as political parties adopted the practices of indigenista institutions, deploying aid through client-leaders who would support their candidates (see Kidd 1995b:64–69). As indigenous leaders came to serve as the "seal of legitimacy" for diverse indigenistas' visions of development, they also became the target of attacks that were ultimately aimed at delegitimizing their circumstantial *patrones* by association. These attacks were framed in terms of the authenticity of these leaders.

During the early years of API, the indigenous organization of national scope, indigenistas of diverse convictions, from military officers who were members of INDI to the critical indigenistas who had formed Marandú, collaborated, assisting indigenous leaders through a variety of programs such as land purchases, vaccination campaigns, and a national census of indigenous populations (see Horst 1998:260, 284; Renshaw 1996:21–23; Instituto Nacional del Indígena 1981). Yet beneath the collaborative facade each indigenista sector was cultivating API's leaders to promote their own agendas. According to Horst (1998:256–63, 283–84), who bases his analysis on documents produced by critical indigenistas and interviews he conducted in 1995, INDI's top officers took a mixed approach, both threatening coercive measures and offering economic enticements, such as providing salaries to API's leaders, in order to (successfully) co-opt them. However, if one considers other information and the views of API's indigenous leaders at the time, the practices of critical indigenistas did not differ much from those of the integrationist sector. According to these former leaders, as they gathered confidence in themselves and nudged API in the direction they considered best, the critical indigenistas working as technical support staff began to obstruct the actions they proposed. When critical indigenistas denied their support for those actions they considered erroneous, the leaders of the API started to lean on staff members from the governmental INDI to carry out those actions.

The attitude of the critical indigenistas is not surprising if one considers Horst's evaluation that, not withstanding the inspiration they derived from the Barbados Declaration, the people who formed Marandú (and later the technical support staff of API) were "eager to communicate [their] own agenda to their native audience, sometimes even to the exclusion of Indigenous peoples' interests" and "presented issues from the perspective of what non-Indians believed the Indigenous peoples should know" (Horst 1998:226). Indeed, this attitude underlies attacks that Marandú's director, Miguel Chase-Sardi, unleashed on API's leaders. For example, he asserted that the problems with API originated in one of Marandú's "big mistakes," which was to "accept leaders who were not [authentic indigenous] leaders," since these "leaders, sent by the communities . . . were mostly those individuals who were more apt to relate with the national society. Therefore, they were the most acculturated individuals [who had] acquired the guile of Paraguayan politicians . . . and had lost the indigenous concept of leadership, which is to act as a servant and distributor of goods among [their] people" (Chase-Sardi 1981:160; Susnik and Chase-Sardi 1995:331).

When indigenous leaders did not match expectations of how an authentic indigenous leader should behave, they were not only left without support, but also accused by their former mentors of stealing money from API.[16] Without denying that some leaders were effectively co-opted by INDI and turned into mere functionaries who worried mainly about their salaries, many leaders were (and still are) convinced that working from within the state could render results that could not be otherwise achieved. Intolerant attitudes on the part of the critical indigenistas toward these positions only reinforced indigenous leaders' perceptions that all indigenistas (whether integrationist or critical) were *patrones* with their own agendas. One Ebitoso leader, who experienced first-hand API's emergence and fall from grace, expressed this eloquently: "I have worked with every one of the indigenista institutions with presence in the Chaco. The one thing I learned from them was: me, me and me."[17]

With the granting of constitutional status to the idea that indigenous communities have the right to lands in quantity and quality enough to ensure the conservation and development of their own ways of life, controversies about authenticity increasingly revolved around the hunter-gatherer paradigm.[18] The core of these controversies concern whether or not indigenous peoples of the Chaco are authentically hunter-gatherers. In the current debates about sustainable development, competing indigenista institutions mobilize the imaginations Indigenous Peoples, Environment, and Risk in ways that reveal traces of the modernist and rupturist stories of globalization. Thus, they have something in common: they leave little space for indigenous peoples to proceed with their lives according to their own stories and imaginations. As Renshaw, who was involved with project Marandú and, later, with API and INDI, expressed, after many years of involvement with the Paraguayan indigenista field, "There have been some advances in the last few years . . . but until now the voices that are more clearly heard are those of the indigenista interlocutors" (1996:9).

Signs of Changes?

My story thus far has much imprecision and leaves many questions unanswered. Nevertheless, I have provided a basic understanding of how the conditions of possibility for this story came into being. Indians, Nature, and Progress, central imaginations of the modern myth, have mutated into Indigenous Peoples, Environment, and Risk. This has taken place in part through translations, contention, articulation, and resonance produced as governmental institutions and social movements struggled over and negotiated in multiscalar settings the consequences of state-led development. In Paraguay, given the capacity that the indigenous-rights and the human-rights networks had to influence the flow of external development aid critical for the Stroessner regime, the entire indigenista field had to open up to those emerging imaginations. In other words, even the integrationist indigenistas have to grapple with imaginations that command respect for the autonomy of Indigenous Peoples and the Environment; hence their claims to also support visions of sustainable development. Notions of sustainable development, with their implicit claim to respect the autonomy of what and who were formerly mere objects of development, has compelled not only critical indigenistas but also those espousing an implicit integrationist agenda to legitimize their visions of development by recruiting indigenous client-leaders to lend their voices to those visions. This has put the spotlight on issues of authenticity that have remained a pervasive feature of the political field in which indigenous peoples are immersed in Paraguay. Lately, the politics of authenticity has been expressed through the continuing debates among indigenistas on whether or not indigenous peoples of the Chaco are hunter-gatherers and on what consequences this may have for their development. The striking feature of these debates is their lack of participating indigenous peoples. They appear only as the objects of the debates, not as debating subjects. This means that, despite the (corpo)realization of the global condition, with its openings to notions of generalized autonomy—including that of former "objects"—the Yshiro have to struggle hard to articulate the new authorized imaginations (Indigenous Peoples, Environment, and Risk) in ways that will allow for more symmetrical interconnections to develop between the yrmo and the modern world.

What I call the global condition has been (corpo)realizing through the struggle of (some) humans and the nonhumans who are making increasingly visible the pluriverse invisibilized by modernity. As Latour has argued (1999, 2004), nonhumans are very powerful, and their rebellion against the objectifying project of modernity is enormously mobilizing for humans. Bringing back into view their agency, they have put into question the great divide between nature and culture and lent further weight to the challenging of the colonial difference between modernity and its others. Thus, the struggle I refer to reveals the increasing difficulties the modern project finds in its attempt to treat human and nonhuman others as mere objects without agency of their own. This is important because for over five hundred years the pluriverse has been invisibilized by modernity's imposing claims of universality. Hence, many of the "crises" that moderns now experience as globalization (i.e., the incapacity of modern institutions to address a global problematic that appears to them as radical uncertainty and proliferating risks) can be seen as the symptoms of the unruly diversity inherent in a fully agentive pluriverse. But these crises can be also seen as the unprecedented opportunity for moderns to consider seriously the need to move beyond modernity. While there are indications that this might be taking place in some corners, the dominant trend seems to go in the direction of reinstating modernity even when it is rejected. This is evident in the debates about different notions of sustainable development in the Paraguayan indigenista field, where even those espousing stances that can be related to the rupturist story of globalization end up enacting globality as modernity. Moralities play a fundamental role in this process.

2 *Porowo*/Moralities

Esnwherta said to the Yshiro: "Because you killed my children [the Anabsero] now you have to take their place. You will relate to the new generations as they related to you. And you will do it exactly as they did, otherwise you are all going to die." That's the responsibility that Esnwherta gave to the *tobich oso* [the initiated men].
—Keiwe, *Esnwherta au'oso*

This sense of responsibility, of course, is a metaphor that denies closure; the actions, the connections, and intentions are not causal but obscure ceremonies.
—Gerald Vizenor, *Authored Animals*

For a long time I had noticed that in matters of morality one must sometimes follow opinions that one knows to be quite uncertain, just as if they were indubitable.... [B]ut, because I then desired to devote myself exclusively to the search for the truth, I thought it necessary ... that I reject as absolutely false everything in which I could imagine the least doubt, in order to see whether, after this process, something in my beliefs remained that was entirely indubitable.
—Rene Descartes, *Discourse on the Method of Rightly Conducting One's Reason and Seeking Truth in the Sciences*

Descartes's malin genie has always been with us, in one disguise or another, his presence confirmed by ever renewed desperate attempts to annihilate the threat of relativism, as if no such attempts have ever been undertaken in the past. Modernity was lived in a haunted house.
—Zygmunt Bauman, *The Fall of the Legislator*

Four Enacting the Yrmo

In the early 1980s, a group of Ebitoso leaders from Diana and Ylhirta (the two existing Ebitoso communities at the time) sought to obtain, from the Paraguayan government, legal property of 21,000 hectares of land in the place known as Ynishta.[1] All these leaders stood out in their communities because of their variously privileged positions within diverse patronage networks. Some were well connected with integrationist indigenista institutions, while others were better connected with critical indigenistas.

According to INDI's interpretation of Law 904/81, indigenous leaders must gather at least two hundred families in order to make a community big enough to claim this amount of land. After most Ebitoso had signed the petition, the number of signatures still fell short. A group of leaders decided to ask their ancestral rivals, the Tomaraho, for their signatures. Although the Tomaraho were not sure if they would actually move to the new lands, their elders thought that it was a good idea to be part of the land claim; if they eventually decided to leave their settlement in San Carlos, they would have a place to go. The necessary number of signatures was thus collected, and the next step was to elect leaders who INDI would legally recognize and who would act as interlocutors during the land claim. The election, held in 1984, took place only in the Ebitoso communities (Stunnenberg 1993:229). These communities chose the legal leaders from the group of leaders and influential individuals who were carrying forward the land claims. Those elected were relatively more literate, more fluent in the official languages, and more familiar with the intricacies of the Stroessner's bureaucracy. These "literate" individuals won the election in part because those who voted were the more literate community members, who understood better what was at stake in the election. However, it was not literacy per se but kinship that defined the election outcome.

As a strategy to promote literacy and the gospel, the New Tribes missionaries provided aid primarily to those families who sent their children to school and Bible study groups. Over time, descendants of those families continued to send their own children to school, such that eventually those who were more literate tended to be closely related. In other words, to say that the more literate individuals voted for the most literate leaders is tantamount to saying that those leaders were elected by their closer relatives.

In 1985, several families from Diana and a few from Ylhirta moved to the new settlement in Ynishta (see map 2). The elected leaders told their community members that in the new settlement the Ebitoso would be able to live as they chose, without the interference of missionaries, military, or local *patrones*. They enticed people to move to Ynishta with two promises: that the exploitative relations with Paraguayan *patrones* would be mitigated and that a "development project" was to be financed by the indigenistas who worked in the state INDI and API, the indigenous organization of national scope. The development project turned out to be a cooperative store that the leaders would manage and that, in theory, would replace the aid provided by Paraguayan *patrones*. The store would provide credit to the Ebitoso and thus allow them to break from debt-bondage relations with Paraguayan *patrones*. However, given the circumstances in which the new community was created, the legal leaders themselves became *patrones* of sorts. Nevertheless, important differences existed between the quasi-patronage system in Ynishta and the patronage networks operating in Diana and Ylhirta. In effect, excepting the missionaries network that operated according to a different economy of demands, the patronage networks connected to commercial hunting were built on the basis of a system of debt-bondage that worked as long as four conditions were met: (1) *patrones* had discretionary power to decide whether or not they would grant credit to an Ebitoso individual; (2) the Ebitoso had no effective means to pressure *patrones* for credit; (3) *patrones* operated more or less as a common front, so that no debtor could switch patron without paying his or her debt; and

(4) the local authorities actively dissuaded the Yshiro from attempting to withdraw from debt-bondage relations without paying their debts.

None of these conditions were fully met in the case of the cooperative store located in the new community. In contrast to Paraguayan *patrones*, the leaders' discretionary power to grant or deny credit was limited by INDI and API, which tied further economic support for development projects to the economic performance of the cooperative. These institutions expected that the cooperative would be run according to a logic of management mainly concerned with the self-preservation of the enterprise. Meeting this demand was important for the leaders of Ynishta, because without a steady flow of financial support from those institutions, their leadership would be at risk. Also in contrast to Paraguayan *patrones*, the leaders were more susceptible to the influence of kin, especially since it was hard for them to convince people that the aid provided by indigenista institutions had to be treated according to an "economy of demands" governing more "business-like" patronage networks. As a result, the demands of INDI and API were strongly countered by the demands of the leaders' kin (in essence, the whole community), who kept asking for more credit. In addition, the leaders could not use violence to coerce the community into being loyal to the cooperative and paying their debts.

By 1986, the leaders began to see that if they kept giving credits on request, the cooperative would go bankrupt. Yet kin pressures for credit increases did not relent. Thus, the leaders first refused credit to their most distant relatives, who were in a weaker position to pressure them. Then they followed suit with progressively closer kin. Doing this, the leaders forestalled the collapse of the cooperative for three years, but also eroded their own base of support. When the cooperative finally went bankrupt, so did their leadership.

Before what ultimately happened with the cooperative, the first individuals and families to whom the legal leaders denied credit were adversely affected. These individuals and families had to reconnect with their former Paraguayan *patrones*, who were offended at having been abandoned by their clients. Thus, in several cases these Ebitoso had to endure especially difficult conditions in order to obtain credit from affronted *patrones*. Some of the influential individuals, who had lost the election for legal leadership, were among this group of people. These influential individuals still had contacts with indigenista institutions, and some of them took the newly disenfranchised group's complaints to INDI and API, thus becoming their spokespersons.

These institutions requested from the legal leaders an explanation as to why they were denying credit to some community members. The leaders answered that they had suspended credit to those with large debts who were not paying them back. If these individuals were complaining, the leaders claimed, it was because they were illiterate and backward, and thus did not understand how the cooperative worked. Many staff members found these assertions to be believable because, in fact, the first people to whom the leaders denied credit were among the less literate members of the community. But if the people without credit were illiterate, this was due to the correlation between kinship and literacy. In other words, they were denied credit not because they were illiterate and ignorant, but because they were among the more distant relatives of the legal leaders. Nevertheless, by this time (early 1986), indigenistas maintaining a strong critical stance had begun to distance themselves from API, and thus INDI's integrationist approach had become dominant in the former organization; in this context, the explanation provided by the leaders was accepted by API without further questions. These events and the processes that ensued help illuminate the intersection between what I call different moral logics and the situated moralities arising from them.

The way in which white settlers imagined Indians and Nature prefigured the ways in which they thought they should treat them: they should develop them. Development was a moral imagination insofar as it implicitly addressed a central moral question: what is the right thing to do (with the Indians and Nature)? The Cartesian project "haunted" this question with the demand of certainty, a certainty that could be produced only according to the logic of a regime of truth in which the starting assumption was the ontological separation of world and word (or nature and culture). With its foundations in the sixteenth century, but with increasing intensity and widening scope from the eighteenth, this regime of truth has claimed to relegate moral stances to the back-room of beliefs, while actually reformulating them as matters of "fact" (see Docherty 1993:10; Larmore 1996:89–117; Latour 1999). In this regime of truth, facts have displaced gods, ancestors, spirits, and custom as the source of moral answers. Therefore, this regime of truth would answer the question of what is the right thing to do with Indians and Nature as follows: know with certainty what they are and you will know what is the right thing to do with them!

According to this logic, facts (reality) speak for themselves and moral stances automatically derive from them. Implicit in this logic are two related ideas: first, that the (would-be-known) object and the (knowing) subject are self-contained entities, that is, that they pre-exist their mutual relation; second, that moralities derived from self-contained external objects are beyond doubt because they are not distorted by the subject's interests, but are purely "objective." Given its grounding on Cartesian dualism, and given its moral significance, I call this reasoning Cartesian moral logic. By using the term "moral logic," I do not refer to specific moral stances; I refer instead to the logical procedure by which one arrives at a moral stance. In this sense, the moral stances adopted by many Yshiro often signal a relational moral logic that, unlike Cartesian moral logic, does not see self-contained entities as the source for moral stances. Rather, it is the specific web of relations that give shape to the knower as part of the yrmo that must be carefully observed in order to obtain highly contextual clues to determining appropriate stances and conduct.

Moral stances are situated. That is, they are the product of specific circumstances, historical and otherwise. This poses a methodological problem: how to distinguish between moral stances that are in practice entangled with one another without having to, in each case, give a detailed account of the circumstances from which they emerge? Using moral logics as a common thread or point of reference reveals a central difference between specific moral stances that, being enacted in a field marked by steep asymmetries, tend to appear indistinguishable, thereby reinforcing the invisibility of the yrmo.

Relations Make Entities

It would be erroneous to assume that the explanations the legal leaders gave to INDI and API regarding their management of credits were produced with Machiavellian insight in order to imitate the vision of development that had become dominant in those institutions. In fact, these kinds of explanations continue to be common among those who have managed cooperative stores in Yshiro communities. Over a dozen cooperative stores have opened and closed in different Yshiro communities since 1986 without achieving long-term sustainability. Individuals who have acted as storekeepers are usually chosen, by the communities or the funding organization, from among the most literate members of a given community. These storekeepers often explain that the cooperative under their charge failed because their fellow community members were illiterate (*no son letrados*) and could not understand how it should work. This sort of explanation reflects situated moralities arising from the intersection between Cartesian and relational moral logics.

In 1999, an environmental NGO provided funds for the opening of a cooperative store in one of the Ebitoso communities. To avoid repeating the failure of past cooperative stores, the NGO staff and the leaders of the community agreed in a public meeting that credit should not be extended to anybody. The aim of the cooperative, it was said, was to provide food at the cheapest price in the area, not to provide food through credit when there was no money available. After less than a month, many people started to voice anger because the storekeeper kept to the rule of not giving credit. As the storekeeper thought that the offended parties would listen to me, he asked me to talk to some of them and explain again why he could not provide credit. I took great pains to explain the rationale of momentarily suspending their demands on the storekeeper. In this way, I argued, the store would remain open and would be able to keep providing food at cheaper prices than could be found at the Paraguayan stores. Ginés, an Ebitoso elder in his sixties, after listening to me silently, told me the following story.

At its beginning it was not like this. Then, *porosht* [God] made man and woman with black beeswax. The people were black. God told somebody that he was going to send big rain and that everything and everybody was going to die, except those who made an oven with mud and entered into it. Some people did this and killed *amyrmyt bahlut* [the great armadillo] and fed on it during those days that the rain poured. There were some other people who ran into the bush to save their life. After the waters drained off, the people came out from the oven. The people who came out of the oven were white and they were very intelligent for they had followed the laws of God. The others who saved themselves in the forest, but did not follow God's laws, kept being black and not very intelligent. In those times, there was still a tree that connected the earth with the sky. People would go up to the sky through the tree and would gather the honey that was all over the place as if it were dew. But it happened that termites began to eat the tree and eventually it fell down. Some people were left up in the sky and the others were left on the earth yearning for the now unreachable sky. Thus, the whites thought and calculated that they could make a tower to reach the sky again and they set out to do it. But when they started to construct the tower they confused each other with their orders and there was no longer any understanding among them. (12 September 1999, field notes)

I was perplexed as to why Ginés told me this story, which seemed to me unrelated to our previous conversation about the store. Only later, it dawned on me where the connection was. This is a puruhle story, which narrates how certain aspects of the yrmo came into being. Puruhle narratives being very flexible, stories or fragments of stories can be arranged so as to convey specific messages. In this case, and without curtailing other resonances and meanings of a very dense narrative, Ginés's story was aimed at contesting my assumption that the problem was about misunderstanding the rationale behind denying store credit. By telling me the story of how "whites" and "blacks" were distinguished, including in this their different intellectual capacities, Ginés was ironically recognizing the "rigorousness" of my arguments, but also the futility of trying to impose them on "different" people. If, by following the laws of God, whites "get things right," while the "others" must go about with their not-so-precise intellects, the story of the tower brings into perspective that one consequence of the whites' reasoning capacities is a lack of mutual understanding. Through his story, Ginés pointed out that the problem was not one of understanding what the cooperative was and how it should work. The problem was that he did not accept the underlying moral logic that positioned the idea of how the cooperative should work (which was based on the idea of what a cooperative is) above the relations that provided the reason for the cooperative to exist in the first place. In other words, it was problematic to try sustaining the cooperative without caring for the relations among community members:

without understanding among them, there would be no community, and without community, there would be no need for a cooperative.

Why do I call this a relational moral logic? As has been discussed with regard to other indigenous groups, relational ontologies open up an "intellectual landscape . . . in which states and substances are replaced by processes and relations" (Descola and Pálsson 1996:12). In these intellectual landscapes, entities exist only as an effect of the relations that constitute them (see Amawtay Wasi 2004; Blaser, Feit, and McRae 2004; Cajete 2000; Descola 1996; Fischer 2001; LaDuke 1999; Viveiros de Castro 2004; Waters 2004a). Given that for many Yshiro "all that exists" coemerges from the relations that are described in puruhle narratives, the source of morality too cannot be other than those relations. Thus, while Cartesian moral logic gives precedence to self-referential entities over relations, a relational moral logic gives precedence to relations over entities. From this perspective, relations are the source of morality, and since relations are always in the making, answers to the moral question of what is the right thing to do are always contextual. For example, in the case of the first cooperative store, the leaders clearly privileged relations over definitions (entities) when closer kin were involved. This underscores that the situatedness of the moralities at stake in the events that took place in Ynishta were in part shaped by the mutual entanglement of Cartesian and relational moral logics.

According to the anthropological literature on the Paraguayan Chaco, most indigenous peoples express the view that, at least ideally, individuals have an obligation to share with all the members of the network that forms a residential group (Renshaw 1996:149; see also Kidd 1999:44–46). However, as Strathern (1996:523) has pointed out, while networks can in theory extend indefinitely, in practice they are "cut" by other networks. Who is within and who is outside a given network of sharing is defined by the kinds of "issues" considered relevant to set the network's reach and its boundaries. In the Yshiro case, diverse issues have intersected at different times, with the networks of sharing giving rise to different forms of sharing. For example, before the missionaries arrived, a network of sharing was delimited through the intersection of the *Esnwherta au'oso*, the relations with the *ukurb'deio* (which, for the moment, can be translated as "supernatural powers"), gender, clan ascription, and age ranks. After the missionaries came and the initiation ritual was abandoned, networks of sharing changed. Age, clan ascription, and even the *Esnwherta au'oso* were no longer central to sharing; rather, kinship based on the nuclear family and patronage relations came to define how sharing should be performed. A similar process of transformation took place when, in Ynishta, the leaders brought the functioning of the cooperative to bear on their sharing (or not sharing) with their relatives.

This form of sharing reveals a morality that is situated at the intersection of the relational and the Cartesian moral logics. In effect, the leaders tried to strike a balance between two different ways of understanding "what is the right thing to do" with regard to sharing the assets of the cooperative. Thus, they gave precedence to relations over self-referential entities (i.e., the proper functioning of the cooperative) when closer relatives were involved, but reversed precedence when dealing with distant relatives. However, soon after the leaders started to do this, the logic that gives primacy to self-referential entities took hold of the unfolding events.

Wututa, the Traditionalist Community

Early in 1986, when the dissidents had started to raise their voices against the legal leaders, a group of critical indigenistas approached some of the dissidents' spokespersons to inquire about the feather paraphernalia the Yshiro used for their rituals. The indigenistas wanted to collect samples for a new museum of popular art (see Ticio Escobar 1999:341–43). The spokespersons suggested that they contact the Tomaraho, who still performed the initiation ritual. The Ebitoso spokespersons also offered to guide the indigenistas to the Tomaraho's camp in the interior of the Chaco. During that visit, the Ebitoso spokespersons convinced the Tomaraho to move to Ynishta and the indigenistas to assist in the process. On their return to Asunción, the indigenistas created an NGO, Comisión de Solidaridad con los Pueblos Indígenas (Commission of Solidarity with Indigenous Peoples, or CSPI), in order to obtain funds for the relocation. When the Tomaraho moved to Ynishta, in May 1986, CSPI provided them with tools, seeds, and food to sustain their families during the initial period in the settlement.

The relocation of the Tomaraho to Ynishta added tensions to an already explosive situation. The legal leaders and their supporters did not welcome the Tomaraho. Although the Tomaraho had legal rights to the land, having given their signatures for the claim, there was a strong feeling among many of the most literate Ebitoso that the Tomaraho did not deserve the land because they had not worked closely in the land claim. The dissident Ebitoso, however, sided with the Tomaraho when these feelings began to surface in discussions and commentaries. In addition, many dissident Ebitoso began to partake in debylylta (the initiation ritual) performed by the Tomaraho. The most literate Ebitoso, still on good terms with the legal leaders, began to insult the dissident Ebitoso by calling them "backward" and "uncivilized." Finally, the dissidents' spokespersons were able to call for a new election of leaders, calculating that, with the vote of the Tomaraho, they would win the election. However, the Ebitoso legal leaders obtained from INDI an order that directed the Tomaraho to choose their own, separate leaders; thus, the legal leaders again won the election.

In the meantime several members of CSPI created another NGO, Ayuda a las Comunidades Indígenas del Paraguay (Aid for Indigenous Communities of Paraguay, or ACIP), to continue support of the Tomaraho. For some of the dissident spokespersons, it seemed evident that ACIP's key staff was primarily interested in the preservation of rituals and other "cultural traits." When they lost the election, these spokespersons convinced ACIP to help their group and the Tomaraho to create a new community where they could practice their "traditions" without interference from the more literate Ebitoso. Thus, in 1987, the Tomaraho and the dissident Ebitoso moved to Wututa, which was within the territory of Ynishta but located fifteen kilometers inland from the main settlement on the banks of the Paraguay River. The new Tomaraho and the Ebitoso settlements, although in proximity to each other, were separate, and although the Ebitoso spokespersons obtained legal recognition of Wututa as a single indigenous community, the Ebitoso and Tomaraho agreed that each group would have its own leaders and would manage its own issues.

In Ynishta and Diana people commented that those who had moved to Wututa were not only backward and illiterate, but also lazy, since the only thing they wanted to do was to "sing" (i.e., perform debylylta) and be photographed by the indigenistas. People from Wututa ridiculed the people of both Ynishta and Diana for trying to be like Paraguayans, but achieving only clumsy results. Given the language used, critical indigenistas connected with ACIP began to see the dispute as one between "traditionalists" and "acculturated" groups (see Chase-Sardi 1987:126; Chase-Sardi, Brun, and Enciso 1990:58–61). From the perspective of the critical indigenistas, the conflict was about traditionalist Ebitoso struggling to retain their indigenousness against the wishes of acculturated Ebitoso (Chase-Sardi, Brun, and Enciso 1990:56; see also Chase-Sardi 1987:125–29; Ticio Escobar 1999: 356–57). Therefore, the critical indigenistas felt that they were helping the traditionalists to become "re-tribalized," whereby they could avoid becoming "a miserable rural lumpen-proletariat" (Chase-Sardi 1987:129). In contrast, from the perspective of the integrationist indigenistas, who by that time controlled INDI and API, the conflict was about a recalcitrant uneducated (i.e., backward) group inhibiting the progress of the more educated (i.e., "developed") Ebitoso. For these integrationist institutions, the alternatives that the Yshiro faced were either to remain backward and forever poor or to become developed and fully participate in the benefits of modernity. Integrationist and critical indigenistas thus understood the conflict in the same way, but with inverse values. Having in common the Cartesian moral logic, both indigenista institutions "translated" a conflict about the relative weight that should be given to relations and entities into a conflict between entities (factions) which were clearly defined by specific "traits": their relation to development and tradition. The leaders of Wututa soon adopted these labels to differentiate their community from those of Ynishta and Diana.

Entities Make Relations

What started as a tension between moral logics soon became a dispute between Ebitoso factions that supposedly possessed distinct defining traits. That is, the dispute quickly came to be framed in terms of Cartesian moral logic, at least to some extent. From the dispute emerged two entities (factions) whose mutual relations were in some circumstances predicated on the traits that defined them. This is most visible, again, in how sharing of resources was performed in the new context.

After the dissidents formed the new community of Wututa, in many cases they came to consider being or not being a traditionalist a relevant criterion to determine with whom they should share their resources. Thus, even as the dissident group openly rejected the imposition of Cartesian logic, they extended the reach of that very logic through their use of "traditionalism" as a relevant criterion for sharing. However, the relative dominance (or the direction of the translation) of one logic over the other was (and is) a matter of contingent circumstances, as is illustrated by how I came to be involved with the traditionalist Ebitoso.

In 1990, while doing undergraduate studies at Universidad de Buenos Aires, I had a summer job as a tourist guide on a cruise ship that traveled the Paraguay River between Asunción and Corumbá in Brazil (see map 1). On these trips, I met some of the "traditionalist leaders" of Wututa who gave talks on their culture and sold handicrafts to the tourists. Through the summer, they told me about their community and the visions that they had for it. I told them about my studies in anthropology and my interest in working with indigenous peoples. By the end of the summer, they had invited me to return to Paraguay and work with their community. I accepted the invitation, and a year later, when I had to prepare my undergraduate thesis, I went to Wututa to do research. During this initial fieldwork, the leaders were explicit about their expectation that my work be useful for the community. We agreed that I would do my best to find funding for certain community projects. I returned to Argentina and spent the next eighteen months finishing my degree and applying for funding for those projects. Meanwhile, the traditionalist leaders began a land claim for 10,000 hectares that included Karcha Bahlut, a highly significant place as it was where the original teachings of the Anabsero had been passed on to the Yshiro, where the Ebitoso came into contact with the whites for the first time, and the site of one of Boggiani's logging camps (see map 2).

In 1993, a contingent of the traditionalist Ebitoso decided to occupy Karcha Bahlut in order to pressure the government for a legal resolution of the land claim. In the same year, we obtained funding for a community project through the Center for Field Research/Earthwatch, an American NGO that connects volunteers with researchers. The project, which lasted until 1997, was atypical in that it was not a development project per se, but a "basic research" project on "traditional knowledge and technologies." The volunteers sent by that organization worked with Yshiro instructors, observing and recording how the Yshiro used different traditional technologies. The volunteers also helped to develop herbariums and ethnotaxonomies that were to be included in an in situ archive and museum to be built by the community as part of the project. Daily wages for Yshiro instructors were budgeted, and the money which came from housing the volunteers was used to purchase ox-carts, cows, boats, and other items necessary for the community.

In this context, somebody invited a nontraditionalist relative from another community to work with a volunteer, which led to many discussions regarding whether being a traditionalist or not should be a relevant criterion for deciding if a relative from another community deserved to share the benefits of the project. In most situations people accepted that a person's traditionalism was not as important as her or his status as a relative, with the persuasion of the traditionalist leaders playing an important role in these outcomes.

Because this was not a development project, the leaders had no pressures to meet established economic goals. The only restriction on how they could use project resources was their own capacity to convince community members to use those resources, which were limited, in certain ways and not others. I soon realized that the leaders were extending their network of supporters by making the benefits of the project reach as far as possible. Although in comparison with "real" development projects this one was modest in terms of its material input, the leaders were eager to make it an example of the benefits that traditionalism could produce. Turning the label of backwardness around, they argued in community meetings that the support of American volunteers showed that *progreso* was predicated on the maintenance and strengthening of Yshiro traditions.

In contrast, when the resources under consideration had to be used according to restrictive criteria established by external funding organizations, the outcomes of these discussions were different. For example, access to credit from the cooperative store set up in Wututa with ACIP's financial support was restricted to the traditionalists, or so argued the leaders acting as storekeepers. Given that ACIP expected the storekeepers to make the store sustainable, the storekeepers ended up using a strategy similar to the one the leaders of Ynishta had used to balance the contradictory demands from external institutions and from kin: they denied credit to some people (usually their more distant relatives). Yet they felt or were pressed to justify their decisions, and I often heard them argue that those to whom they denied credit were not really traditionalists.

Thus, once Wututa was established as a distinct community, even the traditionalist leaders had to operate under constraints much like those faced by the leaders of Ynishta. Edgardo Cordeu, an anthropologist who specializes in Yshiro mythology, has responded to this by suggesting that the similarity of circumstances across the Ebitoso factions reveals Ebitoso traditionalism as "inauthentic." For him, traditionalism has been no more than clever manipulation by the self-fashioned traditionalist leaders of the critical indigenista infatuation with the "other" (see Cordeu 1989b:43–45, 1991b: 10–12, 1999:24–26). Yet some of the events leading to the emergence of traditionalism go well beyond any leader's capacity to manipulate them. Moreover, they actually go beyond any human capacity to do so.

Powers and Relations

Don Veneto Vera, an Ebitoso konsaha (shaman) in his sixties, was relatively well off in Puerto Diana, having a few cows and acting as an herbalist healer. Yet, tired of the poor treatment of the New Tribes missionaries, he was among those who moved from Puerto Diana to Ynishta in 1985. In 1986, when the Tomaraho arrived, he joined a group of Ebitoso men who frequented the Tomaraho's tobich. Don Veneto explained to me, in Spanish, "I liked to go see those *tobich'oso* (the ones from the tobich) because *me hallaba*" (lit. "I found myself"; it also connotes entertainment and enjoyment). At the beginning, he took part in the rituals performed by the Tomaraho as an observer. Soon, however, ukurb'deio (supernatural powers) began to visit him (and other Ebitoso participants) while he was sleeping.

For many Yshiro, there are a number of relevant interlocutors in human-nonhuman relations. These include the Anabsero, *porosht* (God), and *diguichibio* (spirits and ghosts). What modern knowledge categorizes as natural phenomena (rain, thunder, etc.) and celestial bodies, the Yshiro consider also to be fully agentive beings. An important category of nonhumans is the bahlut, the first exemplar of a species. Since plants and animals are like splinters of the bahlut, it is with them and not with individual plants or animals that relevant relations are established. Nonhumans of all kinds are usually referred to with the general label *ukurb'deio*, which can be translated as "power," "capacity," and "potency." When Don Veneto started to dream, ukurb'deio invited him to enter into closer relationships with them.

Initially, the guidance of Tomaraho elders was critical, because Don Veneto could not clearly understand what ukurb'deio were telling him during his dreams. Later, as he started to understand, the ukurb'deio began to instruct him directly.

The transformations that Don Veneto has undergone as a result of these relations are visible to his neighbors. On the one hand, they point out that he is now poorer because he does not try to make as much money, and the little that he has is spent to purchase alcohol. On the other hand, several of them recognize that Don Veneto now has "powers." When I asked Don Veneto if he considered himself to be economically worse off than before, he answered affirmatively and explained that this was due to the demands imposed on him by the ukurb'deio. Failing to respond to these demands is very dangerous. Nevertheless, Don Veneto does not complain much because, while he does not have time to make money, the ukurb'deio make sure that his family remains provided for. Once, while we were out hunting, he said, "I never come back to my home without something to eat. Every time I go hunting, I already know where I will find my prey. The ukurb'deio tell me. They give me that animal. We are never hungry in my home." His family is also provided for by the gifts from people whom Don Veneto has cured of disease. If his family is poor, he told me, it is a sign of how little knowledge the Yshiro of today have of the ukurb'deio.

> These people [most Ebitoso] do not know that they can hunt and fish because we [konsaho] talk with the ukurb'deio. We sing what they tell us to sing so that there will be plenty of animals and fish. If we don't sing there will be drought, or flood, or the animals will go away. . . . We sing and they say, "Don Veneto is singing all day; Don Veneto is borrachón (drunkard); Don Veneto does not want to work." They have no respect. They should be sharing their food with my family for it is because we [konsaho] sing that they can eat well. (7 November 1999, tape recording)

The agreement established with the ukurb'deio is based on the understanding that Don Veneto must follow their instructions strictly, or he will die or get sick. In turn, the ukurb'deio give him varous capacities that are beneficial for the community. Among these powers are control over rain and mosquitoes, and the power to bring fish to the surface, to attract certain animals, and to cure diseases. The instructions and demands of the ukurb'deio are varied, ranging from restrictions on the consumption of certain species, to the performance of rituals that contribute to the reproduction of humans and nonhumans, to fasting, singing, and according to Don Veneto, the consumption of alcohol to enhance visionary dreams.

Through Don Veneto and other people who have relations with ukurb'deio, a (re)new(ed) network connecting humans and nonhumans emerged. This network had important effects on how some Ebitoso relate to each other. For example, if an individual is prohibited from consuming certain species or parts of an animal, that individual may share those species or parts with people who can consume them. Don Veneto's healing powers cannot be "bought," but, at the discretion of the "patient," they must be reciprocated with gifts. In turn, the performance of rituals demanded by the ukurb'deio often requires Don Veneto to enlist the aid of those who belong to those networks of reciprocity. In short, through a connection with the ukurb'deio, a group of the Ebitoso have woven and reinvigorated the network of reciprocity that extends across the human–nonhuman divide. This network can be seen as an aspect of traditionalism that is far removed from any single human's capacity to manipulate. This is a heterogeneous network involving nonhumans with their own characteristics and volition, and with an enormous power to mobilize humans.

Not everybody enters into these kinds of human–nonhuman relations. Some people are never approached by ukurb'deio in their dreams. Some are never invited to establish deeper relations with them. Some people do not accept the offers. Relations between humans and nonhumans are not fixed; rather, they are contingent on particular conditions. Whether such relations develop depends on the availability of guidance to interpret dreams, on the quality of those interpretations, on the willingness of both ukurb'deio and human to establish a closer relationship, and on the clarity of their mutual communication. In any case, the general status of these relations is not irrelevant, for they profoundly impinge on the overall health of the yrmo.

In Wututa, a general respect or appreciation for the "old ways" did not result in a community free from conflicts. In fact, new and different tensions and conflicts appeared, because not everybody participated in the emerging network connecting human and nonhumans. Disagreements arose about which ritual procedures were appropriate and which were not. To this day, some Ebitoso elders affirm that the Tomaraho do not perform rituals properly and also complain about the new Ebitoso konsaho's use of alcohol in the tobich. Fearing the likely negative consequences of incorrectly performed rituals, these elders refuse to participate in them. The Tomaraho and Ebitoso practitioners scorn the elders as being *evangelio* (evangelists). Other conflicts arose because some people claimed that certain tasks needed to sustain the network of reciprocity connecting humans to nonhumans interfered with the performance of other tasks by which the community obtained market goods. For instance, some leaders complained that rituals interfered with the economic activities (agriculture) being financed by ACIP, and thus the community was risking the loss of aid. At the same time, other leaders complained that the organization's key staff implicitly promoted the performance of rituals to the detriment of economic activities.

All these conflicts were at the root of the final demise of Wututa. The group of Ebitoso who moved from Wututa to Karcha Bahlut in 1993 was formed mostly, but not only, by people who were part of the newly emerging network of reciprocity brokered by Don Veneto. Between 1994 and 1995, Wututa was finally abandoned as a place of settlement. The Tomaraho, who had complained about their conflicts with some Ebitoso neighbors, obtained their own lands and moved to Pitiantuta with ACIP's support. The Ebitoso who had remained in Wututa scattered between Ynishta and Puerto Diana.

As the leaders who had initially invited me moved to Karcha Bahlut in 1993, I decided to follow them and their group. Don Veneto was among them. In 1995, he began to invite me to the meetings that a group of men organized in a tobich that they had opened nearby. When I returned the following year, Bruno Barras, one of the leaders who had taken up permanent residence in Asunción, met me at this city's airport. He informed me that a group of journalists, artists, and members of the Paraguayan parliament were going to visit Karcha Bahlut in order to witness the first debylylta to be performed solely by the Ebitoso since 1956. On my arrival in Karcha Bahlut, Don Veneto explained to me that some Anabsero had visited him in his dreams and had instructed him to find a boy to go through the initiation. Given that nobody seemed willing to offer his or her child for such an experiment, Don Veneto selected his own grandchild in spite of the fact that he was only nine years old (traditionally, boys were initiated when they entered puberty).

The ceremony was performed at the end of July 1996 and was partially witnessed by the leaders' Paraguayan guests. The leaders did not miss the opportunity to signal to their guests the religious importance of Karcha Bahlut and how badly the community needed to have the land as legal property. In 1998, the community received the titles of the land. Since then, over forty young Ebitoso males, from nine to twenty years of age, have been initiated, with effects reaching beyond Karcha Bahlut.

Asymmetrical Translations

A development project, the cooperative store, which started in Ynishta with the support of indigenista institutions, ignited a confrontation in which the relative preponderance of different moral logics was at stake. A relational moral logic, which was concerned with the effects and duties arising from relations, found its limit in its intersection with a Cartesian moral logic, which was concerned with the responsibilities and duties arising from the "nature" (i.e., definition) of entities. However, these different moral logics, which I neatly distinguish in words, are actually very much entangled with each other. The circumstances in which these entanglements occur (their constraining and enabling character) ground situated moralities in concrete practices. This disallows easy generalizations that would conflate the relational moral logic with "traditionalism" and the Cartesian moral logic with "acculturation."

Both Ebitoso factions were dependent on development aid from indigenista *patrones*. This made them, and particularly their leaders, susceptible to the Cartesian moral logic implicit in their *patrones'* demands for sound economic management of project resources. Yet both set of leaders had to also operate within the constraints imposed by the relational moral logic implicit in the demands of their kin. Precisely because of these similarities, the boundaries of these "factions" are much more blurry than it might at first appear. Cartesian moral logic and relational moral logics are embedded in the concrete practices of both factions.

The difference between these moral logics cannot be accounted for by assuming purity in their concrete enactments; rather, their difference emerges from their diverse genealogies and, more important, from how they "see" what they see, and with what results. The difference between these moral logics is a subtle one because both perceive entities and relations. However, while the Cartesian moral logic sees relations as emerging from self-referential entities that enter into contact with each other, the relational moral logic sees entities as emerging from relations. The Cartesian moral logic is incapable of addressing the political, ethical, and epistemological conundrums that characterize the global condition, or at least is incapable of doing so in a way that will allow globality to be performed as an alternative to modernity. The relational moral logic, in contrast, contains precisely this promise, not least because it accounts for the agency and autonomy of purpose of nonhumans. This is a point that must not be taken lightly since the urgency and obstinacy of nonhumans' purposes offer a powerful reminder that politics are not only the business of humans.

The asymmetry between these different moral logics allows that, in concrete practices, conducts shaped by the relational logic can be easily translated into the terms of the Cartesian logic. As with the emergence of the Ebitoso factions and their use of traits to define their mutual relations, these translations may actually deepen the grasp of one logic in detriment of the other. But these asymmetrical translations between logics cannot be understood if one focuses only on the Yshiro. Actually, the translations presented in this chapter probably would have not taken place if the indigenista institutions had not been somehow involved. Their role in these events was critical since it was through their demands, and their capacity to make those demands pressing for the Yshiro, that the direction of the translation between moral logics mostly favored the Cartesian. For the most part, translations in the other direction, that is translations that would strengthen and further stabilize the yrmo, go no farther than the Yshiro communities. Rather, the Yshiro's highly contextual practices, informed by the relational moral logic that suffuses the yrmo, are consistently translated into immutable traits graspable for a Cartesian moral logic concerned primarily with entities.

D espite their grounding in a common moral logic, the critical and integrationist indigenistas that observed the conflict in Ynishta enacted different moral stances that positioned them on opposing sides of a dramatic plot involving dire alternatives. These stances arose from the intersection between their baseline Cartesian moral logic and the networks in which each one of these indigenista stances took shape. In the mid-1980s, when the split in Ynishta happened, integrationist and critical stances were still operating with different imaginations. The former upheld the imagination Indians, which supported the idea that the right thing to do with "Indians" was to develop them by transforming and fully incorporating them (along with Nature) into the modern(izing) national society. The latter, in contrast, was already operating with (and contributing to the authorization of) the increasingly stable imagination Indigenous Peoples, which supported the idea that the right thing to do was to promote their sustainable development, understood as the preservation of their cultural traditions and the environment in which they lived.

Over the years, the decreasing dominance of the imagination Indians, and its eventual displacement by the imagination Indigenous Peoples, has come to be understood as a "moral improvement." For example, an index of the end of the hegemonic coincidence was the emergence of the idea that exercising pedagogic violence was no longer the right thing to do to Indians. From the dominant Cartesian perspective, this would suggest that the moralities applied in relation to the Indians improved because it was "learned" that representations of the Indians as savages, backward and the like, were not accurate; Indians (now indigenous peoples) were actually people who lived in harmony with nature, who cherished egalitarianism, and so on. This (supposedly more accurate) "representation" of the Indians requires another (improved) moral imagination: not development but sustainable development. Yet, rather than having achieved a more accurate representation of the "object" Indians, one is in fact dealing with an altogether different reality, with other objects, subjects, and moral stances. This new reality contains some promises for furthering the pluriverse, but also reveals the profound grasp that the modern regime of truth has on many of us, a symptom of which is this paradox: while the new moral imagination sustainable development embodies seemingly contradictory moral stances regarding what to do with indigenous peoples, ultimately these stances end up producing similar results.

Knowing

Critical indigenismo spearheaded in Paraguay the process of authorizing the imagination Indigenous Peoples and contributed also to authorize its "siblings," Environment and Risk. This process began at the height of the Southern Cone's civil unrest in the late 1960s and early 1970s, and therefore, radical ideals about the role of intellectuals in the transformation of an unjust society, which were popular on the Left at the time, nourished the thought and actions of these indigenistas. Central tenets of this perspective included the notion that knowledge is not neutral, that subordinated people's knowledge is crucial for their own liberation, and that the most fruitful position that intellectuals could adopt in relation to subordinate groups was not as vanguards but as interlocutors and catalysts for their knowledge (see Fals-Borda 1977; Freire 1970).

These ideas were the foundation of the Barbados Declaration (International Work Group for Indigenous Affairs 1971), which called on anthropology to commit itself to the struggle for the liberation of indigenous peoples and forcefully reclaimed the need to respect indigenous peoples' cultures. Interestingly, Miguel Bartolomé, Miguel Chase-Sardi, and Georg Grunberg, three of the eleven signatories of the document, worked at some point in Paraguay. Moreover, Adolfo Colombres, one of the theorists of *antropología de apoyo,* the version of engaged anthropology that emerged from this milieu, was also associated with Marandú—the project that in the early 1970s was aimed at preparing cadres of indigenous leaders in Paraguay—and with the people who later formed CSPI, the NGO that supported the move of the Tomaraho to Ynishta (see Chase-Sardi and Colombres 1975; Colombres 1982, 1992:9).[1]

Although some of those who formed the radical sector of indigenismo were professional anthropologists, the majority were active and interested citizens who were not, or not mainly, affiliated with the academy. Thus, the intellectual production of critical indigenistas was geared more toward political mobilization than toward satisfying academic criteria of scientific validity. Moreover, for this sector, so-called scientific neutrality amounted to nothing but an endorsement of the status quo. For example, several years after the end of the turbulent 1970s, Miguel Bartolomé still condemned a group of anthropologists from Centro Argentino de Etnología Americana (CAEA), who worked in Paraguay, because of their lack of political or humanitarian involvement with indigenous peoples, and qualified them as "avid purchasers of myths" (1989:416).

Underlying the politics of involvement or detachment that divided the anthropological waters was an implicit chasm between radically different positions toward knowledge. In contrast to the "scientism" of CAEA, for the anthropologists connected to Marandú, "the scientific value of an interpretation is not as important as is its mobilizing capacity and its political efficacy. This kind of anthropology also searches for scientific objectivity, but the burning needs of the colonized people are not subordinated to it. The task is to . . . search for the interpretation that is more favorable to the group, although without moving far from what is real and true" (Colombres 1992:160).

In the 1970s, this stance was tenable in the context of grassroots political organizing or of working with members of the growing international indigenous advocacy network, such as IWGIA and Survival International. For example, Chase-Sardi recalled that in 1972, when to gather support for Marandú he presented similar ideas in Stockholm, at the UN Conference on the Human Environment, the only one who understood and supported the position was Peter Aaby of IWGIA (Susnik and Chase-Sardi 1995:326). However, this "lenience" toward "scientific objectivity" diminished as the indigenous advocacy network began to build connections with international development institutions. In addition, the rising tide of repression in the Southern Cone also pushed a realignment of discourses of social commitment along more scientific and apparently neutral lines. As all of Paraguay's neighboring countries fell under military dictatorships and state terror, many intellectuals were killed, disappeared, or had to flee. Those who remained in the region had no choice but to become more "pragmatic" and less openly political. The discourse of development and connections with development institutions provided this pragmatist cloak, but not without a price: these institutions required that indigenistas' actions be guided by objective "scientific knowledge." This is how applied anthropology inspired in Anglo-American traditions, where an expert's authority was largely based on his or her "scientific" methodologies (see Grillo 1985; Ferguson 1997; Shore and Wright 1997), took hold in the mid- to late 1970s.

Given that it must be instrumental in guiding interventions, knowledge produced for consumption within development institutions is characterized by the assumption that there is an objective world that is "not just knowable but knowable in positivist, empiricist terms," and thus complex situations "are reified into objectivized categories" (Stirrat 2000:36; see also Ferguson 1990; Arturo Escobar 1995). As professional applied anthropologists produced texts about the situation of the indigenous peoples of the Chaco, this kind of objectivist rhetoric displaced earlier nonprofessional but openly engaged political discourse. While nonprofessionals' writings and activities did not disappear, "professional anthropologists" began to set the terms with which the situation of indigenous peoples was to be described, analyzed, and addressed.

Nevertheless, the professional anthropologists' objectivist discourse did not diminish the radical political underpinnings of many of the critical indigenistas' visions of sustainable development. As newly arrived professional anthropologists mingled with local indigenistas, elements of the previously explicit political views were to some extent incorporated into the new "scientific" views that were becoming dominant in development circles. In the new configuration of expert knowledge, antropología de apoyo's idea that indigenous peoples had to be engaged dialogically was accommodated along with the bottom-up approach that started to be favored by development institutions in the late 1970s (see Rahnema 1992; Finnemore 1997:210–11). Likewise, the view that indigenous cultures should be respected also fit well with the view, increasingly accepted in development circles, that indigenous cultures were ecologically sound and therefore useful for sustainable development.

In 1987, when the conflict in Ynishta caused the split between two Ebitoso factions, there was already a consensus among anthropologists of the Chaco that respecting the hunter-gatherer traditions and ways of life that indigenous peoples were supposedly trying to retain should be a central component in relations between indigenous and non-indigenous peoples as mediated through sustainable development (see Renshaw 1996; Von Bremen 1987; Gómez-Perasso 1987). Although many of these concerned intellectuals shared with antropología de apoyo the idea that preoccupation with the objectivity of knowledge was secondary, they also shared or were aware of what Hornborg (1994) calls globalized "standards of public credibility" that conflate authenticity with self-referentiality and autonomy. For this reason, they portrayed the emergence of Ebitoso traditionalism as the flourishing of a dormant seed that had always been there and therefore as a process that, at its core, had no connection with their own intervention (see Ticio Escobar 1999:357).

Through the years and as the demands for objectivity have become more pressing, this kind of argument has been refined and sophisticated by applied anthropologists through a series of propositions about what constitutes the "indigenousness" of indigenous peoples of the Chaco and about what consequences for proper actions are derived from these "facts." One of these general propositions, implicit throughout entire texts regarding the relations between indigenous and non-indigenous peoples, is that indigenous peoples are the unwilling victims of a process of colonization solely driven by the whites (victimizers). With these roles in place, it follows almost automatically that narratives about the colonization of the Chaco constitute "romances of resistance" (Abu-Lughod 1990), where the complexity of the process, including ways in which different moral logics interact with each other to produce unforeseen effects, is lost. These romances of resistance get their dramatic effect from a storyline that stresses the endurance of "core traits" of indigenous cultures against all odds.

The endurance of these core traits precisely constitutes the second general proposition about indigenous peoples of the Chaco. The trait most often cited is indigenous peoples' morality, which according to several authors is clearly distinguishable from the individualistic Western one. This morality expresses itself most visibly in the economic relations among indigenous peoples (moral economy) and between humans and nature (moral ecology). For example, the moral economy of the Chaco indigenous peoples is supposedly characterized by an equalitarian ethic of sharing which, at least ideally, prescribes the obligation to share with the entire residential group (Renshaw 1996:149; Kidd 1999:44–46). Kidd describes an example of this moral economy.

> Food that enters the household is pooled, and all members have free access to it. . . . [Visitors receive] food whenever people [from the household] eat. It is within the household that children are raised, and this is described by the Enxet [indigenous people from the southern part of the Paraguayan Chaco] as "caring for them." . . . Personal, nonconsumable property is freely lent and borrowed [within the household], often without having to ask permission. . . . Between households, there is a great deal of voluntary sharing of food. This is regarded as an expression of love between people and usually takes place among close kin. . . . Among the Enxet . . . the creation of love is synonymous with the creation of social relationships. (Kidd 1999:45)

Indigenous peoples' moral ecology, in turn, is characterized by a refusal to transform the environment. According to Von Bremen, hunter-gatherers maintain the idea that the resources that sustain their livelihood are abundant enough.

> [They] do not worry about their reproduction . . . because they consider themselves an integral part of the environment. . . . [E]ach natural and cultural phenomena has specific functions that were determined in a past without time. . . . [To] survive in such a world the most important thing . . . is to know, more than anything else, the characteristic qualities [of those phenomena]. . . . Thus, the fundamental objective [in the life] of the hunter-gatherers . . . is to conserve the world such as it is. (Von Bremen 1987:13–14; see also a more recent statement of these ideas in Von Bremen 2000)

In these narratives, what distinguishes indigenous from non-indigenous peoples (or authentic from non-authentic indigenous peoples), aside from whether they fulfill the role of victims or of victimizers, is morality. In principle, what is different seems to be the content of these contrasting moralities, but a closer look reveals otherwise. For example, consider Kidd's depiction of "authentic indigenous morality," where the indigenousness of sharing only emerges from a rhetoric that exoticizes practices that, at least as they are described, the proverbial "Western person" could not fail but to find familiar. In the same vein, consider Von Bremen's depiction of indigenous peoples' "mission in life," a depiction that, aside from being grounded by a formulaic recognition of the nondualistic perspective, does not differ much from some versions of Western deep ecology.

Then where does the difference lie? It lies in the implicit assumption that indigenous moralities are essences out of history. Von Bremen argues that "even a hundred years of colonial history in the Chaco have not eliminated these mechanisms [i.e., the moral ecology of the hunter-gatherers] from the indigenous peoples' behavior" (Von Bremen 1987:10). Kidd, in turn, says that in spite of colonization, exploitation, and missionary indoctrination, the Enxet "have managed to maintain *an authentic indigenous morality*" (Kidd 1999:38, emphasis added). This reification of indigenous peoples' difference is not mainly the result of "outmoded theoretical" positions unaware of the "constructionist turn" in anthropology; rather, it is the result of positions whose coordinates are determined by the development industry's demands for clear-cut and manageable categories, the commitment to cultural diversity, and the Cartesian moral logic.[2] The intersection of these coordinates produce stances that, while they hint at the rupturist story of globalization by seeking to open a space for radical difference, ultimately reinforce the modernist story by reenacting the subject-object divide.

Even as ideas of respect for and dialogue with the "others" signal possible pathways beyond modernity, the reification of difference turns out to be the loop through which one returns to modernity. But this is a dynamic that is not limited to development practitioners, for it is the dominant moral logic that ultimately imposes its imprimatur on the most varied sets of moral stances. My own previous work is an example of this as well. Although I was under no pressure to produce clear-cut and manageable categories, and thus could be more attentive to "the constructionist turn" in academia, I was also committed to social justice and cultural difference—

CHAPTER 5

however "constructed" that difference might be. Consequently, when analyzing the emergence of traditionalism among the Ebitoso, I understood the "invention of tradition" to operate as a more or less conscious strategy to struggle against domination (see Blaser 1992, 1994). In other words, I reified cultural difference as a strategy, which was in turn just a symptom of the underlying fact driving the Yshiro behavior, that is, domination. But the facts that define authentic indigenousness or that explain indigenous behavior are themselves symptoms of a modern knowledge practice that needs such facts precisely because they provide the answer to the question about which relations are appropriate between "us" and indigenous peoples.

In Paraguay, the propositions that define indigenous peoples as victims, as essentially egalitarian, and as spontaneous ecologists have their corollaries in assertions about what legislation and forms of development are most appropriate for indigenous peoples so defined (see Von Bremen 1987, 1994; Kidd 1995a, 1995b; Stahl 1993; Grunberg 1997). The power of these assertions comes from the truth supposedly inscribed in the very being of indigenous peoples. In other words, experts observe certain facts that, above and beyond what indigenous peoples could say about themselves, define what indigenous peoples are. What indigenous peoples might say in this respect is taken, at best, as an index of more profound realities, such as unconscious moralities, underlying economic structures, and the like, which are accessible only to the expert, who would prescribe the proper course of action.

Perhaps the most clearly articulated example of this was provided by Georg Grunberg (1997), who, building on the main tenets of the hunter-gatherer paradigm, proposed a model of sustainable development adapted to the cultural traits that characterize this "way of life": a diversified economy that combines "traditional" hunting-gathering activities in the forest with "modern" gathering activities such as working for development projects, for the ecotourism industry, or for the custody of protected areas. Regardless of the particular circumstances of each group (i.e., the relative predominance of traditional or modern hunting-gathering activities), the inescapable precondition for this kind of project is to ensure land holdings large enough to sustain their characteristically indigenous ways of life without degrading the environment (see also Von Bremen 1994; Kidd 1995a; Serafina Alvarez 1995; Grunberg 1997).

Critical indigenistas successfully furthered this vision of development when the constitutional assembly included in the constitution of 1992 an article explicitly linking the ways of life of particular indigenous communities to the amount of land to which they were entitled. The success of this legislation demonstrates that as the new imaginations Indigenous Peoples, Environment, and Risk became further (corpo)realized, they increasingly shaped the practices of the entire network that linked local indigenista NGOs to international development institutions and donor governments of Western Europe and North America. These imaginations have come to shape even the *integrationist* agenda, but with a twist: integration is promoted not on the basis of knowing what is best for indigenous peoples, but on the basis that no one can know it.

Not Knowing (. . . But Knowing)

For major landowners in the Chaco, the constitutional standing accorded to indigenous rights represented a threat to their interests. Until 1992, landowners averted the risk of expropriation in favor of indigenous peoples by claiming that Law 904/81 could not overwrite their constitutional rights to private property (Prieto and Bragayrac 1995:66). The constitution of 1992 changed this situation completely; with the codification of indigenous rights came a more palpable threat of expropriation for major landowners. As the new constitution was being approved, the main lobbying organization of the landowners, Asociación Rural del Paraguay (ARP), began a campaign against the land claims of indigenous peoples, arguing that "a programme of anti-progress [was] being dealt with to destroy all that the daring pioneers ha[d] conquered in the Chaco [*sic*]" (quoted in Kidd 1995b:72). As land claims and pressures on the Paraguayan government mounted, ARP created an indigenista institution, ARP's Commission on Indigenous Affairs, which began a campaign to "inform the public opinion" about the "reality of the Chaco."

This reality was described in a document, produced in 1994, entitled *Tierras del Chaco para indígenas y campesinos* (Lands in the Chaco for indigenous peoples and peasants), wherein ARP made public its vision of development for the Chaco. The document argued that land claims had paralyzed the economy of the Chaco, that they were unrealistic, and that they responded to the designs of anthropologists and foreigners who wanted to convert the Chaco into an "anthropological exhibit of hunter-gatherers." The central aim of the document was to attack the two main arguments of the critical indigenistas: that the amount of land requested by indigenous peoples was connected to their ways of life, and that these ways of life were more suitable for environmental protection. ARP argued that indigenous peoples were no longer hunter-gatherers and that they were being forced to live as hunter-gatherers against their desires. This was evident, ARP asserted, in their ongoing demands for schools, hospitals, and jobs, and in the depletion of natural resources on the lands that they already possessed (see Asociación Rural del Paraguay 1994).

ARP thus cast doubts on the accuracy of the hunter-gatherer paradigm in guiding interventions. The alternative they presented for achieving the sustainable development of indigenous peoples was based not in the provision of lands but in increased integration of the Chaco into the national and the global market, boosting thus the regional economy and starting the trickle-down process, all of which would open for indigenous peoples a wider arch of life's choices. In ARP's view, the market, and not expert knowledge, was the best mechanism for sorting out what kind of development indigenous peoples should pursue. In fact, the document clearly stated that while indigenous peoples should have a say about their own development, the most important thing was "not to leave indigenous development at the whim of the theories sustained by anthropologists hired by NGOs and some religious orders" (Asociación Rural del Paraguay 1994:309). In short, while respect for cultural differences was touted as important, those differences were conceived as objects amenable to market integration (Asociación Rural del Paraguay 1994:106–8).

Certainly, this was a very interested reading of the "reality of the Chaco," and attuned, as far as possible, to the neoliberal rhetoric of respect for the cultural differences and autonomous decision-making that emerged along with the authorization of the imagination Indigenous Peoples. The full extent to which this was rhetoric alone is revealed by the blatant ethnocentric and evolutionist views that persistently resurface in the document. Nevertheless, although ARP's use of neoliberal rhetoric was circumstantial and interested, it is important to examine it more thoroughly because it reveals the logic through which integrationist agendas have been redefined under the global condition.

Neoliberal prescriptions emerge from a core set of ideas first put forward by Friedrich Hayek in a form that one might call a theory of the market society. This theory is a metahistory of progress in which the modern capitalist society is said to be the result of an evolutionary process through which societies obeying certain social rules, mainly the unhindered expression of self-interest, have prevailed and expanded. While these rules may not have been chosen consciously, the groups who observed them, however unconsciously, were more successful in increasing their numbers than those who did not (Hayek 1973:251; see also Tomlinson 1990:43–44). These rules emerged at the cost of suppressing two moral instincts supposedly ingrained in human nature: solidarity and altruism. According to Hayek, these moral instincts had been useful at other stages in the evolution of society, but they now threatened the harsh but ultimately more adaptive order of the market society (see Gamble 1996:27–31). Why is the market society considered to be more adaptive? Because by promoting the liberty of its members, it ensures life for larger populations. But liberty, here, is more than a value; it is a central mechanism that ensures the survival of the market society. Hayek sees liberty as synonymous with autonomous decision-making. And why is such autonomy critical to the order of the market? Because humans cannot know with certainty what is the right thing to do in order to achieve their own life objectives and to ensure their own welfare (self-interest). Yet if in their ignorance individuals attend to their own business without imposing their visions on others, the aggregate result is that the more adaptive order (i.e., the market) continually reemerges (see Tomlinson 1990:17–66; Gamble 1996:41–44).

Although for Hayek, the market society is the peak of social evolution, its order comes under threat when the two moral instincts, altruism and solidarity, are allowed to make their way into state policy. This occurs when those who believe that human reasoning capacities can grasp the complexity of society begin to dictate, through state intervention, a specific direction to human affairs (redistribution, for example). This unavoidably involves the violation of autonomy and ultimately leads to the demise of the market society and the benefits it produces. Consequently, Hayek proposes a program of action to manage this risk: anoint market dynamics as the overarching rationale which subsumes all other rationales informing social relations (Hayek 1973; see also Kukathas 1989:1–19).

From the core tenets of neoliberalism emerge three points worth further discussion. The first point involves the central role that risk plays in the market-society theory. According to Hayek, modern society has reached the peak of (social) evolution, yet, if it does not contain humans' atavistic moral instincts (altruism and solidarity), it runs the risk of losing all that has been achieved. In other words, the main thrust of the prescription is to prevent this risk. In this sense, it is evident that neoliberalism is very much attuned to the *esprit du temps*. While it is true that *The Road to Serfdom* (1944), Hayek's first statement on the risks faced by the market society, was published long before the emergence of what Beck calls the risk society, it is also true that Hayek's ideas were not recruited for programmatic agendas until the 1970s. As Jobert (1994a:20) has pointed out, the rise of neoliberalism was associated with perceived constraints on economic growth and capital accumulation that started in the 1970s. But these perceived constraints were part of a wider sense of dissonance between what was expected of modern institutions and what in fact resulted. The impact and popularity of the famous report *The Limits to Growth* (Meadows et al. 1975), which made obvious that the environment asserted its agency through the limits it imposed on "modern man's pursuit of progress," is an example of this. In short, the market-society theory gained currency in the 1970s not only because it made economic sense to some, but also because it made sense in a general climate where risk and uncertainty had begun to overshadow ideas of progress and certainty. And it made sense precisely because it addressed the question of how to know and act in a context of radical uncertainty and impending risks.

The second point involves the logic through which Hayek arrives at neoliberal prescriptions. To the question of how to know what is the right thing to do, Hayek responds with a procedure, a mechanism: the market. His governmental prescription is premised on his claim that human intervention in the dynamics of the market society (a dynamics that has evolved without conscious human intervention) will produce enormous afflictions, because humans cannot know anything with certainty. Thus, the proper way to address such a risk is to put market dynamics above the always insufficient cognitive capacities of humans and to let this mechanism sort out the contending claims of a society with different individual conceptions of a good life. This recommendation does not directly address the truth or the good of competing claims; rather, uncertainty about these issues is taken to be ontological. Yet it is implicit that the truth and the good is whatever comes out of the market dynamic through which all contending claims have to be sorted out (see Szerszynski 1996:108–17). The appearance that this procedural answer to the question of how to know does not make substantive claims about reality rests in a contradiction, and in this contradiction rests its truth-power. The contradiction becomes evident if one asks how Hayek can know that his own prescription represents the best way to act. Is it because his prescription derives from the certainty that society operates in the way he says it does? But has he not argued that human knowledge is always uncertain? Or is only *some* human knowledge uncertain, but not his? Through this self-reflexive inconsistency the market-society theory reinstates, at a higher level of abstraction, the ontological divide between (knowing) subject and (known) object and thus reiterates the possibility of claiming absolute certainty without being called into question. Now the knowing subject is located at a metalevel from which it legislates how the (objectified) subjects who make up the world are to sort out their mutually contending "subjectivities." Of course, as the modern regime of truth requires certainty, which is equated with a well-established relation of objectivity, the knowing metasubjects are never implicated in the reality being described. The consequence of this non-implication is typical of the modern regime of truth: the denial of politics as the opportunity to dispute and negotiate fundamental moral claims.

The third point to be made about neoliberal prescriptions concerns the centrality that autonomy and participation have in them. Given the dynamics of the market society, autonomous decision-making is key to ensuring that this "higher" social order reproduces itself once and again. It is therefore no surprise that neoliberalism has been quick to fashion itself as a governmental rationality that is hospitable to the regained autonomy of Indigenous Peoples and the Environment (as is reflected in the temporal coincidence of neoliberal reforms and the inclusion of environmental and indigenous concerns in Latin American constitutions). Moreover, neoliberalism actively seeks to turn all kinds of entities into active participants (as autonomous decision-makers) of the market dynamics. Yet the incorporation of new autonomous decision-making participants requires assurances that none of the decisions made will challenge the predetermined boundaries of the specific kind of autonomy offered by the market. Here is where the ghostly presence of the modern "metasubject" is key, for it is precisely as the invisible frame/legislator that the modern regime of truth redeploys itself in the global condition. The neoliberal logic of framing suffuses throughout contemporary development discourses and practices that target the Yshiro and other indigenous peoples, from the market-society theory that informs them, to the policy framework into which these theories are translated, to the actual techniques used to translate those policy frameworks into specific interventions.[3]

The "unruly behavior" of Indians-turned-Indigenous Peoples, who found in the global condition an opening to make their "subjectiveness" visible to the modern eye, has brought to the forefront the problem of how to integrate (human) "others" into the represented body-politic while at the same time respecting their differences. The response has been multiculturalism, a "technique" that consists in carving out a space for difference within society. In this way, (human) others are incorporated within the global society (supposedly) without having to be transformed in order to fit. For example, amid an overwhelming set of policies that assume that development is dependent on the integration of every country into the market economy, the European Union states, in its framework document about development cooperation and Indigenous Peoples, that many "indigenous economies are oriented towards subsistence rather than the market economy," and that given the pressures that are making these economies harder to sustain, development cooperation should "support indigenous peoples in their efforts to consolidate their economies" (European Commission 1998:5). Moreover, the development of indigenous peoples "should be based on their own diverse values, visions and priorities, bringing out the full potential of indigenous culture" (European Commission 1998:2). Thus, the idea of integration into the benefits of the global society through development no longer requires that the other be disciplined and transformed into the "same." Rather, it is implicitly asserted that the global society can welcome difference and heterogeneity within itself. Yet the space carved out for the display of difference is framed by a larger logic which is not up for negotiation.

In effect, the economic systems, values, visions, and priorities of "indigenous cultures" are tolerated as long as they do not disrupt the wider logic of the market, promoted by neoliberalism as the founding pillar of "global society."

Although they stand at apparently opposite ends, both critical and (neoliberal) integrationist indigenismo end up responding in similar ways to the imagination Indigenous Peoples and its autonomy. Both claim to embrace and respect it, while finding ways to circumvent and deny it. In the disregard for the autonomy of indigenous peoples and what they could say about themselves and the world is implicit the idea that facts (accessible only to the modern, or the "meta-modern," subject) speak by themselves, and the assumption, perhaps the hope, that these facts can conciliate dissension and silence opposition (see Latour 1999:216–57). As Bauman (1993) says, the threat of relativism is always haunting the modern house. However, the production of "facts" neither brings peace nor settles the debates and controversies of the indigenista field. Rather, it intensifies them by obscuring the central problem: that as long as it is assumed that the facts that constitute the reality of indigenous peoples speak by themselves, there is no need to speak *with* indigenous peoples. In this way, even though many experts and institutions from the Paraguayan indigenista field have contributed to shape a propitious terrain to break from modernity, refusing a dialogue that could liberate the pluriverse from the constraints of universalism repeatedly betrays this possibility.

One must not overlook that many deeply committed critical indigenistas have made great personal sacrifices to support indigenous peoples for many years and under the hardest political circumstances.[4] Thus, they have built the kind of deep and respectful relations with the actual indigenous peoples of the Chaco that I am trying to build as well. The refusal to dialogue in a way that could free the pluriverse occurs only in the moment in which these relations are translated into "knowledge," be it in the form of development reports or ethnographies for academics and the wider public. But this is not a minor problem. Indeed, this contradiction reveals the insurmountable limitation faced by intramodern attempts at overcoming the asymmetries produced by modernity/coloniality, for it is not by knowing the human and nonhuman others but by relating to them in other ways that one can overcome these asymmetries.

Relating

But where am I in this story of knowledge and moralities? I started my undergraduate studies at Universidad de Buenos Aires, Argentina, in 1985, a year or so after the military dictatorship (1976–83) came to an end. With the return of exiled academics and a general rejection of all that was associated with the dictatorship years, a Marxist-inspired anthropology became dominant. Although unstated, the idea that being committed to social justice and anticapitalist struggles was a requirement to authorize anthropological knowledge also became dominant. In this context, models of a detached and politically neutral anthropology were pushed to the fringes. In principle, the same did not happen with the objectivist undertones implicit in the idea that the contribution of the discipline to social struggles was to "unveil" the reality of capitalist domination. However, by the late 1980s, poststructural critiques of objectivist approaches began to make headway in some university circles. This, together with the demise of the communist bloc, the anticlimactic experience of the Argentinian democracy (which did not deliver as expected), and the changing conditions of academic work under International Monetary Fund–backed structural adjustment induced a profound reconsideration of the meanings, possibilities, and venues for academic political commitments.

When I began my work with the Yshiro, in 1991, I was not under any concrete pressure to produce instrumental knowledge, beyond a vague moral imperative to be of service to "their cause"—which, I assumed, was more or less similar to that of most oppressed rural people living under capitalist conditions. However, I was not connected to any formally organized political group that would compel me to translate that imperative into a well-defined agenda. Earthwatch and the Argentinian National Council for Scientific Research, the institutions that financed my research at different points between 1992 and 1997, were interested in the "pure" (i.e., academic) aspects of my research, rather than in its practical "secondary effects." In contrast, the Ebitoso leaders who had invited me to work with their community did have practical demands. But these were not about the knowledge I could produce; rather, they were about the skills I could lend for the purpose of obtaining resources that would benefit their community and also enhance their position as leaders. Thus, I soon found myself developing a research agenda focused on processes to which I was clearly contributing.

As I became more familiar with some of the Yshiro, their language, and the contexts of their actions and discourses, the grounds on which my perception of their situation rested shifted. I could not avoid noticing the contradictions between my understanding of their situation and their own understandings. By 1993, I was acquainted with antropología de apoyo, which gave me a roadmap of sorts for my hazy political commitments. Among the postulates of antropología de apoyo was that the anthropologist should contribute to the revalorization of the indigenous peoples' own culture and knowledge, and should "transfer to the oppressed the most important result of the discipline," which was "the description of the mechanisms by which they have been exploited and degraded for centuries. . . . [The anthropologist] must limit herself or himself to informing and putting in the oppressed group's hands the theoretical elements that will allow them to become conscious of their own reality and all that is at stake in it. This transfer will stimulate a change in the group, a process in which the role of the anthropologist will diminish until it disappears" (Colombres 1992:158). Thus, in addition to thinking that I was contributing to the revalorization of the Ebitoso's own culture by collecting information on their "traditional knowledge" and assisting the people of Karcha Bahlut in the construction of their museum, I intended to transfer to them "the most important results of the discipline." Here is where I started to sense the presence of the yrmo, the first hint of its existence coming, of course, as an "anomaly."

The anomaly, from my perspective, was that many Yshiro refused to see themselves as victims of white capitalist exploitation or to understand their reality as the result of a relation between opposing sides. To my renderings of their reality in those terms, my Yshiro interlocutors countered with stories that emphasized their roles as active and willing participants in establishing relations with the whites. Many Yshiro narratives about the contact portray the Yshiro as active and willing parties in establishing bonds of reciprocity with the whites, although it is often pointed out that this bond of reciprocity was, and continues to be, betrayed by many of them. Thus, in contrast to narratives that implicitly delineate the roles of victims and victimizers, Yshiro narratives focus on how their relation with the whites changed and as a result produced their existing mutual roles. Some Yshiro intellectuals stress that justice consists in changing the current relations by rebuilding bonds of reciprocity so that unequal parties might again become equals.

Instead of perceiving that these stories embodied critiques which were grounded in a different moral logic, I tended to understand the "soft criticism" of my Yshiro interlocutors in terms of more or less explicit versions of the idea of hegemonic processes and false consciousness. It was not until 1995, when I encountered critiques of Cartesian dualism (Latour 1993), feminist theorizing on positionality and situatedness (Haraway 1991; de Lauretis 1990; Joan W. Scott 1992), and Native American ontologies as they are expressed in contemporary Native American literature (Silko 1977; Scott Momaday 1989; Vizenor 1994), that I began to consider the possibility that the perspectives held by some Yshiro, which I saw as resulting from hegemonic processes and ultimately as a kind of false consciousness, might manifest a world with an ontology and moral logic different from the one in which I was operating. This led me to question the very assumptions on which my explanations of, and relation to, the Yshiro reality rested. Of course, this kind of self-reflexive "turn" had already been well established as an authorizing condition for disciplinary knowledge. Moreover, the terrain in which I was operating, shaped by the emergence of the new authorized imaginations (Indigenous Peoples, Environment, and Risk), had already predisposed me for a more "dialogic" approach to research.

As I began to pay attention to the different grounds from which I and my Yshiro interlocutors analyzed the asymmetrical field in which we were all immersed, I felt that my "ears and eyes opened" to the existence of another world, and communication with my interlocutors improved. Becoming aware of the presence of the *yrmo* not only allowed me to be more receptive to what people said or did, but also shifted my understanding of the contradictions that I felt about being an observer of processes in which I was actively involved. Although it took a long time, many of these contradictions fell into place when Don Veneto told me that he had saved my life, thereby pushing me to profoundly reconsider my epistemological assumptions and my ontological commitment to a regime of truth that only succeeded in reproducing the very hierarchies that my Yshiro friends and acquaintances were trying to dismantle.

Experiences like the one I had with Don Veneto and witnessing the invisibilizing and decorporealizing effect that the indigenistas' (and, up to then, my own) ways of knowing (or not knowing) had on the yrmo changed my "political" commitment. What started as a combination of academic demands and vague political imperatives to help a hypothetical cause has become a far more complex engagement. I have come to conceive my involvement with the Yshiro, and my analysis and writing about this involvement, as moments of a larger collective performance by which a not-yet-well-defined globality is taking shape. In effect, I see my task as concerned with performing, along with some Yshiro and non-Yshiro intellectuals and social movements with whom I feel a commonality of intention, a pluriverse of "worlds and knowledges otherwise." Of course, to paraphrase an old Marxist dictum, these performances are possible only to the extent allowed by conditions that are not of our choosing. What kind of globality we perform depends on how we deal with those conditions.

One constraining condition that is not (entirely) of our choosing is the dominance of the modern regime of truth (and its associated moral logic); the profound hold that it has on some of us imposes limits on any attempt to transcend it from inside. Another condition that is not of our choosing is what I call the global condition, but this turns out to be somehow enabling for the project of performing the pluriverse, but only if we can escape from the hold of the modern regime of truth. Here is where relating is critical. The two meanings of the term *relating* are for my project indivisible. On the one hand, relating means connecting, being associated, attached, and concerned. On the other hand, it means storytelling, narrating, and communicating (in this inflection, the English verb *relate* is close to the Spanish *relatar*). In the modern regime of truth, knowing (including knowing what is the right thing to do) takes place only when the knowing subject relates to the knowable object without attachment, with the distance of objectivity. Supposedly, this relation produces knowledge, something that according to this regime of truth is clearly distinguishable from stories.

For those of us who have been raised and educated in that regime, shedding this profoundly embodied conception of knowledge and truth can take place only through practice, which means one must stop knowing in the above sense and start relating. As I was somehow compelled to do this by my Yshiro interlocutors, I came to appreciate the epistemological and political possibilities of the relational world in which many of them live. A feature of this world is that what they call knowledge precisely implies enmeshing oneself in potentially transformative relations with human and nonhuman others. Thus, it is never expected that knowledge will bring closure (or certainty), only a deeper understanding of the unending responsibility of using eiwo (the capacity for distinction-making) to relate (in both its senses) the stuff that makes up the yrmo into a meaningful world. In this understanding, the quality of knowing, which is the same as the quality of relating, can be gauged by its effects. Does this knowledge/relation contribute to weave a livable world where differences (of location and not of value) are protected from the negative potency of wozosh?[5]

I speak of my own and other actors' moral stances and enunciative positions at this point in the story because, as Yshiro intellectuals would stress, only by telling first how these stances came out of the primordial indistinction of the puruhle (i.e., by tracing their genealogy) can I engage them properly in the present (the azle stage/dimension). That is, only after narrating how my own moral stance and enunciative position have come into being through the same process that other moral stances and enunciative positions have done so could I engage those other stances without implying that my evaluation and ways of relating (to) them is detached and somehow objective. In effect, as indicated by the relation between puruhle and porowo (in their triple character as stages, dimensions, and narrative corpuses), spelling out genealogies is never simply the enunciation of something that happened in the past, unrelated to the moral stance from which one narrates these genealogies and to the purposes of the narration. Different ways of telling the genealogy of the global condition, including my own way of telling it, make sense only in the context of the moral stances that I have tried to make explicit, and both the genealogies and moral stances are at the basis of the conflicts (and the story) upon which I will focus on in Part III.

My telling of this story is a situated performance that emerges from intersecting "threads" such as the relational moral logic I experienced in the Yshiro communities and the changing disciplinary and political paradigms (fueled by the global condition) that made me prone to dialogical engagements. This particular conjunction of threads has been enabling in that it has given me the space and opportunity to be transformed by my relations with Yshiro intellectuals. However, the asymmetries that curtail and narrow the spaces for the yrmo to be performed exceed my immediate interactions with the Yshiro, and even those that mark the relations between indigenous and non-indigenous peoples in Paraguay. These asymmetries are ingrained in the modern way of knowing. Thus, I strive to contribute to the efforts that some Yshiro leaders and intellectuals are making to strengthen the yrmo, by contaminating my knowledge practices with their relational logic, hoping that, in turn, I will be able to contaminate that of my readers. The unhindered performance of the relationality implicit in many Yshiro practices might be critically important in learning how to enact globality as a pluriverse.

The problematic posed by the global condition, in which the subject-object divide becomes blurred, is precisely how one can know in such a context. Thus far, the dominant response has addressed this problematic by claiming to recognize uncertainty, while in practice enacting notions of certainty and objectivity. As in the case of Paraguayan indigenistas, the shift from an integrationist paradigm to one that respects indigenous peoples' autonomy (translated into respect for their cultural differences) has no correspondence in terms of a shift in the epistemological and moral stances of experts vis-à-vis indigenous peoples. The "difference" inherent in the performance of relationality is constantly translated and tamed into the reified categories with which the Cartesian moral logic can operate. This is one of the ways in which modernity redeploys itself as globality in concrete practices: experts talk, analyze, and propose blueprints for a new relation with the others of modernity, but they do so in a way that reproduces the modernist pattern of relations and reinstates the colonial difference, all the while eschewing politics or, what is the same, the possibility of negotiating the way in which diverse worlds will articulate with each other. In contrast, the relational moral logic embodied by many Yshiro and other indigenous peoples operates on the basis of relational knowledge that is necessarily contextual, partial, and, therefore, always open to be revised in lieu of new experiences being brought into the relations that make up knowledge. This is a moral logic that, not being constrained, lends itself well to perform pluriversality.[6] However, whether this moral logic will expand or will keep being constrained depends in part on how processes of translations are understood and enacted.

3   *Azle*/Translations

Translation looms large among the cultural practices that
at once join and separate us.
—Lawrence Venuti, *The Scandals of Translation*

The work of translation is a work of epistemological and
democratic imagination, aiming to construct new and
plural conceptions of social emancipation upon the
ruins of the automatic social emancipation of
the modernist project.
—Boaventura de Sousa Santos, "The Future
of the World Social Forum"

Behind the Cartesian moral logic that seeks in "reality out there" the ultimate response, one that will settle dissension and end conflict, is lurking the threat of relativism. In effect, if there is no objective reality out there providing the universal ground that would bridge narrow subjectivities, what could possibly forestall the chaos of absolute moral relativism and the death sentence this would imply for politics? Relativism or universalism: these are the only options that the modern myth and its constitution offer.

From a relativist standpoint, nature (or the reality/world out there) is either out of reach or nothing but the reflected image of our own cultural and subjective projections (see figure 1). Therefore, all that exists are cultures which, without the common ground of nature, are incommensurable and incommunicable. The result is absolute relativism. In the second scenario, different cultures have access (however partial and skewed) to nature and thus to a common ground that allows for mutual commensurability and communication. In effect, by having the world out there as a common ground, different cultures can be claimed to be at least partially equivalent. Many modern "experts" (be they academics or activists) would nowadays explicitly claim adherence to the notion that all cultures are more or less equally partial and skewed in their access to nature (or the world out there). However, in their actual knowing practices, they implicitly assert a privileged access to the world out there by enacting universalist claims in the form of ultimate causes, underlying structures, or what have you that are accessible only to the expert's eyes. In this way, rather than simply claiming partial equivalence with

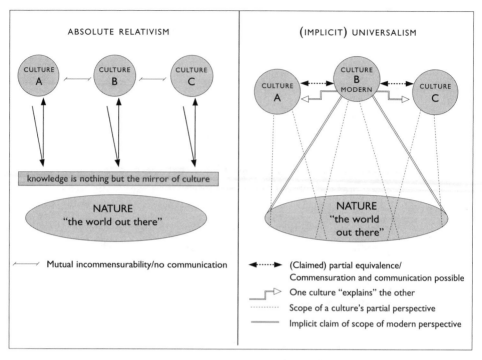

ABSOLUTE RELATIVISM

(IMPLICIT) UNIVERSALISM

CULTURE A

CULTURE B

CULTURE C

knowledge is nothing but the mirror of culture

NATURE
"the world out there"

CULTURE A

CULTURE B MODERN

CULTURE C

NATURE
"the world out there"

Mutual incommensurability/no communication

(Claimed) partial equivalence/ Commensuration and communication possible

One culture "explains" the other

Scope of a culture's partial perspective

Implicit claim of scope of modern perspective

Figure 1. Two forms of conceiving the modern constitution's nature–culture divide.

other "cultures," modern experts end up explaining those other cultures according to modern parameters. Yet, revealingly, making this point is usually equated with arguing for relativism. This makes evident that the modern constitution allows only a very narrow space for conceiving differences in moral and political terms. The terms are so narrow that if a difference is radical, it is considered intractable. Hence, the constant search for some sort of common ground, a universal that will offer an escape from relativism. In the absence of such common ground there cannot exist communication and politics. But what determines communication and politics to be dependent on some form of universalism? What I call the logic of representation, that is, the imperative to conceive and perform translation as the establishment of a chain of equivalences grounded in an assumed world out there.

According to the *Oxford English Dictionary*, the word *translation* connotes the movement, displacement, and change of something which never-

CHAPTER 6

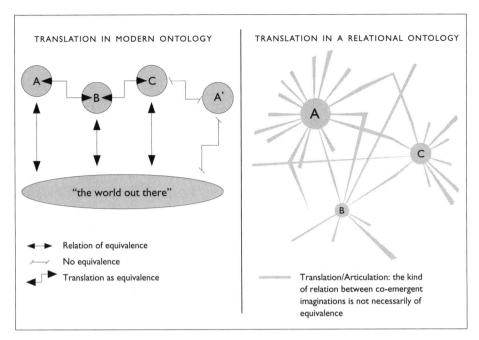

TRANSLATION IN MODERN ONTOLOGY

TRANSLATION IN A RELATIONAL ONTOLOGY

"the world out there"

◄—► Relation of equivalence
⌐—⌐ No equivalence
◄⌐ Translation as equivalence

Translation/Articulation: the kind of relation between co-emergent imaginations is not necessarily of equivalence

Figure 2. The two versions of translation.

theless manages to retain its original properties. In other words, translation occurs when in the movement or change from A to B a property is kept constant in order that equivalence between the former and the latter can be claimed.

From the perspective of the relational ontology I am trying to enact, and building on ANT (see Latour 1999), translation is the process by which imaginations come into being. In contrast to the modern constitution's ontological split between nature and culture, the starting point for the relational ontology is a network in which the points of articulation between different threads or communicating conduits constitute the imaginations A, B, and C (see the right side of figure 2). What gets translated (moved, circulated) among the threads that compose this network is the "vital energy" that gives (corpo)reality to imaginations. The imagination A is constituted by a larger number of articulations (i.e., intersecting threads) than imagination B, which means that imagination A is more (corpo)real than imagination B. It is their mutual articulations that make imaginations (corpo)real, and the same is true for the realities/worlds that a group of imaginations shape. Articulations are the result of the work of translation, that is, of mutual accommodation between intersecting threads in such a way that they eventually become entangled in a mutually reinforcing exchange of vital energy. Thus, from a relational perspective, translation is fundamentally a mechanism of reality-making.

In contrast, from a modernist perspective based on the logic of representation, translation is a mechanism to establish equivalences between representations and an already existing external reality. In effect, as Liu (1999:20) has pointed out, in its common usage translation involves the transfer of the "transcendental signified" from one language to another. The transcendental signified is precisely the claimed original equivalence between world and its representation. It is this equivalence, rather than a generic vital energy, that must remain constant and be circulated through the translation from language A to B and C. The assumed world out there is what operates as the *common measure* (or referent) that allows different representations (or languages) to be thought of as *commensurable*, and possibly as mutually equivalent (see the left side of figure 2).

Under the logic of representation, communication is also predominantly conceived as the movement or circulation of a transcendental signified. Thus, communication is also a form of translation. One can say that communication has effectively taken place when speaker A's proposition about the world out there has been moved or circulated onto speakers B and C in such a way that the propositions the latter speakers hear and produce in response are somehow equivalent to the original (see left side of figure 2). Thus, if speaker A were to say, "The world is blue," communication would be deemed to have occurred if speakers B and C were to respond by referencing the world that A says is blue (either by embracing or refuting the proposition). But were the latter speakers to respond without reference to such world (e.g., in response one of them says, "Dogs bark") communication would be deemed to have failed. In other words, for communication to occur, the propositions generated by those communicating must be somehow equivalent, even while they differ. Furthermore, this equivalence can only be established if there is a common measure behind all the propositions: the world out there. This is why in the modern regime of truth the idea that there is no world out there operating as the common ground (i.e., the idea of incommensurability) is taken to be synonymous to incommunicability and absolute relativism.

Seen from the perspective of a relational ontology, translation under the logic of representation appears to be a very peculiar way of performing reality. As is the case with any imagination, those imaginations performed under the logic of representation remain or become (corpo)real by increasing the number of articulations that form them, yet in this particular case the articulations must be performed as equivalences. Thus, translation becomes overridden by the concern with streamlining, subordinating, or eliminating anything that disrupt the chains of equivalences that have as central referent an authorized imagination or, what is the same, a representation deemed to be the accurate equivalent of reality out there. If one returns to the left side of figure 2, which depicts translation under the logic of representation, and supposes that proposition A ("the world is blue") is deemed an accurate representation of the world, translating proposition A into B and C (which stand for differently formulated propositions) implies keeping constant the original equivalence between reality and its representation so that in different ways all the propositions are saying the same thing. If any new proposition emerging from translation were to say, "The world is red," the chain of equivalences between differently formulated propositions would be broken, and the original equivalence between proposition A and the reality/world would be challenged. Since proposition A is already established as an accurate representation (i.e., is an authorized imagination), the tendency is for new additions to the chain of equivalences being produced through translation to be streamlined so that no disruption occurs and further (corpo)reality is brought to the whole chain of equivalences. In this case, proposition A' ("the world is red") will be discarded as an inaccurate representation of the world out there. If A' were to have said, "Dogs bark," it would not have been considered worth "rational" debate, since it does not reference the world out there, over which one can disagree if it is blue or red. This is precisely what happens when the pluriverse manifests.

In this part of the book I look into how translations based on the logic of representation work to (corpo)realize the modernist story of globalization, and how these translations are disrupted by the Yshiro's performance of the *yrmo*. The focus and anchor of the analysis is the deployment of the neoliberal agenda of global development—one of the most concrete and powerful performances of the modernist story of globalization—as this was translated into a specific development project targeting the indigenous peoples of the Paraguayan Chaco. This chapter begins with the process of translation through which this project was brought into being.

Streamlining a Sustainable Development Project

Since the 1980s, Western European governments and the institutional ancestors of what would become the European Union (EU) increasingly embraced the neoliberal idea that market dynamics provide the best framework for sustainable development (see Leys 2001; Jobert 1994). Thus, implementing what some called the "New Policy Agenda" of global development (Edwards and Hulme 1996) became a condition developing countries had to meet in order to receive aid credits and loans from the governments of "developed" countries and multilateral institutions. By the mid-1980s, several Western European countries individually or through the EU became involved with the democratization and economic integration processes undertaken in the Mercosur countries. This encouraged the creation of close ties between both blocs in the governmental, nongovernmental, and private sectors. As a result the EU, and some member countries on their own, soon became the primary extraregional market, the largest external investor, and the main bilateral aid donor for Mercosur countries, all of which gave the EU important leverage to influence these countries' transitions to democracy (see Freres 1998, 2000; Muñoz 2001).

In 1992, through a "framework agreement for cooperation," the EU promised to help Paraguay address the economic and social challenges associated with the return to democracy. The agreement established as areas of cooperation the usual targets of neoliberal reform, that is, state rationalization, economic liberalization, decentralization, democratization, and the like (see European Economic Community 1992). In this way, the agreement sought to extend the reach (and therefore the corporeality) of neoliberalism—and by extension the modernist story of globalization—by translating to the Paraguayan context the neoliberal prescriptions already embraced by the EU. The production of specific projects and policies was the next stage in this process of translation. But this had to proceed so as to ensure that the chain of equivalences connecting neoliberal prescriptions,

EU policy frameworks, and Paraguayan policy frameworks would not be challenged. In other words, in their specificity as representations of a given reality, the policies or projects into which the agreement would be translated should not contradict the original claimed equivalence between the world out there and neoliberal prescriptions.

In May 1992, the Paraguayan government created a commission that would draft a proposal for the sustainable development of the Paraguayan Chaco, to be presented for funding to the EU. According to the government, the project was necessary because the region's "environment, flora and wildlife are in danger of being damaged if measures are not taken to impede a process of generalized depredation," and because "the Chaco represents for [Paraguay] an important economic reserve given the potential of its natural resources" (Gobierno del Paraguay 1992). No mention was made in this document of the indigenous peoples of the Chaco. In parallel, EU personnel prepared the framework for a technical mission that would have as its task to seek concordance between the objectives of the Paraguayans and the objectives of the EU. In contrast to the Paraguayan counterpart, the framework prepared by EU personnel did mention indigenous peoples, as it established that "the purpose of the project [was] to execute simultaneously two interacting actions: protect the forest habitat of Indigenous peoples and consequently protect their way of life" (SETA 1992:A1). The justification of the project was that the Chaco was under "excessive and irrational exploitation of natural resources" perpetrated mainly by "the big agro-industrial enterprises and multinationals whose main objective is to maximize production" and which are in "total contradiction with the Indigenous culture still existing, essentially a [culture of] forest-dwellers and agriculturalists" (SETA 1992:A1–2).

From its inception, the work of translation necessary to bring into being the would-be project was besieged by the potentially contradictory views that the Paraguayan government and the EU have about the needs of the Chaco. The technical mission's task was threefold: (1) it had to articulate these disparate views and objectives in a common denominator; (2) this common denominator had to be compatible with the cooperation agreement (and the whole chain of equivalences that constituted it); and (3) the common denominator had to be inscribed in a document that would act both as a diagnostic of the problem and as a preliminary project proposal to be sent to the European Commission (the EU's government executive branch) for preparation of a final project proposal. The initial contradiction between the objectives of the EU and the Paraguayan government evolved and impacted the process of translation as the latter unfolded through the Paraguayan indigenista field.

Draft Proposal

In July 1992, the EU technical mission, composed of a team of experts from the Spanish consulting firm SETA arrived in Asunción. As the framework of their contract indicated, SETA had one month to evaluate the proposal made by the Paraguayan commission, visit the Chaco region, collect information on its population and geography, and interview "stakeholders" other than the government before starting to draft their diagnostic and preliminary proposal. In evaluating the proposal presented by the Paraguayan commission, SETA concluded that it did not reflect an overarching vision of development adequate to the Chaco's reality and therefore rejected most of it (SETA 1992:II-18–20). The vision that the Paraguayan commission presented was connected to growing trade among the Mercosur; thus, the Paraguayan government's intention was to "effectively incorporate the Chaco, a national patrimony with a productive potential little exploited, into the economic and social development of the country" (SETA 1992:II-1). Yet, for SETA, economic liberalization contributed to the increasing deterioration of the Chaco's environment. Moreover, the consultants determined that the existing model of growth, based on the expansion of the agricultural frontier to increase outputs for export, was reaching its limit (SETA 1992: I-2).

During SETA's visit to Paraguay, its members came across several critical indigenista NGOs that forcefully argued that projects involving indigenous peoples in the Chaco must address their land claims. Thus, when SETA drafted the preliminary proposal to be presented to the EC, the first objective they set for the would-be project was to support the settlement of indigenous peoples and landless peasants on their own lands (SETA 1992: III-2). Furthermore, in April 1993, two representatives of critical indigenista NGOs visited the person in charge of processing SETA's proposal within the EC office in Brussels and insisted that the resolution of land claims had to remain a central aspect of the project.

Also in 1993, the engineer Juan Carlos Wasmosy became the first civilian president of Paraguay in more than four decades. He came to power amid the tensions of the transition that followed Stroessner's overthrow and tried to advance neoliberal reforms based on a very delicate "governability pact" with opposition forces both within and outside the Colorado Party. Many of the leading figures of those forces were landowners whose properties were being claimed by indigenous peoples or were legal advisors representing landowners in their struggles against indigenous peoples' claims.[1] The critical indigenista NGOs saw the close connections between landowners and the new administration as a potential obstacle to manifesting their visions of sustainable development, which were based on obtaining large tracts of land for indigenous peoples. In this context, the proposed, EU-financed project appeared to be a potential source of leverage for removing this obstacle.

The critical indigenistas first asked the EU to establish as a precondition for giving the Paraguayan government funding for the development of the Chaco that all standing indigenous peoples' land claims should be solved. They also demanded that the Paraguayan government allocate financial resources from the national budget to pay for purchases and expropriations of lands for indigenous peoples. Thus, critical indigenistas sought to intervene in the process by which the Paraguayan government and the EU were translating their agreement for cooperation into a specific project. The critical indigenistas' ultimate aim was that this project be a translation of their vision of sustainable development. The situation thus created was one in which two "projects of translation" (the governmental and the critical indigenista) encountered each other in the proposed project as it emerged. In this way, the governmental translation was affected by controversies over different visions of development taking place in the indigenista field, and conversely, those controversies were strongly impacted by the ongoing process of translating the bilateral cooperation agreement into a specific project.

Given the centrality that equivalences have in translations operating under the logic of representation, it is not surprising that the critical NGOs drew attention to the fact that the rationale behind the requested preconditions echoed that of the framework drafted by EU personnel in 1992: the sustainability of the environment was predicated on a form of land use that was characteristic of indigenous peoples' ways of life, which in turn could only be preserved if indigenous peoples had enough land. Furthermore, attempting to build another equivalence (now in relation to the Paraguayan legal framework), the critical NGOs pointed out that owning enough land was part of the indigenous rights granted by the new constitution. As the EC was preparing the proposal for approval by the Council of Europe (the EU governmental institution where governments of member states are represented) and by the Paraguayan government, IWGIA and Survival International, two European-based NGOs that were part of the international indigenous-rights network, advised the critical indigenistas to lobby the EC through representatives of the member states in the Council of Europe and the European Parliament. In early 1994, critical indigenistas sent letters stating their views to various EU institutions and representatives, asking them to pressure the EC to introduce in the official proposal the precondition about land claims. In July 1994, these efforts bore some fruit: the Asia and Latin America (ALA) committee took notice of certain issues the critical indigenistas had raised. The ALA committee, formed by representatives of the EU member states, was in charge of overseeing the EC's management of development projects in Asia and Latin America. As such, it had the power to modify or suspend specific projects. In this role, the ALA committee ordered the EC to incorporate as a precondition of its proposal that the Paraguayan government allocate a portion of its national budget for the expropriation and purchase of lands on behalf of indigenous peoples.

Soon after, a draft of the EC's proposal began to circulate. In this version much of the language and diagnostic of the SETA proposal had been retained. Thus, the draft included the idea that economic liberalization was the basis of the environmental degradation of the Paraguayan Chaco. Moreover, it pointed out that in order to prevent further environmental degradation it was critical to preserve the way of life of the indigenous population of the area (European Commission 1994). In a meeting in September 1994, ALA committee members adhered to the draft proposal, but asked that a further precondition be added: that indigenous peoples be consulted regarding their development needs. The draft proposal traced a series of phases through which the project would have to be designed and implemented: phase 1, or the consultive phase (eighteen months), during which indigenous peoples would have to be consulted to prepare a Global Operative Plan (GOP) and the Paraguayan government would have to settle the land claims; phase 2, or the operational phase (four years), during which the actions proposed in the GOP would be implemented; and phase 3, or the transference phase (one year), during which the European personnel would transfer the management of the process of development to the "target population." The draft proposal stipulated that total funding for the project would be the equivalent of 14 million euros, yet disbursements at the consultive phase were to be minimal, and no further disbursement was to proceed until the land issue was resolved.[2]

Final Proposal

The wording of the draft proposal and the EU's implicit pressure on the Paraguayan government to solve the land claims infuriated the landowners. In answering, the powerful landowners' association Asociación Rural del Paraguay (ARP) raised protests against the land claims and the critical indigenista vision of development, specifically arguing that indigenous peoples did not need large tracts of land because they were not hunter-gatherers. In addition, ARP echoed the argument that had been raised during the Earth Summit in Rio (1992) by some governments of developing countries, that is, that environmental concerns were used by developed countries to lay claims over natural resources that they had depleted at home but which were still abundant in underdeveloped countries. For example, ARP claimed that the EU supported the campaigns for lands carried out by "anthropologists and foreigners" because by "forcing the developing nations to convert their [sic] indigenous peoples into hunter-gatherers, they [Europeans] save themselves from the ecological dangers that they have created" (Asociación Rural del Paraguay 1994:110). As a solution, ARP proposed the creation of a special commission that would be in charge of steering the development of indigenous peoples in the Chaco. This commission was to be composed of integrationist indigenista institutions such as INDI (representing indigenous peoples' interests), ARP, ASCIM (the Paraguayan Mennonite agency for indigenous development), and certain institutions related to the Anglican and Catholic Churches. Indigenous peoples were to be consulted, but the priority was "not to leave indigenous development at the whim of the theories sustained by anthropologists hired by NGOs and some religious orders" (Asociación Rural del Paraguay 1994:309).

At this point, it was becoming evident that the strategy pursued by the critical indigenistas to (corpo)realize their vision of development (i.e., making the proposed project into its equivalent) had brought their preexisting dispute with integrationist indigenistas into the process of translation started by the EU and the Paraguayan government. Three translations were now at work in the crafting of the proposed project: the governmental, the critical, and the ARP/integrationist indigenista. Both the critical indigenistas and ARP claimed that their visions of development were based on accurate representation and assessment of the "real situation of indigenous peoples"; thus, both would test the "accuracy" of whatever proposal came out of the process of translation initiated by the Paraguayan government and the EU, and, by extension, both would test the whole chain of equivalences in which this proposal would become a link.

At the beginning of 1995, the Paraguayan minister of foreign affairs declared to the press, while at the World Economic Forum in Davos, that solving the total outstanding land claims (around 900,000 hectares by that time) was "a complete fantasy" (press release, United Press International, 30 January 1995). In the same meeting, President Wasmosy said that the NGOs "talk about ecology and rights . . . but say things that are not really true" (press release, United Press International, 30 January 1995). The same press report commented that these declarations had caused dismay among the EC officials working on the project, who declared: "No land, no project." Seeking to verify that this was the EC's position, the critical NGOs asked for an official clarification. To their consternation, the EC responded that if the Paraguayan government solved those land claims that would allow the settlement of nine specific indigenous communities, they would consider the preconditions fulfilled.[3]

Immediately, the NGOs began a campaign to force the EC to accept the criteria that all outstanding land claims be solved in order to consider the preconditions satisfied. Prompted by the coalition of Paraguayan and European NGOs, members of the European Parliament (MEPs) exerted pressure on the EC. An Enxet leader also traveled to Europe to exert pressure on the

EC. However, the EC staff evaded the MEPs' questions and told the visiting Enxet leader that land claims were an issue internal to Paraguay.[4] Finally, just before the proposal was officially endorsed by the Paraguayan government and the EU, in December 1995, a final version of it was circulated. The language and intent of Prodechaco, as the proposal-cum-project was to be known, more than confirmed the critical NGOs' fears. Not only did the issue of the land precondition remain unclear, but the very language of the proposal in its final drafting unashamedly reflects the intervention of ARP. As a comparison with the earlier EC draft proposal and the document with which ARP responded to that proposal shows, the final proposal was clearly meant to appease the landowners' lobby.

For example, the first EC draft proposal stated that the project sought, "on the basis of the active participation of the autochthonous population, to create productive activities without prejudice to the natural environment and respecting the rights of the Indigenous population" (European Commission 1994). To this the landowners' ARP responded that "natives of the Chaco are those inhabitants that have lived in the area for several generations . . . Indigenous, non-indigenous, Mennonites, etc. A group [of inhabitants] must not be benefited at the expense of another group that has been in the area for fewer generations" (Asociación Rural del Paraguay 1994:117). Thus, the final official version of the project was amended as follows: "On the basis of the active participation *of all the sectors* of the autochthonous population . . . [the project will] create productive activities without prejudice to the natural environment *with a special focus on the indigenous population, [but] taking into account the rights of all inhabitants of the Chaco*" (European Commission and Gobierno del Paraguay 1995:2, emphasis added).

Similarly, with regard to who should steer the project, the EC's initial draft proposed to form an advisory committee that "will be composed of governmental institutions [ministries], the target population and *indigenista* institutions not dependent on the government [i.e., NGOs]" (European Commission 1994:3). However, for ARP it was critical "not to leave indigenous development to the whim of the theories sustained by anthropologists hired by NGOs and some religious orders" (Asociación Rural del Paraguay 1994:309). The final proposal stated that the advisory committee was to be composed "of governmental institutions [ministries] and the target population" (European Commission and Gobierno del Paraguay 1995:3). NGOs were not even mentioned.

Yet the most appalling aspect of the changes adopted by the EC in its final proposal was in language that surfaced at different points in the document. This language was so blatant in its ethnocentrism that one cannot avoid thinking that the actual document of the final proposal must have been written by an ARP member. In the EC's initial draft, the need for the project was justified in the following terms: "The activities of hunting, fishing and gathering . . . and a rudimentary agriculture were well adapted to the natural environment. [However,] since the beginning of the century . . . almost all the land of the Chaco had been given away to benefit foreign and national entrepreneurs (loggers and ranchers). An important part of the Indigenous population was exterminated and the survivors, expelled by the new proprietors, find themselves in a very precarious situation and without land" (European Commission 1994:1). To this diagnostic of the situation of indigenous peoples, ARP responded,

> It is a beautiful myth to believe that indigenous peoples do not abuse nature. . . . [The idea] of a "minimalist economy of an egalitarian society" [citing the anthropologist Stephen W. Kidd] fiddles with absurdity when man [sic] has no longer the dexterity of the hunter. . . . This expresses our thinking about relations with indigenous peoples: we share the same moral convictions about how backward races must be treated. . . . [O]ur civilization must not step on traditional cultures, but respect for these must not be an excuse to keep these peoples apart from change and progress." (Asociación Rural del Paraguay 1994:107, 143)

Echoing this thinking the EC's final proposal reads,

> The activities of hunting, fishing and gathering, . . . and an *extremely* rudimentary agriculture were well adapted [to a situation in which] *the population was minimal, but demographic growth makes it unviable nowadays. These [indigenous] populations nevertheless are characterized by extremely precarious conditions in terms of health, housing, and education. All this impedes their integration into the living conditions minimally guaranteed by the National Constitution. [Thus,] they must be integrated into civilization.* (European Commission and Gobierno del Paraguay 1995:1, emphasis added)

Of course, the final proposal also had input from the Paraguayan government, which is most evident in the change of positions adopted toward "economic liberalization." In the first version of the proposal drafted by the "experts" of SETA, it was asserted that the environmental problems of Paraguay resulted from economic liberalization. This assertion remained in the first draft proposal, but in the final version the degradation of the environment, and the consequent need for the project, was blamed on the "protectionism of the industrialized countries and the subsidies to agricultural products" (see European Commission and Gobierno del Paraguay 1995:1).

The first EC draft proposal, heavily influenced by the critical NGOs, was hotly contested by ARP and the Paraguayan government, an indication that the latter considered the proposal not to be equivalent to its own goals of development. This lack of equivalence interrupted and threatened equivalences already established between Paraguayan and EU policy frameworks, particularly those connected to the economic aspects of the transition. The process of economic integration prescribed by neoliberalism, and implicitly or explicitly required by the EU policy on cooperation, was central in the cooperation agreement (see European Economic Community 1992). Moreover, the economic aspects of the transition were a point of interest for European investors with capacity to influence EU policy. The Paraguayan government, in turn, was easily influenced by the key players in the pact of governability, such as the landowners who saw Paraguay's integration into Mercosur as an opportunity to accommodate an increased agroindustrial output. In this context the first EC draft proposal constituted a nuisance for the smooth negotiation of more "substantive" issues, including large investments in infrastructure and the privatization of state-owned services. As the critical indigenista vision of environmental sustainability *by means* of protecting indigenous peoples' ways of life had contentious implications (i.e., land claims) for the relations between powerful Paraguayan and European interest groups, Prodechaco took shape with a very weak commitment to this "means" for achieving sustainability.

The changes incorporated into the final proposal reflect how the process of translation was streamlined so that Prodechaco would become a link conducive to strengthening two sets of established equivalences: on the one hand, the equivalence of interests between powerful interest groups on both sides of the bilateral relation; on the other hand, the chain of equivalences connecting the project all the way back to neoliberal postulates and the modernist story of globalization. Prodechaco's very existence depended on keeping these chains of equivalences free from disruption. This required Prodechaco to be kept at arm's length from the land issue and its associated dispute about visions of development.

Land and Participation . . . but Just a Little

In April 1996, the first seismic movement generated by the unsolved tensions of the "democratic transition" was felt when General Oviedo, a leading figure in the coup against Stroessner, attempted to topple Wasmosy's government. The attempted coup was a turf war between Oviedo and Wasmosy, in which the former used all available populist rhetorical ammunition to gather public support. For a population who had lived for thirty-four years under an extremely pervasive patronage system, the prospects of a shrinking state and privatization schemes were frightening. Based on a populist discourse, and by attacking the privatization plans that Wasmosy was trying to implement, Oviedo gathered significant support from sectors of the population directly or indirectly dependent on the state for their livelihood. Nevertheless, the strong external support that Wasmosy received from the United States, the EU, and especially the Mercosur governments proved effective in disarticulating the alliance that Oviedo had formed with some sectors of Paraguay's dominant groups. This support ultimately deactivated the coup, although without resolving the tensions that generated it (see Costa and Ayala Bogarin 1996; Oviedo 1997; Wasmosy 1998; Narvaez Arza 1998). These events helped to make Wasmosy appear to be a guarantee that democracy and economic reforms would continue in Paraguay.

Such was the political situation in Paraguay when the first two European experts of the U.K.-based consortium that had won the contract to execute the project arrived, in November 1996.[5] The central task these experts were to carry out during the "consultive phase" was to prepare the Global Operative Plan (GOP). The GOP had to serve several functions simultaneously: as an evaluation of the situation of indigenous peoples in the Chaco; as a study of how the land claims had been addressed by the Paraguayan government during phase 1; as a roadmap for the actions to be implemented in the next phase; and as a self-reflexive report on how the roadmap had resulted from consultations with indigenous peoples and local experts on the topic of indigenous development.

The revision and approval of the GOP by the Paraguayan government, the European Commission, and the ALA committee was set as a gate through which the project had to pass in order to continue into the next phase. Thus, in spite of the changes introduced in the final official version of the project proposal, the critical indigenistas remained hopeful, because the precondition that the Paraguayan government had to settle indigenous peoples' land claims remained. Nowhere in the proposal was it clearly stated how many of the land claims had to be settled, yet the critical NGOs believed that they could convince the ALA committee to adopt the position that the precondition would be met only by settling all of them. There were reasons to be hopeful. One of the two experts who arrived in November 1996 was Georg Grunberg, a signatory of the Barbados Declaration who had extensive experience in Paraguay. For the critical indigenistas, this was an auspicious development, since they knew that Grunberg shared their views on development. However, hope lasted only briefly.

Early in 1997 Grunberg was fired at the request of the EC, which in turn claimed that the Paraguayan government had made the request. The weak justifications given by the Paraguayan government and the EC could not disguise the fact that Grunberg had been fired because people at both institutions were concerned that he would create problems when the GOP was sent to the ALA committee for review.[6] From the perspective of the members of the Paraguayan government and the EC most interested in the project (the ministry of agriculture and the EC's South American Unit, respectively), the position that the ALA committee was to adopt regarding the land claims remained uncertain. If the European staff of Prodechaco were to submit an unfavorable report regarding the land claims, the ALA committee could suspend the project. Grunberg's ideas about sustainable development seem to have worried the Paraguayan government and the EC staff enough to fire him preemptively.

Soon after Grunberg left Paraguay, the remaining Paraguayan and European staff of Prodechaco held preparatory meetings for the elaboration of the GOP. The critical NGOs were invited to participate in several workshops. In response, they demanded that Prodechaco clearly state its position regarding the land precondition: did Prodechaco agree that the precondition required all land claims to be settled by the Paraguayan government? Was Prodechaco to inform the ALA committee if the Paraguayan government did not fulfill this precondition?[7] Prodechaco responded to these questions by saying that it was only a "technical project," without the authority to evaluate the performance of the Paraguayan government regarding the land claims. Yet the critical NGOs knew that Prodechaco was carrying out a study of the land-tenure situation.

Given the answer to their questions, the NGOs suspected that Prodechaco would downplay how many of the land claims were unresolved. Therefore, the NGOs asked the ALA committee to order an independent evaluation of the Paraguayan government's performance regarding the land claims. They had reason to think that without this independent review the ALA committee would consider the Paraguayan government to have fulfilled the precondition on land claims despite outstanding land claims. Among these reasons were the likelihood that Prodechaco would produce a biased report and the fact that the Paraguayan government had bought a large amount of land for indigenous peoples. Since 1995, responding to the original pressures from the EU, the Paraguayan government had allocated a line in the national budget to buy land for indigenous peoples, and INDI had bought 400,000 hectares of land for this purpose. However, as research by Stephen Kidd (1997b) showed, those purchases were part of fraudulent operations organized by landowners, staff from the state INDI, and some indigenous individuals. Around 67 percent of those lands had not been claimed by indigenous communities, and, worse, they were either unwanted scraps of land, poor in quality, far from water sources, or subject to floods. In other words, these were lands that indigenous communities were unlikely to ever occupy.

As the end of the consultive phase and evaluation of the preconditions approached, in mid-1998, the critical NGOs claimed that neither they nor the indigenous communities had been granted nearly enough participation in the elaboration of the GOP. In the eighteen months of this phase, only four meetings, lasting one day each, had been organized with indigenous peoples. These meetings were held in different areas of the Chaco, and most indigenous communities therefore met with Prodechaco only once, if at all. In the span of a single encounter, it was assumed, indigenous participants would be able to grasp the objective of the project and then to articulate their "development needs" in relation to that objective. Furthermore, once the GOP was drafted, in early 1998, no one outside Prodechaco was allowed to see it. Responding to requests from the NGOs, Prodechaco informed them that once the GOP was approved by the Paraguayan government and the EC, it would be distributed for consultation in "order to establish cooperation criteria and lines of participatory action for its execution."[8] In other words, participation was welcome only to implement in the "'operative phase" the plan that had been designed behind closed doors in the "consultive phase."

Considering their lack of access and the land situation, the critical NGOs asked the ALA committee not to approve the commencement of the second phase.[9] In July 1998, the EC persuaded the ALA committee that the operational phase should not be delayed, although under pressure by the U.K. delegation the committee did agree that an independent report on the land situation should be provided.[10] This meant that final approval for the GOP was delayed, yet Prodechaco was allowed to implement the actions proposed in it.

In September 1998, John Palmer, an anthropologist hired by the EC to carry out the independent evaluation of the land-claims situation, arrived in Paraguay. His report, presented in April 1999, arrived at conclusions similar to those that had been published by the critical NGOs (see Kidd 1997b; Lackner 1998), that is, that the amount of land reported by Prodechaco as the property of indigenous peoples was inflated and that the method of calculation ran counter to the spirit of the project. "If it does not take into account the communities' land claims as opposed to bureaucratic calculations based on doubtful data," argued Palmer, "it must be supposed that Prodechaco's interest in relation to indigenous peoples territorial rights does not go beyond securing for itself a minimal space required for agricultural development projects—in this way excluding the [traditional] economy of the indigenous peoples."[11]

In July 1999, the ALA Committee summoned a European Commission representative and asked many questions about the project that could not be answered, allegedly because the person directly in charge of the "Paraguayan desk" was on vacation. The committee members decided to put their questions in writing and sent them to Prodechaco's co-directors who would have to respond them in person in the following meeting of September

1999.[12] Prodechaco's co-directors went to Brussels to meet with the ALA Committee knowing that this would be their final showdown with the critical NGOs' lobby and that the survival of Prodechaco was at stake.

The critical NGOs had been able to get the ALA committee members to raise a series of questions that contested the extent to which both preconditions—land and participation in the design of the GOP—had been fulfilled. Prodechaco responded that some land claims were still unresolved for three reasons: first, the landowners' refusal to sell, combined with the refusal of (critical) supporting NGOs to accept alternative acquisitions; second, expropriation involved a lengthy administrative process; and third, the inefficiency and irregularities of INDI's past administrations had delayed the purchases (Prodechaco 1999).[13] The differences existing between Prodechaco's and other reports about the amount of lands necessary for indigenous peoples' development were explained on the basis that other reports had tried to include the issue of land quality. Prodechaco argued that these reports did not specify what they meant by quality of land. That is, the quality of land could be measured only in relation to specific purposes such as hunting-gathering, livestock farming, or agriculture. Prodechaco claimed that there was no research done about which one of these activities was the "chosen developmental strategy of each community" and, therefore, the criteria of quality was preposterous (Prodechaco 1999).[14]

In relation to the issue of participation, and in contrast to the critical NGOs' claims, Prodechaco argued that NGOs were participating in the project and gave the example of ASCIM (the Mennonite agency dealing with indigenous peoples). According to Prodechaco NGOs like European Survival International and their Paraguayan partners did not want to have working relations with the project because they were "opposed to development projects for Indigenous peoples . . . [for] radical philosophical reasons" (Prodechaco 1999). Other Paraguayan NGOs did not want to work with Prodechaco "in the clear hope that the project funds could be re-channeled through the NGO sector" (Prodechaco 1999). Another point raised by Prodechaco was that a distinction had to be made between indigenistas (run by non-indigenous peoples) and properly indigenous organizations, and it argued that in contrast to the former, the project had always had good and fluid relations with indigenous organizations (Prodechaco 1999).

Prodechaco thus presented the indigenous land problem not as a systemic problem (i.e., as the result of the unofficial but operative policy of the Paraguayan state), but as a contingent one. It blamed the lack of resolution of land claims on lengthy bureaucratic procedures, the idiosyncrasies of landowners, and critical indigenistas, as well as on specific acts of corruption within INDI, but not on the Paraguayan government's lack of political will to overcome these problems. Prodechaco also undermined the value of the critical NGOs as valid interlocutors for the kind of issue the committee was evaluating. In effect, in not-so-veiled terms, it implied that the critical NGOs would be dissatisfied regardless of what Prodechaco could accomplish, because they were against the very idea of development. It made no mention of the fact that the critical NGOs were proposing alternative forms of development.

It is ironic that Prodechaco could present what clearly amounted to admitting the failure of the participation precondition as an argument to undermine the claims made by the critical NGOs. By arguing that the amount of lands demanded by critical indigenistas was preposterous because nobody knew which developmental strategy the indigenous communities had chosen, Prodechaco indirectly acknowledged that its proposed action plan was not the result of consultations with the indigenous communities. Yet, with its feeble response, the ALA committee deemed the preconditions fulfilled and authorized Prodechaco to proceed.

Translation Instability and Streamlining

Prodechaco's existence depended on its capacity to distance itself from the land issue. This "requirement" was the source of Grunberg's dismissal and of Prodechaco's refusal to evaluate in the GOP the Paraguayan government's performance regarding land claims. The actions of the EC and the Paraguayan government, as well as those of Prodechaco once the process of translation brought it into being, demonstrate that those links that are already part of a chain of equivalences have a vested interest in streamlining new articulations/translations so that they do not disrupt the existing chain. Under the logic of representation, extending the chain of equivalences without disruption is key to lending (corpo)reality to a given imagination, which thus can claim to be an accurate representation of the world out there. Nevertheless, adding a new imagination to an existing chain of equivalences can have very uncertain consequences, for there is no guarantee that these additions will not introduce "intractable" dissonances and, thus, instability and disruption. Yet, in spite of the uncertainty and instability that translation might bring into existing imaginations (claiming to be accurate representations), the very (corpo)reality of the latter depend on the ongoing addition of new links that this process achieves. In the next chapter we will see how Prodechaco addressed the need to translate—and therefore extend and stabilize—itself into concrete interventions, while trying to control the instability introduced by this process of linking into the chain of equivalences.

The first thing that Prodechaco did once it came into being was to produce its own vision of development in the form of the Global Operative Plan (GOP), which continued the process of translating the chain of equivalences connecting the project, powerful interest groups, neoliberal prescriptions, and modernity-cum-globality. This translation was critical to further (corpo)realize Prodechaco and the whole chain of which it was a part. As a new vision of development, the GOP had to become authorized. Under the logic of representation, to do so, Prodechaco would have to be convinced that the GOP accurately represented the reality at hand, that is, the "situation of indigenous peoples of the Chaco." One of the preconditions set by the ALA committee stipulated that indigenous peoples participate in the making of this particular representation and in designing the action plan proposed to address it. Hence, Prodechaco produced the GOP not only under the logic of representation, but also under the logic of participation. But what does the logic of participation entail? In development, participation and representation appear as closely related concepts: if representation means that one thing stands for something else in a relation of equivalence, surely the optimal equivalence would be a thing standing for itself. From this perspective, participation in development projects takes place if the target population represents itself in the development process.

Constrained by these two logics, Prodechaco struggled to translate into the GOP the chain of equivalences it was part of. The demand that indigenous peoples participate in making this representation of their own situation introduced a destabilizing factor into the existing chain of equivalences. Prodechaco dealt with this potential threat by envisioning its mandate as helping indigenous communities to represent themselves "accurately"—another instance of streamlining, though the "objects" in this case are not documents but communities. Before entering into this discussion, I must address some changes that took place in the Yshiro area during the 1990s. Information about these changes and their effects is needed to understand how Prodechaco blended the logics of representation and participation in a plan whose objective was to make the Yshiro communities (and other communities) into new links of the chain of equivalences that gave (corpo)reality to the modernist story of globalization.

Leveling Hierarchies

Many things changed in the Yshiro area as the Paraguayan transition advanced and the integration of Paraguay into Mercosur deepened. New economic enterprises emerged alongside new sociopolitical dynamics, including, for example, the growth of an economy built on low-capital commercial fishing. In 1990, and as fishing stocks dwindled in the southern parts of the Paraguay River, Paraguayan fishermen appeared in greater numbers in the area of Alto Paraguay. These fishermen were soon followed by intermediaries in the fish market, who saw a better profit in dealing directly with the Yshiro.[1] As the presence of these intermediaries (often called *patrones*) increased the demand for fish, more Yshiro turned to fishing as their main source of cash. Parallel to the growth of the "fishing economy," an increasing number of Brazilian entrepreneurs bought lands in the area. In contrast to the previous owners, who had used the lands for real-estate speculation, these entrepreneurs clear-cut the forest for cattle ranching and did not tolerate Yshiro individuals hunting on their properties.

These processes were accompanied by important changes in patronage networks. Although in the "fishing economy" debt-bondage practices persisted to some extent, certain critical differences were introduced. Trading fish did not require large amounts of capital, a thorough knowledge of the area, or complex connections with local and national authorities; therefore, myriad "fishing *patrones*" from southern towns appeared. These new *pa-*

trones competed with the old local *patrones*, each striving to have the largest number of Yshiro individuals working on their behalf. By 1996 some Yshiro had themselves become fishing *patrones*, using the little capital they had built on the basis of steady salaries as public employees. Increasing competition for land and natural resources pushed many Yshiro, especially young women, to migrate to Asunción for employment opportunities. Thus, some women also became more independent from patronage networks, or at least from those that more directly affected the everyday life of the communities. Given that migrant workers and fishermen were not dependent on particular *patrones*, by the late 1990s most Yshiro had a higher degree of economic independence in relation to particular Paraguayan *patrones* than they had ever had.

All these changes had important consequences for how the Yshiro imagined themselves, their desires, and the problems they faced. Many older Yshiro interpreted these changes as being connected to the end of the Stroessner regime and the subsequent diminution of the aid (medicines, food, clothing, and the like) circulating in patronage networks. A few months after the attempted coup of General Oviedo, in 1996, Don Clemente, an Ebitoso elder in his late sixties, who had once been well situated in these networks because of his connections with the local Colorado Party and military authorities in Bahía Negra, ruminated:

> We indigenous peoples don't need fancy clothes, bicycles, or luxuries. We just need our lives to be long. That's what we need. We do not need to be millionaires. We need a government that once in a while sends somebody to visit us and see if we need hospitals or schools or work. That's what we need from a government . . . that's why sometimes we miss General Stroessner. . . . He gave us many things, land, clothes, medicines. . . . [President] Wasmosy knows very well that we are poor, but once he won the election he left the people. Then we do not know who will be fair with us, who can help us. We think that perhaps Oviedo will be like Stroessner. (15 June 1996, tape recording)

Like Don Clemente, many other people, especially those past their forties, experienced the loosening of the patronage networks with anxiety and an increased sense of insecurity in terms of their livelihood. Thus, many of them expressed their desire for the government to have a stronger presence in the area. They complained that "the *seccional* (the Colorado Party's local cell) does not receive aid on our behalf anymore," and they asked, "Where is the government?" Many cherished the memories of a time in which *patrones* were plentiful.

This anxiety was not shared by the *cultureros* (a term the traditionalist Ebitoso coined to refer to themselves). Many of them also noted the changes in the patronage networks and the dwindling circulation of aid, but as Doña Tama, an Ebitoso woman in her late fifties, explained, "We are poor, but we always have something to eat. Look at my family, they never go hungry. Those people say 'we are poor, we have nothing to eat' because they do not know the bush, they do not know where to look for food." In reference to the cultureros, her husband, Tito, explained,

> Here everybody knows, *costales y vangelio* [Pentecostals and Evangelists] want to get the children into their church. When the meeting in the church finishes, they come here and tell us we have to leave this [culture]. We say no, if they want to watch, watch. We are all in our culture. We are always looking for [sustenance] little by little. No fights, no discussions. That's how we do things. When we meet in the *tobich* we bring the *weterak* [newly initiated] to the bush to look for *mbuzu* [eel], *ñandu* [ostrich], and *carpincho* [capibara]; all together, young and old. Then we return and we sing and stay all night. . . . We teach our children. Look at that youngster [pointing to a young male of around fifteen years of age]. He does not know how to look for [subsistence], yet he knows how to fuck. If he goes looking for a woman, then his father will have to support them both, and their baby, because the son does not know how to look for food. And if there is something, we share. If I get something, I have to give a little to my neighbor. If he is lucky tomorrow, he will give me [some]. You don't look for food only for yourself, it is for everybody. That's what we do. Teach our children. *Wetete* must learn his work. It is not like going to watch TV.[2] That's not work. Those young people go watch [TV] and come back late. In the morning they sleep while the father and mother are looking for food. And the children call their father *sham* [brother] and their mother *nam* [sister]. It changes all, they have another understanding. They no longer have respect for their mother and their father. The children do not look for water, do not make fire.

The mother has to bring the water, cook their food, wash their clothes. The only thing she does not do is wipe their asses. . . . That's why we want to have our own land, where we can stay without troubles. We can grow some vegetables, go hunting, and have our *cultura*. (16 May 1999, tape recording)

By the mid-1990s, the cultureros had come to rely more on hunting, gathering, fishing, and gardening for direct consumption. Only occasionally would some of them take up a changa (casual labor) in order to obtain money for buying market goods. Thus, they were relatively independent from *patrones*. What allowed this group to maintain their independence from *patrones* was, as Doña Tama and Don Tito explained, their *cultura*. Cultura is much more than the debylylta (initiation ritual); it is the whole livelihood that debylylta structures. Debylylta establishes gender and age distinctions with specific duties and responsibilities, and thus contributes to "producing" young adults able to fulfill their obligations toward their families and residential group. In addition, the relations that cultureros establish with the ukurb'deio (nonhuman powers) also involve training the younger generations on how to secure their subsistence from the bush and from the river.

However, by the late 1990s the cultureros had begun to find it increasingly difficult to live their cultura. As Don Tito's remarks underscore, their neighbors had begun to press them into abandoning their ritual practices, and the introduction of mass-media technology was luring their youth away from their responsibilities. In addition, an emerging group of Ebitoso had become much more aggressive toward the cultureros, and as some of these individuals reached leadership, the cultureros were threatened with expulsion from the communities where they resided. Thus, from the perspective of Don Tito and other cultureros living in Diana and Ynishta, obtaining lands for themselves was essential.

The emerging Ebitoso group that had turned aggressive toward the cultureros was composed of Pentecostals and what I call "small Yshiro entrepreneurs." Several contradictory accounts describe the origins of the Ebitoso Pentecostal group, but, in any case, it is clear that not until after 1994 were their numbers substantial enough to harass the cultureros. The small entrepreneurs had been slowly forming since the Ebitoso settled Ynishta. A few of them were able to gather a little capital to buy cows and enlarge their stock by grazing them on the lands of the communities. Later this group was enlarged by the Yshiro fishing *patrones*. Most of the small entrepreneurs obtained their initial capital from steady incomes either as teachers, as health auxiliaries in the communities, or as state employees in Paraguayan towns neighboring Diana and Ylhirta. With their access to financial resources, these people became influential individuals in their communities and were at times elected legal leaders. Yet the always limited authority of influential individuals, in association with the changes that had affected the wider patronage networks since the end of the Stroessner regime, meant that in the late 1990s legal leaderships based on patronage relations were considerably weakened.

Two vignettes serve to illustrate the visions held by some of these small entrepreneurs about themselves, their desires, and the problems they faced. Teresa Payá, a thirty-eight-year-old Ebitoso teacher, was in 2000 one of Diana's leaders. Her husband, Gaspar, a forty-year-old Ebitoso, was one of the few Yshiro hired on a permanent basis by a nearby ranch. Their steady income had allowed them to purchase a refrigerator, a TV set, and a VCR. With these technologies, they turned their three-room house into a home theater, where they showed videos rented from a store in Bahía Negra and sold fresh beverages to the public. During a visit in 1999, and as I was preparing my backpack to return to my home in Karcha Bahlut, they were showing a documentary on the Amazon. Those in attendance included Antonina (Teresa's sixty-something-year-old mother), Gaspar, three of Teresa's children, and five or six other visitors. Suddenly, Antonina yelled out to me, "Mario, Mario, come to see this!" "What is it? I have to finish my packing," I answered, still concentrated on collecting my things. "You are an anthropologist, come see the Indians!" I could not help but notice the irony, and looking at her sitting in the front row, I said, "What do you think I have been doing since April?" There was a moment of perplexity, and then everyone burst into laughter. Gaspar, always ready for a joke, started to scream "Uuuuhh" while beating his mouth, mimicking the "Indians" of Old Hollywood's Westerns, which they rented from Bahía Negra. Teresa, who was in the kitchen, said, laughing, "What a *totila* [crazy, clown] you are, my mom is talking about *indios ité* [in Guarani *ité* means "accurate, pure, exact, real"), *indios atrasados* [backward Indians]."

On another occasion, I met Lamberto on the boat that makes weekly trips between Bahía Negra and Concepción City. In his late forties and one of the first legal leaders of Ynishta, Lamberto was relatively well-off, possessing a couple dozen cows and a small store. As was usual when we met, we quickly launched into a conversation about the communities. I was telling him about some ideas that the current legal leaders were discussing, when he interrupted me, saying, "Do not forget that it is difficult to trust the Indians ... they just want to get *provista* [goods] today and then they don't want to work. They do not think about planning what they are going to do tomorrow; they just worry for today ... that's what the anthropologists say." I was struck to hear Lamberto reiterating features of the hunter-gatherer paradigm. I asked whether that was the way he behaved, to which he replied no. "Then, aren't you an indigenous person?" I continued. "Perhaps I have become more like a Paraguayan," he concluded with a crooked smile.

In both instances my interlocutors expressed their sense of a lack of correspondence between dominant views of indigenous peoples and their own lived experiences. With the socioeconomic and political changes that had taken place in the Yshiro communities, images of indigenous peoples—as hunter-gatherers, extremely poor, and dependent on Paraguayan *patrones*—had become incommensurate with how many of these small entrepreneurs experienced themselves. For many of these Ebitoso, the dominant images of indigenous peoples constituted a central problem. For example, Teresa and Maria Romero, a thirty-six-year-old teacher who belonged to the group that had become intermediaries in the fishing business and was the wife of the head leader in Ynishta, were struggling to get rid of a Paraguayan supervisor from Bahía Negra. They resented the fact that although they each had more training and credentials than their supervisor, the ministry of education did not consider them well-suited to run their own schools without Paraguayan supervision because they were indigenous women. But instead of contesting the images of indigenous peoples as backward, Teresa and Maria labeled other Yshiro as the "real Indians" and attempted to distance themselves from those Yshiro. Thus, unsurprisingly, they resented the cultureros who reinforced the image of the Yshiro as "backward Indians." In fact, they often complained that the cultureros were a "drag" on progress because they did not send their children to school and always disputed what the *más letrados* (those with higher levels of literacy) said and did.

The changes that took place from the mid-1980s onward meant for most Yshiro greater economic independence from particular *patrones*, but also increased competition for resources. Relative independence therefore did not prompt widespread nostalgia of the kind Don Clement expressed concerning the old *patrones*, who had provided some degree of economic security. Rather, Paraguayan and Brazilian *patrones* were viewed as competitors who were after the same resources the Yshiro needed to survive. Given the increased visibility indigenous peoples acquired during the constitutional debates in 1992 and the intensification of flows of information between the communities and the capital city, former Paraguayan *patrones* were prevented from using the most blatant forms of coercion that had been at their disposal during the Stroessner regime. Thus, *patrones* had difficulties not only in controlling the Yshiro and keeping them in debt-bondage relations, but also in discouraging them from becoming competitors for the same natural resources. This created resentment among Paraguayan *patrones*, who often voiced, in the presence of Yshiro individuals, their opposition to the government dispensation of lands to indigenous peoples. They argued that those lands would go to waste because indigenous peoples did not work the land. Modesto Martinez, a close Ebitoso friend of mine, who was in his early forties at the time, demonstrated familiarity with these stereotypes in his description of how some Yshiro leaders had agreed to give the hearts of palm trees to a processing factory.

> They [the leaders] did not call for a meeting. They just let those who wanted to cut the trees to do it . . . for nothing. Those trees have a lot of value. You can make handicrafts, hats, baskets, our houses. . . . They are worth a lot more than their hearts. But they cut everything. And we must be very careful what we do with the land because the new generations of the Paraguayans will criticize how we use the land and will try to take the land away from us. We must be prepared to face that attack, because the Paraguayans say that the government gives land to the indigenous peoples for no purpose, that they do not work it. The Paraguayans want to take our land from us so that they can sell it to the Brazilians, and we depend on our land. (16 May 1999, tape recording)

Modesto not only repeated the commentaries expressed by Paraguayans neighboring the Yshiro communities, but also, unknowingly, echoed the arguments raised by the ARP in order to deny indigenous peoples' need for more land (see Asociación Rural del Paraguay 1994).

For people like Modesto, who had experienced ten to fifteen years of fending for themselves and their families without depending on strong patronage networks, the increased competition for natural resources became a central preoccupation. Modesto wondered how to face this situation.

> Nowadays people don't care for their community, [they] just care for themselves. . . . I have never been a leader, but if I were, I would say that we need to work by ourselves. . . . We need to be productive because there are many elders who have nothing and we have no work to give them. And the people don't think and the Paraguayans come to fool us. Not long ago a guy from INDI came and said, "What do you need? Because I have a project that will come out in six months . . . I come to take note of your opinions. What do you want?" That's what he said, this Paraguayan by the name of Hugo who came from INDI. He said that in August we will have the project, but he never returned. We do not ask for anything. We are just used to the Paraguayans coming and asking, "What do you want?" And we say, "We want this or this." But they say, "No, no, that's too little." So somebody asks for an oxcart, and the other for cows, and the Paraguayans say, "Yes, yes, what else?" So we ask for a motorboat for medical emergencies. . . . You see, we are not the ones who ask for projects, they are the ones who come, the politicians, too. They all come and ask, "What do you want?" But all those things are not true. They just come to get our signatures and then they eat all the projects [pocket the funding]. They probably make arrangements with the leaders and they eat all of it. I say, I have not been a leader yet, but I say that we have to do it ourselves. The Paraguayans lie to us. I met that Hugo guy in INDI once. He almost stepped on my foot and did not recognize me. And I gave him a liter of honey because he had come to help us [laughing]. What a fool! (16 May 1999, tape recording)

As Modesto's comments underscore, demands for state aid did not disappear, but cynicism about it was rampant. In contrast to the Stroessner era, the increased flows of people and information between the communities and Asunción had provided many Yshiro with a wider understanding of the state's operations and its apparent displays of generosity. This knowledge also fueled cynicism about the legal leaders' role in the patronage networks.

Internal hierarchies were further flattened as an effect of increased economic independence from patronage networks, making it very hard for any particular group among the Yshiro to press on another group their own imaginations of themselves, their desires, and the problems faced. Thus, the loosening of patronage networks was accompanied by increasing instability for legal leaders, who were voted in and out of their positions with astonishing celerity. For a time, the intensification of centrifugal forces which had been operating since the whites had settled the area appeared to be largely irrelevant for most people in the communities. However, as Modesto's comments imply, by the late 1990s it had become clear to some Yshiro that it would become increasingly difficult to face the emerging challenges to their subsistence base without curbing those forces.

In any case, in August 1997, the Yshiro participated in one of the workshops Prodechaco organized in order to consult with indigenous communities regarding their development needs. Apparently, Prodechaco's staff interpreted the leveling tendencies operating in the communities as a lack of clear mechanisms of representation. This "lack" would become a central concern of Prodechaco.

Seeking the Right Links

When one analyzes the early documents and proposals related to Prodechaco, it is evident that those who drafted them assumed that non-indigenous NGOs had a greater capacity to produce "accurate" representations of indigenous peoples than indigenous peoples themselves. For example, during the mission carried out by SETA in 1992, only four indigenous individuals were among the 118 individuals interviewed in the process of preparing the first proposal of what would become Prodechaco (see SETA 1992:IV/1–IV/6). Later, in the technical proposal made by the consortium who won the contract to carry out the project, it was clearly stated that participation of the "marginalised people in the planning stages of intervention . . . would be achieved mainly by using national and international NGOs working with [them]" (Halcrow Rural Management / Natural Resource Institute 1995:19). In this sense, non-indigenous NGOs appeared, in principle, to be the perfect link that could articulate the reality of indigenous peoples via the chain of equivalences that had been extended and further (corpo)realized with the creation of Prodechaco.

Although after the firing of Grunberg it had become clear that the Paraguayan government and the EC would not allow the land issue pushed by the critical indigenistas to be part of the project, Prodechaco staff still hoped that by involving those NGOs in the workshops leading to the GOP, they could save the reputation and legitimacy of the project in front of European observers such as NGOs, members of the European Parliament, and, more important, the ALA committee that would make the final decision on whether Prodechaco would proceed following the end of the consultive phase. However, most of the critical NGOs did not take the bait and refused to participate in the workshops unless Prodechaco adopted the position that all the indigenous peoples' land claims had to be solved by the Paraguayan government. For Prodechaco, this was impossible to do without risking its own existence. Thus, the project found itself facing a dilemma: how to produce a legitimate GOP while disregarding those organizations that had been foreseen as the ones that would provide the project with accurate representations and be the appropriate vehicles for participation.

This dilemma was compounded by another problem. While Prodechaco was preparing the GOP, the hunter-gatherer paradigm used by the critical indigenistas continued to serve as the "most accurate representation" of indigenous peoples of the Chaco. Consultants contracted by Prodechaco to elaborate the GOP basically restated the idea that indigenous peoples of the Chaco were (essentially) hunter-gatherers (see Prodechaco 1998b). Moreover, these ideas were being used to train project staff on how to deal with indigenous peoples. This was risky: the more the hunter-gatherer paradigm was legitimized by Prodechaco's own hired experts, the more elements the critical NGOs had to dispute the project's commitment to the interests of indigenous peoples. In effect, the critical NGOs argued that by trying to downplay indigenous peoples' land needs, Prodechaco was showing a lack of interest in preserving their ways of life. Given that Prodechaco could not address the land-claim issue (at least if its staff did not want to be fired like Grunberg), it found itself compelled to produce alternative representations of the indigenous reality on which to base the GOP. In short, Prodechaco had to find the "right link" for helping it to further translate the chain of which it was itself part. This link had to solve both the problem of representation and the problem of participation, and the solution came in the form of a new imagination.

In August 1997, some Yshiro went to the only participatory workshop organized by Prodechaco in Alto Paraguay, where the Paraguayan co-director explained that Prodechaco was not, at that point, designing any concrete project.[3] Rather, he said, Prodechaco wanted to discuss with indigenous peoples how it could help them in their development. Having delivered these explanations, the co-directors invited participants to speak. A man was the first to respond: "We want 500 rolls of wire for a fence, and also shovels and drills." Then a woman read a list: "Forty rolls of wire, 150 metal plaques for roofing, 55 milking cows and bulls for each family, chairs for the church, and two mares." Several other individuals followed suit in the same fashion.

If one analyzes this occurrence in relation to Modesto's comments on how politicians and state agents came to the communities promising development projects, it is not hard to understand why the people responded to Prodechaco's call for participation in this way, informed as they were by previous experiences with development projects. Later during that workshop, people from the communities got into a heated discussion. While the topic of the discussion was Prodechaco's decision to hire, without consultations, two former Yshiro leaders residing in Asunción to conduct a census of the indigenous communities of Alto Paraguay, the discussion itself reflected the flattening of hierarchies within the Yshiro communities. The participants complained that many other people in the communities could have done the job, but that the same individuals were always hired by projects and indigenistas who considered them representative of the Yshiro. Many argued that it would be more fair to allow community members themselves to decide who should take a given task or assignment. Finally, they agreed to send a formal letter to the Prodechaco co-directors requesting that they consult with the communities before making decisions that concerned those communities.[4]

This kind of experience did not seem to prompt Prodecho to question its process of participation. Rather, Prodechaco interpreted these complaints as an indication that the communities suffered from a lack of "mechanisms of effective representation and self-management." In fact, Prodechaco saw this lack as the "problem beneath all the other perceived problems for the development of Indigenous peoples of the Chaco" (Prodechaco 1998a:104). In addition, Prodechaco held the critical indigenista NGOs partially responsible for this problem. A section of the GOP, titled *Prodechaco: Analysis of the Problems*, stated that the indigenous peoples' reputation as the hunters and gatherers of development projects resulted from the state of poverty in which they were immersed. Poverty left indigenous peoples no alternative but to take whatever people of "good will" gave them, a condition that, the argument continued, only strengthened the relations of dependency that indigenous peoples had with strangers. Dependency, in turn, impeded the development of a clear structure of leadership and local government able to steer the process of development (Prodechaco 1998a:102–4).

In a separate memorandum attached to the GOP, the European co-director of Prodechaco was even more explicit.

> Despite the popularity of Prodechaco with the target population, there remains entrenched opposition from some NGOs. Their position is that . . . Indigenous communities still need protection from outside influence. . . . [E]xperience has shown that it is exceedingly difficult to "protect" unsophisticated Indigenous populations from exploitation by both the unscrupulous and the *well intentioned*. In these circumstances, unless the communities themselves are assisted to develop the social, *representational* and technical skills to voice and defend their own interests . . . their continued exploitation . . . is inevitable.[5]

The hunter-gatherer paradigm was unsuitable to represent indigenous peoples in the way that Prodechaco needed in order to keep itself and the chain of equivalences of which it was part free from disruption. Thus, Prodechaco produced an alternative imagination claiming not only that indigenistas did not represent indigenous peoples accurately, but also that they were at the core of the "development problem" of the Chaco. Prodechaco then concluded that if "well intentioned" NGOs could not represent indigenous peoples accurately, indigenous peoples would have to represent themselves.

Yet the indigenous peoples for the most part lacked the "representational skills" that would make them good links in the chain from which Prodechaco emerged. That is, they could not produce representations of themselves and their situation that were workable (i.e., nondisruptive) for Prodechaco. The solution was to redefine the objective of Prodechaco: now a central objective of the project would be to develop the representational skills of the communities. In this way, in a single move, the new imagination Indigenous-Peoples-Lacking-Representational-Skills eliminated the NGOs as accurate representatives of indigenous peoples and gave Prodechaco an objective that circumvented the land issue associated with the hunter-gatherer paradigm.

Prodechaco planned a series of learning stages through which communities would become able to represent themselves accurately (i.e., to become a nondisruptive link). The series began with "community formation," which involved learning how to express the problems of the community in the form of plans and projects, and developing the skills necessary to manage those projects. Supposedly, the exercise of these capacities through planning would promote self-determination, and self-determination would in turn "signal" Prodechaco to disburse financial resources to be managed by the communities (Prodechaco 1998a:115–16).

The planned stages, from community formation to self-determination, clearly support the argument that by helping communities to acquire "representational skills," Prodechaco intended to make indigenous communities new links that would extend with minimal distortion the chain of equivalences of which the project was part. Prodechaco could not add to the chain just any link; each link had to be carefully formed or shaped in advance. This posed a challenge for Prodechaco. On the one hand, according to the logic of representation, Prodechaco had to teach indigenous communities how to represent themselves accurately. On the other hand, according to the logic of participation (and its implicit claim of respect for autonomous decision-making), Prodechaco had to be able to claim with at least a minimum of plausibility that the "philosophy of the project [was] not to carry out activities that would modify the indigenous culture" (Prodechaco 1998a:103). The challenge was thus to produce the link required by Prodechaco through indigenous peoples' own autonomous decisions and participation.

The way in which the communities were invited to participate illustrates how framing helps to streamline "autonomous decision-making" by apparently noncoercive means. In the workshop organized in Alto Paraguay, this invitation was delivered in the following manner: "We are here not to distribute goods. . . . We just want to facilitate your own development, steered by yourself. Of course, you will need skill development . . . and participation is essential. *If you want to work with the project, well, here we are, but if you have other ideas, so be it.*" This way of inviting participation disregarded Prodechaco's own view that "structural poverty" would push indigenous peoples to accept whatever they were offered—including whatever Prodechaco offered them. In this circumstance, Prodechaco's idea that indigenous peoples were completely autonomous to accept or not accept the invitation to participate in community formation was willingly blind to the coerciveness of the situation. It is true that participation was enticed through the promise of financial aid; however, participation was also coerced by the implication that Prodechaco could choose simply to do nothing for indigenous peoples if they did not pursue community formation. Thus, a coercive situation already present (such as the critical problems faced by indigenous peoples) is used as a tool to discipline indigenous peoples into certain desired forms or conducts. The fact that these "tools" are already present lends the intervention an appearance of being noncoercive, and those who use these tools seem to not be implicated in the "autonomous" decisions of the target population.

"An Order Functional to the Wider Order of the World"

Faced with the need for articulations that would translate and extend the chain linking Prodechaco, neoliberalism, and the modernist story of globalization into "the real situation of Indigenous peoples," Prodechaco initially identified non-indigenous NGOs as suitable for the task. That is, from the very beginning, indigenous peoples and their imaginations were not considered appropriate to further articulate/translate this chain. However, when it became clear that the critical NGOs and their conceptions of the hunter-gatherer paradigm were in fact not suitable for this purpose, Prodechaco found no other alternative than resorting to indigenous communities as links. Yet, from Prodechaco's perspective, indigenous peoples lacked the necessary representational skills; that is, it was not clear that they would produce representations that were nondisruptive of the chain being translated and extended.

Prodechaco staff perceived this "lack" as an urgent problem in dire need of resolution. As one Prodechaco staff member said, "I know that what we are doing here is to create a certain order that is functional to the wider order of the world. The best we can accomplish is that this more circumscribed order shelters the communities from the worse impacts of the wider order.... But the truth is that if the communities do not develop these [representational] skills, they will disappear as distinct communities as globalization advances" (4 March 2000, field notes). From this staff member's perspective, the only way the Yshiro could survive was to learn from Prodechaco how to represent themselves in a way that was comprehensible for "the wider order of the world." In other words, the "autonomy" of the Yshiro communities could be preserved only if the Yshiro became integrated as a nondisruptive link in the dominant chain of which Prodechaco was part. It is notable that for the people of Prodechaco the genealogy of the imagination Indigenous-Peoples-Lacking-Representational-Skills quickly became invisible. In effect, Prodechaco's staff soon forgot that this imagination had emerged from the constraints created by the refusal of the most important indigenista NGOs to participate in the project and by the project's own pressing need to produce new articulations with indigenous communities in order to become more stable and to avoid being characterized as just another desk project without connection to the "reality of indigenous peoples." The eagerness with which the new objective of Prodechaco was embraced by its personnel signals the (corpo)reality that the new imagination acquired: this (imagination) "fact" provided an unmistakable answer as to what was the right thing to do.

Concern for the autonomy of indigenous peoples and the preservation of their cultural diversity is an inherent aspect of this imagination. Yet autonomy and multiculturalism are also components of neoliberal governmentality insofar as they do not threaten the chain of equivalences that give (corpo)reality to that governmentality and to the modernist story of globalization associated with it. This is evident in Prodechaco's intention to shape the Yshiro communities in specific ways. Indeed, the community formation promoted by Prodechaco sought to enact the Zapatista slogan "a world in which many worlds fit," but with a twist: by not only attempting to control the introduction of instability into the chain of equivalences it was extending, but also pushing indigenous communities to discipline themselves in (superficially) "culturally diverse" ways that were compatible with (and would reinforce) the chain of equivalences leading all the way back to the modernist story of globalization.

However, demands for and promotion of autonomy and cultural differences have a doubled-edged character, for they open up spaces of uncertainty. In the same way that Prodechaco conceived the situation of indigenous communities as problematic because they could not readily offer themselves as the right links for the chain it was extending, some Yshiro intellectuals began to problematize their situation according to their own preoccupations with the state of the yrmo. By the mid- to late 1990s some of them had already begun to foresee that the centrifugal forces operating in their communities would constitute an enormous handicap in the near future. Among them were the traditionalist leaders, who, when informed of the existence of Prodechaco, began to plot a different goal for it. Shortly after the participatory workshop in Alto Paraguay, one of them contacted me and asked for a "special favor": could I do research about this project? He said the Yshiro leaders wanted me to find out all that I could about Prodechaco's functioning, who was in charge of it in Europe, how it could be lobbied, and so on. He ended the conversation by saying, "This time we [the communities] are going to suck a lot of milk from this tit before the Paraguayans finish it all."

While I was in Europe doing research on Prodechaco, another round of seismic movements of the Paraguayan
transition took place in Asunción. On 23 March 1999, the Paraguayan vice-president, Luis Maria Argaña, was assassinated. This
occurred in the midst of an impeachment process that he had
promoted against the recently elected president, Raul Cubas
Grau, for freeing the former general Lino Oviedo, who had been
detained for the attempted coup of 1996. The killing of Argaña
unleashed five days of public demonstrations, and several dem-
onstrators were killed or wounded when police and paramilitary
forces shot into the crowds. After the Brazilian government convinced President Cubas Grau to resign in order to avoid a blood-
bath and Lino Oviedo was granted asylum in Argentina, the head
of parliament, Luis Gonzales Macchi, formed a "government of
unity" with the main political parties (see Bergonzi 2001; Abente
1999).

The new government quickly began to replace officials in state
agencies, including INDI. The first step the new president of INDI
took was to bring indigenous leaders to Asunción for a meeting.
Thus, when I arrived in Asunción in late April 1999, all twelve
legal leaders from the Ebitoso communities were there. Bruno
Barras, the former traditionalist leader who resided in Asunción,
organized a meeting so that I could report to the leaders what
I had found out about Prodechaco. The meeting stretched over
two days and was attended by the current legal leaders and several other Yshiro observers who for one reason or another were
in Asunción at the time. Bruno opened the first meeting by in-
troducing me to those who did not know me personally, then

talked about his experiences when he visited Canada for a conference in 1998, where he had met Cree and Iroquois leaders, and toured the Six Nations reserve in Southern Ontario.

> I went [to Canada] and there were Six Nations and Cree, and an indigenous woman that was an anthropologist! Look at this, university professor! And at night we went to the university where the indigenous youth, who are also students, danced their ritual dances. They follow the culture of their elders. They have no shame in it. And all the professors were very grateful to them that they showed their dance to them. . . . This is the great mistake of many of us who want to embrace the ways of the Paraguayans and deprecate our own knowledge. Because it is only through our own knowledge, our culture, that we are respected as a people. With this we are granted our rights as indigenous peoples . . . that's how we got Karcha Bahlut. . . . Mario was telling me that it is very difficult to [politically] do anything on your own, and I was telling him that perhaps that's the reason why our ancestors always joined in the *tobich* and through it kept united. . . . The problem is that we have left these practices; that's why we have so many problems, because each one pulls in their own direction. That's why we have to do as the ancient ones did before. We have to work together. (29 May 1999, tape recording)

All the leaders and most observers who spoke afterward made more or less the same argument, locating the root of many contemporary problems in the loss of the unity that, they said, had characterized their ancestors. However, when I told them that Prodechaco was not planning to start with "concrete projects" for Alto Paraguay precisely because they thought that communities in that region lacked solid organizations, the leaders pointed out that most indigenous communities in the Chaco were in similar situations and that factionalism and unstable leadership were common everywhere. The difference, one leader said, was that, excepting those in Alto Paraguay, the other indigenous communities in the Chaco were governed by non-indigenous NGOs. He added, "Prodechaco is following the easiest road. At the beginning Prodechaco said that they wanted to work directly with the communities, but now they are working with the Mennonites [ASCIM], the Catholic Church, and other NGOs."

As the meeting continued into its second day, the leaders grew convinced that a common organization was needed in order to address the challenges posed by changes undergone in the last fifteen years by the country, in general, and Alto Paraguay, in particular. It was clear for them that these challenges could not be addressed by individual factions or by recourse to the known patronage networks. In fact, this visit to Asunción had shown the legal leaders (most of them recently elected) that old patronage networks were almost useless; none of them were going to return home with any form of aid to distribute among community members. However, meeting participants pointed out that although the idea of creating a common organization had been circulating for two or three years, it had never translated into action because of what seemed to be enormous obstacles. Among these were the divisions within the communities, the lack of trust toward legal leaders, and external interferences which exacerbated these other problems.

In this context, the leaders viewed the possibility of tapping into the resources of Prodechaco to boost their leadership and to mobilize the communities in the direction of unity as a great opportunity. But it was also clear that they would be able to obtain resources from Prodechaco only by addressing this institution's concern with the Yshiro's supposed lack of organizational and representational skills. After the meeting, some leaders and I had an informal interview with the co-directors of Prodechaco, who, faced with the leaders' demands, recognized that Prodechaco was not yet ready to start community formation in Alto Paraguay. However, they promised that if the Yshiro created their organization, some concrete projects would start immediately.

I was asked by the leaders to visit each community, speak with the people, and collect their impressions of the proposed organization. After that, I was to collaborate with the leaders to organize discussions in each community, from which, it was hoped, a clear mandate for the creation of the organization would emerge. As these discussions advanced, the leaders would keep meeting in order to draft the statute of the envisioned pan-Yshiro organization. From May to September 1999, the legal leaders and I traveled between the Yshiro communities, and between these communities and Asunción. We held communal meetings and interviewed INDI officials, critical NGOs, and Prodechaco staff. Every trip between locations was meant to bring the pan-Yshiro organization to life by articulating different imaginations together. In this process, the imagination Yshiro Nation came into being.

Addressing Internal Divisions: "Diablos" and "Costales"

During our conversations in Asunción, the leaders had identified the division of the Ebitoso along religious lines as one of the main obstacles in the path toward creating Unión de las Comunidades Indígenas de la Nación Yshir (UCINY), as the pan-Yshiro organization was to be called. This was not the only division, but it appeared to be one of the more intractable. As the community meetings and workshops got under way, in May 1999, it became clear to me that for most people, these divisions had their origin in the arrival of the missionaries and their gospel. For one reason or another, most Ebitoso had converted to the Christian faith. Adults who at that time (the 1950s) had been raised in contact with the puruhle and porowo narratives tried to elaborate commonalities between these narratives and biblical ones. From these attempts, two ideas spread among the Ebitoso: first, that the Bible (particularly the Ten Commandments) was equivalent in almost every way to the *Esnwherta au'oso*, except that the latter did not talk of a Lord Jesus; second, that all things related to the Anabsero and the rituals were "diabolic." Yet, the idea of the diabolic has for some Yshiro, especially elders, a very specific meaning. On their arrival, the missionaries told the Yshiro that the indigenous peoples were being decimated by diseases as punishment for tinkering with the devil and engaging in diabolical activities (i.e., the initiation ritual); the missionaries then offered the Yshiro a safe place in the church and the Gospel. The suggestions of the missionaries conjoined with the Ebitoso's own understanding that diseases were punishment delivered by the anabser Nemur for performing rituals improperly. Thus, the Ebitoso came to associate the tobich, the ritual, and particularly Nemur with the devil. Yet the devil did not strike those Ebitoso as the personification of evil; rather, it seemed to them that the devil merely enforced the Esnwherta's heavy discipline on the Ebitoso at a moment in their history in which they had become unable to act in accordance with her rules. For example, as Don Veneto explained,

You have God. He is the same as Esnwherta. He has his word [au'oso] that you have to obey. If you do not obey, here comes Nemur, like a policeman. He comes and punishes you. You get sick or you die. Same as the devil. Nemur and devil are the same thing. Here *eiyok tobich'oso, eiyok diablos* [we are the men of the tobich, we are devils]. We are watching the *weterak* [initiated males]. If they do a bad thing, we bring them to the disciplinary place [tobich] and punish them. *Eiyok diablos* [we are devils]. (8 March 2000, tape recording)

In the 1950s, when Nemur seemed to be on the brink of accomplishing his threat of annihilating the Yshiro, some Ebitoso "tested" the refuge offered by the missionaries. Susnik's Ebitoso informants in 1956 and 1968 spoke of *la prueba* (the test) in reference to their abandonment of the initiation ritual (see Susnik 1995:204–5). Today, culturero elders usually narrate their incursions into Christianity as an evaluative period from which they returned disappointed.

In contrast, for some other Ebitoso, especially among the younger generations born after the ritual was abandoned in 1956, the imagery of the devil did connote evil, as did all things related to the ritual. Still, this was a kind of evil with which one could negotiate without necessarily compromising oneself in absolute terms.[1] In any case, this initial difference later became associated with differences between traditionalist ("backward") and acculturated ("developed") factions. With the emergence of the Pentecostal group, these associations were further reinforced. By 1999, every time a Pentecostal or someone who saw cultureros as the embodiment of backwardness became legal leader, he or she would begin to harass the cultureros with threats of expulsion from the communities.

One of these conflicts reached a peak almost at the same time as the leaders began to inform the communities of their intention to create a pan-Yshiro organization. Shortly before my arrival in Paraguay in April 1999, the leaders of Ynishta (all Pentecostals) had said that they would call a general meeting to vote on whether or not the initiation rituals were to be allowed any longer in that community. Given that the cultureros of Ynishta were a minority, they looked for support from the cultureros in the other communities. Therefore, as soon as I arrived in Karcha Bahlut that year, I was summoned to the tobich by Don Veneto, who had already gathered a group of konsaho from Diana, Karcha Bahlut, and Ynishta. They asked me to record a message and some songs, which I was to take to Pai Puku Radio, a station, located in Central Chaco, which transmits messages and music sent by indigenous peoples in their own languages. Certain passages of what the konsaho said as they took turns speaking underscore their perspective on the conflict. Speaking in Yshiro, while the others kept singing in the background, Don Veneto said,

> As you have heard from Ginés there are many good things in our culture . . . we want everybody to hear us. . . . Our mother Esnwherta and her mate, Nemur, had said that culture will be the protection against diseases, against the flood, against the drought. They also said that there must be young people to become *weterak* so that tomorrow when we are all dead there are people left to carry on with debylylta. . . . We do this and I don't understand why there are people who hate us so much . . . I wonder if the preachers fear for their partners, if they fear Don Veneto will fuck them.[2] I want everybody to hear this. I want everybody to know that I have no hatred for any person and that this is the way everybody must be, because that's what our elders taught us. I want everybody to be at ease and united as our ancestors told us. We are *diablos* . . . we sing for the benefit of the community. (1 May 1999, tape recording)[3]

Their emphasis on the need to keep good relations among community members was not just rhetoric for the occasion, but characterized multiple conversations that I had with cultureros on topics ranging from gender relations, to leaders, to younger generations, to the causes of diseases. For example, Modesto, an Ebitoso friend of mine, witnessed a discussion in the tobich of Karcha Bahlut between Don Veneto and a man who had suggested that they should expel a Pentecostal who resided in the community. Modesto described the exchange.

> Don Veneto said [to the man], "You must not speak like this. Each person has his or her own idea of what is the right thing to do . . . but you cannot go into other peoples' houses to take them out and bring them here, [you cannot] speak words that are not proper. I respect them very much even if they are Pentecostal. We must leave each one to do as they

think is better. Those who do not come [to the tobich], do not come. We must not utter bad words about them. . . . One must respect them and watch out what comes out of your mouth, watch your words. Otherwise you can make yours and your fellows' paths diverge, and [not recognizing where the other walks] you may suddenly collide with him or her." (18 August 1999, tape recording)

Don Veneto was implicitly referring to the idea of eiwo, the human capacity to distinguish the positive from the negative. In effect, correct talk is usually taken as a sign of eiwo. Cultureros often insisted on the need to use eiwo in order to be accurate and self-restrained when relating to others (humans or nonhumans). Of course, cultureros criticized costales (Pentecostals) for trying to force them out of their ways. However, most of them rejected the idea of coercing people into abandoning their Christian faiths. The spirit of the "tolerant" attitude displayed by the cultureros is perhaps best captured with the fatalist remark with which Don Tito usually ended his criticism of Pentecostals: "Each one knows what she or he knows and does what she or he does. Some acquire eiwo, others don't."[4]

The conflict between Pentecostals and cultureros quickly became a central topic in discussions about the pan-Yshiro organization. From discussions in formal community meetings and other less formal conversations, I realized that the position adopted by Pentecostal and "entrepreneur" leaders with regard to the cultureros was not supported by many people. Not even in Ynishta, where the majority of Pentecostals lived. One day, after an interview with a group of cultureros in Ynishta, I was discussing with Modesto what I had heard, when he said,

They [cultureros] do as the Yshiro porowo. They have no shame of their culture. They are not ashamed of our language. Hopefully it does not finish. There are Europeans and Paraguayans who like this culture. But nowadays the children of the teachers do not want to speak their own language. Then, it is worthwhile that they [cultureros] keep on with the culture. They have the right. Nobody goes to the costales and says to them, "Why are you screaming?[5] Don't do that!" But when they [cultureros] are singing the costales come and say, "Those devils are singing." Instead of protecting their people and their culture, they reject it. For me that is no good. Otherwise, we have to prohibit everything.

The leaders [of Ynishta] speak bad of the *cultureros* because they do not know. They never come and see. If you want to know you have to come and see. I am not a *tobich'oso* [member of the tobich], but I like to go and see what they do, what they say. I have seen them get together and give advice to the *weterak*. And they said to them, "There are elders who can no longer work but can sing, and they need to eat. So, weterak go look for their food!" They are watching who is old, who is sick, and they say, "Let's send our daughter to ask for food."[6] They are protecting the people, they look after their fellows. It is not just about singing. Look at me, I am almost becoming a Paraguayan. If they do not keep the culture, soon there will be no more Yshiro, and the Paraguayans will come and say, you are not indigenous. So we have to let our people be. Why do we have to abandon the *porongo* [maraca made with gourd] to play guitar? We are *indígenas* [indigenous peoples], we are not Paraguayans. (16 May 1999, tape recording)

Discourses like this were common in Karcha Bahlut, where Modesto lives most of the year, and they echo the language of traditionalist leaders. But in the years between 1991 (when I first stayed in an Yshiro community) and 1999, similar types of discourses had begun to resonate in other communities as well. As the patronage networks loosened, many Yshiro had become more vocal about their feelings that the "Paraguayanization" of the Yshiro was a process with few benefits and many negative effects. In some sense, cultureros and costales were two relatively clearly bounded and proactive responses to these feelings. Individuals from both groups narrated in similar ways how they embraced cultura or *el culto* (the Pentecostal cult), respectively: they pulled themselves out of a life of alienation and senselessness to be reinserted into meaningful networks of sociality. For example, when I asked Don Vierci, a sixty-year-old culturero living in Ynishta, why he had "returned" to the *Esnwherta au'oso*, he responded,

We took that word of God that sister Nora [a New Tribes missionary] brought. They said it was a word that would save us. But we did not get anything from those religions. They say the same things that *Esnwherta au'oso* says, but we did not enjoy the way in which they did it, *no nos hallamos* [we did not find that we were in our own selves/place] when following the missionaries. . . . As the new generations were born, they had nobody to teach them. They only have school. They are *letrados* [literate; deceitful, cunning], but they have no *eiwo*. . . . They have children but do not raise them. Look how many children are around being raised by their grandparents while their father and mothers are partying and getting drunk. That's why we want the younger people to learn and respect the *Esnwherta au'oso*. They learn respect for their elders, they learn *eiwo*. Esnwherta does not want the youth to go around without direction. (12 July 1999, tape recording)

Julio Romero, an Ebitoso man I had known since 1991, embraced Pentecostalism in 1998. In 1999, he explained to me his reasons for converting in terms similar to those in which Don Vierci had spoken of his "return" to the *Esnwherta au'oso*.

I was going around without sense, I worked and spent my money drinking. Always like that, always like that. I fought with my brother. I fought with my friends. I never profited from my work. I was lost. Then, Gregorio [another *costale*] talked to me, "My brother, why are you suffering like this? Why don't you come and receive a gift from God?" He told me that, and I began to go to the temple. And then I received the gift and my mind enlightened. I thought, What is the benefit of drinking? What is the benefit of smoking? What is the benefit of partying? There is no use in that for me. In that moment I accepted the Holy Spirit and escaped the hold of Satan. . . . Now I know the good things from the bad things. The church does not prohibit anything, each one knows what is correct and what is not. The brothers are there to help each other to see the right track, not to prohibit anything. Nobody obliged me to join the church, Gregorio just showed me the door. (9 September 1999, field notes)

When the topic came up in community meetings, most people expressed ambivalence and doubts about the ways in which both the cultureros and the costales addressed feelings of a general social malaise. While some people criticized the cultureros for not following the *Esnwherta au'oso* "properly," they did not disapprove the *Esnwherta au'oso* itself, as Pentecostals did. Rather, most people recognized the problem as the failure to live up to its rules. Moreover, most Ebitoso used the ancient Yshiro as a measure against which to compare the present, and when it came to the quality of social relations (one of the core matters addressed by the *Esnwherta au'oso*), the comparison was clearly favorable to the past. Again and again during the meetings, workshops, and conversations that I witnessed, people repeated what I had heard during the first meeting of the leaders in Asunción: that one of the roots of their contemporary problems was that the Yshiro had lost the sense of unity that their ancestors kept through the tobich.

However, not everybody was happy with the implicit (or assumed) suggestion of "going back" to the rule of the tobich. Many non-Pentecostal Ebitoso women and youth were particularly apprehensive of this since, according to them, the discipline of the tobich implied their exclusion from decision-making and the right of elderly men to exert a heavy control over them. As these concerns were voiced, the leaders who had mentioned the Tobich explained that it was the tobich's spirit of unity that they were looking for through UCINY, not to again organize the Yshiro communities around the tobich. These leaders reassured younger males that nobody would oblige them to join the tobich. The pan-Yshiro organization could be inspired in its unity, but it was an altogether different kind of organization that should include all the Yshiro regardless of religion or gender.

While some consensus was reached regarding these concerns, positions were less workable, especially among the leaders, when it came to what should happen with the initiation rituals. In early July 1999, when the leaders held their first meeting to draft the statutes of the organization, the different stances on this issue came face to face. Babi Ozuna and Alejo Barras, both *tobich'oso* who had been recently elected leaders of Karcha Bahlut, asked what attitude the organization would take toward the performance of debylylta. Intense discussions ensued. Some of the leaders, including the Pentecostals from Ynishta and those who were small entrepreneurs, argued that cultureros and their practices were a hindrance to progress. They said that the cultureros were lazy and did not want to work. They argued that the cultureros were disrespectful of the legal leaders, and that there were individuals from this group who often traveled to Asunción and claimed to be leaders in order to ask for aid. Other leaders contested these ideas, pointing out that cultura had much to offer the Yshiro with regard to their contemporary predicaments and arguing that the practice of going to Asunción to fake leadership was a general one, and not limited to the cultureros. Seeing that conversations were at risk of stalling, a former legal leader proposed that, since issues of *cultura* generated only divisions, they should be left out of the discussions leading to the organization and that legal leaders should decide how to handle this in their own communities. However, the issue of *cultura* soon had to reenter the discussion.

Leadership and Reciprocity

Many Yshiro often refer to their kinship with leaders in order to underline the latter's moral failures. For many of them, leaders fail when they do not recognize connections of reciprocity with their supporter-relatives. In these cases, people do not see the leader primarily as a representative of the community in front of the national society, but as a relative who, with their support, can reach a position from which they can obtain material benefits. Followers expect that the leader will reciprocate their support by sharing with them the benefits of the position and by siding with them in internal disputes. It is telling that the people who express this view of leadership rarely complain if their leader retains some portion of the goods that they supposedly obtained for the whole community. This is seen as the privilege leaders receive from their supporters, a privilege for which they must reciprocate. People with this perspective of leadership usually support an aspiring leader during the election, but almost immediately after the leader is elected, they begin to demand that their support be returned. If in a few weeks the new leader does not respond, his or her supporters will start to raise their voices, calling for another election until the leader is ousted.

This understanding of leadership took shape in part as the patronage networks of the Stroessner period were extended. Therefore, there was relative concordance between demands on leaders and what leaders could actually deliver by being connected to patronage networks. However, when the flows of aid dwindled, this concordance began to disappear, as leaders could not properly reciprocate. In this context, supporters closely observed how much the leaders "ate" (retained) of the few resources obtained from patronage networks. Soon, and following the national trend after the transition, discourses about corruption began to circulate in the communities. In consonance with this, and although many shared the leaders' view that the emerging challenges demanded their unity, most people had reservations regarding the willingness of new and former leaders to reciprocate their support. Common people were particularly skeptical of leaders who had attachments, and some said loyalties, to state institutions, political parties, and indigenista organizations.

Zulma Franco, a thirty-six-year-old Ebitoso woman who is a teacher and who is influential in Ylhirta, articulated these doubts, without ambiguity, during a community meeting.

I am not rejecting anybody, especially people of great intellect like Bruno Barras or Pablo Barboza [former legal leaders, often seen by indigenista institutions as representatives of the Yshiro], but it must be understood that they are tied to the institutions they are part of. Bruno is an employee of INDI, and Pablo is an employee of the Gobernación [Departmental Government]. An employee has a boss to whom he or she is subjected. What the boss says, the employee must do. Sometimes the employee can resist the boss to defend their brothers and sisters but other times he or she cannot. Of course there are many [white] people with goodwill. Nevertheless, we have to be conscious that when somebody provides you with economic resources, like it or not, you have to respond to that provider. We all depend on somebody else, but when you depend on a *patron* you cannot resist them. Because that's the system of the whites—if you do not obey them, they cut "the stream." [You wonder] what the stream is? Economic support. If UCINY is the organization that will defend us against our *ymaho* (adversary), the *maro* (Paraguayan), then its leaders must be free to oppose them, they must have no *patrones*. (July 1999, tape recording)

As people discussed how to rebuild the institution of leadership (and the still unborn UCINY) on grounds different than the usual patronage relations, they started to see their own responsibilities in fostering those relations. Former leaders responded to accusations of being "sell-outs" by giving specific examples of how they had been pushed by their communities to negotiate with Paraguayan *patrones* agreements that the communities later regretted.

Most people were aware that the system of patronage tended to bend the loyalties of leaders toward their *patrones*, but they were also aware that leaders without connections were "useless" for the communities, since they could obtain and give nothing to them. Former leaders, who had more experience with the national society and indigenista institutions, suggested that funding for the functioning of UCINY should come only from foreign organizations without immediate interests in local and national politics. If the organization had its own economic support, the relation with Paraguayan NGOs would be totally different. They also pointed out that in the process of getting this support the viability of the organization depended on how people behaved toward the leaders. Since people publicly acknowledged their responsibilities for pressuring the leaders into patronage relations, a consensus began to emerge that demands on them should be restrained for a time.

As community meetings continued, people began to deplore the initial mistrust and cynicism toward the leaders' effort in eloquent ways. For example, the elder Ginés Rizo pointed out that UCINY was like the baby in the story of the *anhet*, an episode in the puruhle narratives which is associated with a larger story about the origin of death (see Wilbert and Simoneu 1987:131–52). This particular episode speaks of a father and his son who after tasting human flesh transform into winged cannibals who prey on the people. Separated from human contact and without hands, they kidnap an old woman to serve as their cook. After one of their forays, they returned with a pregnant woman and instructed the old woman to open her up and cook the fetus separately. The old woman cooked the placenta instead and hid the baby, who she began to raise and instruct. Whenever the cannibals went to look for new victims, the old woman would take the baby out of his hiding place, feed him special food to make him strong, blow on his limbs to make them grow quickly, and whisper in his ears: "Grow quickly, grow strong, my grandchild. There are these cannibals who prey on our people and they are finishing them off. You must grow and be strong because you are going to save our people from this calamity." In a few months the baby became a strong young adult, and the grandmother began to create and try different weapons for him until she found the appropriate one. When everything was ready, the grandchild ambushed the anhet and his son, and killed them. In the meeting, Ginés Rizo referred to this story, saying,

A baby cannot do anything, it is not only useless but also a burden. Yet when a baby grows, it is the guarantee of survival for his or her people.

This organization has not been born yet, but even when it is born it will just eat, it will produce nothing. This organization is like the baby who killed the *anhet*. What would have happened if the grandmother did not feed the child, if she did not protect him, if she did not instruct him until he was ready? We must be patient. Ask nothing and give everything to this organization, for it will save us from those who feed off us. (15 July 1999, tape recording)

The metaphor of UCINY as a baby became pervasive. For example, I heard somebody criticize those who expressed disbelief toward the organization by saying, "When the mother is pregnant, those who are irresponsible deny their kinship. When the baby is born and everybody sees his or her beauty, men fight each other claiming fatherhood. When the baby is a strong working adult, he or she has lots and lots of relatives." When people went to the leaders to donate money for their trips, some would say, "Here comes the milk for the baby" or "Food for my grandchild."

Conceiving UCINY as a baby was a powerful imagination that compelled people to restrain their demands on the emerging form of collective leadership. At the same time, it transposed to UCINY the idea that the relations between leaders and their supporters are (or must be) based on kinship and its inherent responsibilities. If one considers that, in spite of all its changes, leadership had for a long time been connected to kinship, it is understandable that many people viewed UCINY not as an entity that represented them but as a relative connected to them by relations of reciprocity, not of equivalence. This points to the complexity of the articulation that the Yshiro leaders were trying to perform, for they intended to translate and articulate a world operating on the basis of relationality and reciprocity with a world operating on the basis of representation.

Although speeches like that of Ginés Rizo boosted enthusiasm in the communities to the point that many even gave the little money they had to cover the cost of the leaders' meetings and their travel to and from Asunción, the leaders knew the enthusiasm would not last, because people would not wait long to start making demands on the "baby." They also knew that individuals in the communities would continue to challenge the leadership of the organization as long as governmental and nongovernmental institutions showed that they would give help to whoever claimed to be a leader. Thus, the leaders understood that UCINY would exist only to the extent that it could become a gatekeeper between the Yshiro communities and non-Yshiro institutions. To achieve this, two interconnected challenges had to be overcome: first, the leaders had to convince community members to accept UCINY as the only conduit for relations between the communities and non-Yshiro institutions; second, they had to convince those institutions to treat UCINY as the only valid interlocutor in their relations with the Yshiro communities. These challenges were formidable, because they implied that UCINY had to respond to demands based on quite different assumptions concerning the meaning of leadership (i.e., reciprocity versus representation), because those demands had to be met almost simultaneously, and because the whole idea of UCINY hung on a single thread: Prodechaco's promise of "concrete projects." This promise had to be fulfilled before the people in the communities grew impatient and started to again disparage leaders for their dealings with non-indigenous institutions.

(Corpo)realizing UCINY and the Yshiro Nation

The leaders understood that the establishment of UCINY depended not only on the communities, but also on non-indigenous institutions. For a core group of more experienced leaders, it was evident that the conflict between the cultureros and the Pentecostals and entrepreneurs could not be bypassed by UCINY without having an effect on how the relation with non-Yshiro institutions would unfold. They argued that if UCINY as a whole did not adopt a supportive stance toward the cultureros, the cultureros would mistrust the organization and would continue to pursue their own agendas in Asunción. Why would they trust an entity that was not clearly inclined to reciprocate their support? In addition to their concerns about alienating a sector of the communities, the more experienced leaders worried because they knew that "authentic" leadership was understood by indigenistas in a different way than it was understood in the communities. For indigenistas, the legitimacy of a leadership depended on the degree to which it accurately represented the indigenous communities and their interests. The experienced leaders knew that "accurately representing" a community in front of an indigenista institution meant providing representations that were not in direct and evident collision with that institution's representations of the "real" interests of indigenous communities. In other words, the leaders were aware that their representation should not obviously disrupt the existing chain of equivalences from which different indigenista institutions arose. Thus, if critical indigenistas considered traditionalism to be the realistic solution for indigenous peoples' predicaments, then UCINY had to be able to claim that it represented traditionalists. Similarly, if INDI was invested in an integrationist approach, UCINY would have to claim to represent such agenda in the communities. The challenge was not to generate situations, like a visible conflict, that would situate UCINY clearly in either position.

The less experienced leaders developed an awareness of these complexities as they kept going to Asunción. This was especially so for the Pentecostals, who, for the first time, were exposed in an intensive way to the discourses that circulated in critical indigenista circles, which opened their eyes to the necessity of moderating their position toward the cultureros in order to obtain support for UCINY. Candido Martinez, the Pentecostal leader of Ynishta, who in April 1999 had told the cultureros that their rituals would no longer be allowed, changed his views and at the end of July of that same year expressed to the cultureros that in consideration of the primary goal of empowering UCINY he accepted that nobody should interfere with other people's beliefs.

While most critical indigenistas welcomed the creation of UCINY, they also expressed concerns about the Yshiro leaders' willingness to talk to both critical and integrationist indigenista institutions. Some even suggested, as friendly advice, that I should not trust leaders that I had known for several years, because, purportedly, they were corrupt. When I asked for proof of corruption, I was told that simply it was obvious: these leaders "flirted" with the whole spectrum of indigenista institutions. On another occasion a critical indigenista told me with a wink and without further explanation, "It is very risky for the communities when leaders learn too well how to hunt and gather projects. They become too powerful." In the end, one NGO agreed to advise UCINY on legal matters, in order to obtain legal recognition as a nonprofit organization, but not before one of its staff warned, "If you [the leaders] work with X, which is an ethnocidal organization, I will not work with you."

INDI's response to UCINY was also ambivalent. The leaders wrote a letter to the president of the institution claiming for UCINY the exclusive right to represent the Yshiro people in several matters, including land claims and the adjudication of legal leadership. The leaders argued that having UCINY as the only interlocutor representing the Yshiro would speed up INDI's administrative procedures and thus would contribute to the "development of the communities." INDI's president was inclined to accept the idea, since UCINY could relieve the pressures that indigenous individuals exerted on the staff and the coffers of the institution, yet accepting UCINY as the only interlocutor also meant relinquishing the remote control that INDI exercised within the communities through the legal recognition of leaders. Facing this dilemma, the official attitude was to go halfway: an internal memorandum called to the attention of INDI's staff the fact that UCINY had asked that no aid be granted to Yshiro individuals without its authorization.[7] However, the memorandum made no mention of the most critical areas in which UCINY had requested exclusive rights to represent the Yshiro: the recognition of leaders and land claims. Thus, INDI authorities tried to take whatever advantage they could from UCINY, without taking a clear position on the core of the matter raised by the Yshiro leaders, that is, the exclusivity of UCINY as representative of the Yshiro communities.

The ambivalence of these institutions highlights the self-preserving tendency of chains of equivalences. For both critical indigenistas and INDI, to articulate with an organization that took shape independent of their intervention was a move with uncertain consequences. Such an articulation could bring instability or a threat to the chain of equivalences from which they emerged. In contrast, Prodechaco "responded" to the leaders most readily, in part because (for different reasons) both the leaders and Prodechaco wanted UCINY to become a link in the chain of equivalences that the project was extending, and in part because Prodechaco was confident that, through its plans for community formation, it could control how this link would take shape.

On a trip to Asunción in late August 1999, the leaders and I met with the co-directors of Prodechaco to inform them that the creation of the organization was under way and to obtain a formal commitment that the institution would initiate projects immediately. The leaders thought that support, in some form, should be evident at once as a way to strengthen the confidence of the communities in the organization. The co-directors again stated that because the Yshiro lacked an organization with "representational and managerial skills," Prodechaco could not yet launch concrete projects. The leaders were quick to point out that in this way Prodechaco was pushing communities to search for an NGO to act as an intermediary, which contradicted what Prodechaco had been "preaching" about self-development. Moreover, this appeared to be in contradiction to the "new" objective of Prodechaco, which was to promote the self-reliance and independence of indigenous communities. In the end it was determined that Prodechaco would provide funding for the subsequent meetings and workshops of the nascent organization.

On our return to Alto Paraguay, the leaders made a great display of the support they had received from Prodechaco by organizing new meetings and a tour to present to all the communities a draft of the organization's statutes. This idea had been proposed by the Tomaraho leaders who, in mid-August 1999, joined the Ebitoso effort. The Tomaraho proposed that all the leaders tour the communities together, setting up workshops in each to present the final draft of the organization's statutes for community feedback and as an example of unity. Around twenty individuals, including leaders, advising elders, sailors, and myself, shared a small boat, provided by one of the Yshiro small entrepreneurs, as we traveled from one community to the next during two weeks. In each workshop, the idea that the Yshiro had to learn unity from their ancestors was repeated again and again. Back in the boat and during the long hours of travel, the leaders discussed and reinforced these ideas with each other. As days went by, the conviviality that emerged with the daily jokes and activities among the leaders eased the mistrust between Pentecostal and traditionalist leaders and elders. On 24 September 1999 the legal leaders met in Karcha Bahlut and signed the agreement that approved the statutes and officially created UCINY. In the same meeting, Candido Martinez was appointed general coordinator of UCINY, Alejo Barras its secretary, and Teresa Payá its treasurer. Surrounded by community members, Candido said, "We are not going to discuss and hate each other for [divisive] issues any longer. . . . The well-being of *the Yshiro nation* will come first" (24 September 1999, tape recording).

While Prodechaco planned to translate the chain of equivalences of which it was part through community formation, the Yshiro leaders strived to translate several imaginations that made up the "Yshiro communities" into an organization, UCINY. Before this attempt at translation, the Yshiro communities had been shaped by different imaginations that were unconnected, if not divisive. These imaginations delineated groups and divisions, and also fostered mistrust within those groups toward their leaders. By the late 1990s, the need to articulate and reconnect these imaginations in order to face increasing competition for resources and decreasing attention from the state became a pressing issue. The idea that a pan-Yshiro organization would be a useful way to face these challenges had been circulating for a while when Prodechaco appeared as an opportunity to realize it. In effect, the "concrete projects" promised by Prodechaco appeared as a potential tool that could be used to start articulating the multiplicity of imaginations existing in the communities with one another.

UCINY's objectives, as stated in its statutes, included "to keep and strengthen the cultural and ethnic identity of the Yshiro nation," the "recovery, legalization, and protection of the traditional territory of the Yshiro nation," and the "promotion of the general well-being of the Yshiro nation while preserving the current economic and social system."[8] The emergence of the imagination Yshiro Nation was the result of a long historical process, plus five months of discussions, workshops, and meetings in which different, at times mutually contradicting imaginations related to the ancient and contemporary Yshiro were worked out in order that contemporary Yshiro could begin to perform themselves in ways that were conducive to collective action. However, people did not end up sharing exactly the same imaginations of themselves and the world; instead, through dialogue and conversation, arguments and disputes, and fundamentally engaging with one another, the different groups within the communities translated/articulated those imaginations into a common ground, UCINY and the Yshiro nation. To a great extent, knowing as relating played a central role in this process. Only by enacting what people like Don Veneto and Modesto had been suggesting ("to come and see" and "to respect each other") was it possible to overcome factionalisms that had been sustained on the basis of established definitions of who and what the "others" were. In a way, what happened during the period in which UCINY was being brought into existence can be understood as the enactment and expansion of the relational moral logic to the detriment of the Cartesian moral logic that had taken over the yrmo. In a context of relationality, there was no need to enforce equivalences, because translation was conceived not as being dependent on a preexistent "reality" or common ground (which usually implies the subordination of somebody's reality), but rather as the work of bringing into being such common ground, hence the centrality of engaging one another, especially among the leaders.

But UCINY was not only about articulating Yshiro imaginations. The objective of "preserving the current economic and social system" did not use the word *current* by chance. The idea of a current economic and social system, which is neither a remnant of the past nor the finished product of integrationist designs, addressed the debates around the hunter-gatherer paradigm. These debates face the Yshiro with the dire alternatives of being "real indigenous peoples" or "assimilated indigenous peoples," and thus of having to accept the visions of development attached to either of those imaginations. Precisely in this is where the differences, and asymmetries, between Yshiro ways of going about translation and translations operating under the logic of representation are more evident. Within the communities, the articulation between different imaginations Yshiro performed by different groups depended not on their mutual equivalence but on the material possibilities for engaging one another in a sustained and focused way. In contrast, the articulation between UCINY and non-indigenous institutions was overshadowed by the tacit demand that the former be a nondisruptive link for the existing chain of equivalences that gave life to the latter. In other words, these articulations were overshadowed by the demand that UCINY's "vision of development" be equivalent to those of their non-indigenous interlocutors, or, what is the same, that such vision should reflect the same reality.

UCINY tried to appear as though it at least did not contradict either of those visions. Does this mean that UCINY ended up emerging as a link "functional to the wider order of the world"? In principle it would seem that the answer is yes. Yet UCINY emerged neither from Prodechaco's community formation nor from the designs of INDI or the critical indigenistas.

It emerged from the active engagement of the Yshiro communities and leaders, who for their own purposes actively tapped into the designs of Prodechaco, the critical NGOs, and INDI. The Yshiro leaders' purposes were shaped in part by the imaginations that constituted the yrmo. For this reason, and insofar as it was not necessarily equivalent to them, UCINY (and the imaginations that it articulated) was a potentially disruptive or subversive element in the chain of imaginations giving (corpo)reality to the modernist story of globalization.

When UCINY was created, Prodechaco encouraged the Yshiro leaders to promote discussions in their communities to get a preliminary picture of their situation, define their problems, and propose areas for specific interventions. Once these areas were identified, Prodechaco would start providing the necessary "formation" so that communities could represent and manage those "problem areas" appropriately. By early December 1999, and after a long period of droughts and a seasonal ban on fishing, the Yshiro communities were in a critical economic situation. The Yshiro leaders saw an opportunity to improve the lot of their community through commercial hunting. Although a total hunting ban had been in place since 1996, the leaders had heard on their trips to Asunción that, according to recent studies, capibara (*Hydrochoerus hydrochaeris*), yacare (*caiman sp.*), and anaconda (*Eunectes notaeus*) populations had grown enough to support hunting activities. Moreover, droughts had caused animals to concentrate near the Paraguay River, which made the prospect of (legal) commercial hunting very promising.

In late December 1999, UCINY asked the Paraguayan National Parks and Wildlife Direction (NPD) for permission to hunt capibara, yacare, and anaconda for commercial purposes. However, NPD informed UCINY that it could not authorize commercial hunting, because it lacked the resources to send inspectors to supervise the activity; since Paraguay is a signatory of the Convention on International Trade of Endangered Species (CITES), hides obtained for commercial purposes must be certified and tagged by inspectors in situ. At this point, UCINY requested from Prodechaco that support to organize a hunting season be the project's first intervention in the Yshiro communities. The project's co-directors agreed, but on the condition that the planned activity had to be sustainable, that is, hunting had to be pursued in such a way as to conserve animal populations at a level considered sustainable by biologists. With this condition being agreed on, UCINY and Prodechaco divided tasks: UCINY was to generate a series of discussions to inform the Yshiro communities about the goals of the Sustainable Hunting Program, as the project was called, and to organize activity on the ground, while Prodechaco would arrange with NPD and the Paraguayan chapter of CITES the technical and legal aspects of the program. Prodechaco would later provide technical support in the form of community formation workshops for those individuals chosen by the communities to manage the project.

The events that surrounded the creation, implementation, and aftermath of the hunting program illustrate how Yshiro imaginations are potentially disruptive to or subversive of the chain of equivalences that gives (corpo)reality to the modernist story of globalization but also how this potential is thwarted by those who perform this story.

Changing "Maps" of Control and Surveillance

Although Brazil established protected areas and bans on hunting on their side of the Upper Paraguay River in the early 1980s and Paraguay responded in kind in the late 1980s, Paraguayan "citizens" (mostly the Yshiro) kept hunting illegally on both sides of the river. This was possible with the connivance of local Paraguayan authorities who took part in the illegal trade of animal hides.[1] According to local commentators (indigenous and non-indigenous), this situation gave Brazilian authorities carte blanche to enforce their regulations as they saw fit.

The Brazilian *forestales* (forest-policing forces) counted on the silence of the Paraguayan local authorities to subject the Yshiro to all kinds of abuses. Local authorities in Alto Paraguay were not eager to bring to the public's attention the abusive interventions of Brazilian forces over Paraguayan citizens, because this would have brought attention to their own participation in the breaking of national laws and regulations. Once Yshiro hunters were on Paraguayan territory they were safe, but if they were caught by the Brazilian forestales, there was nothing their family or friends could do for them, because the Paraguayan authorities would not even bother asking the Brazilian authorities about the situation of these Paraguayan citizens.

Yshiro hunters still recall that repression by the Brazilian forestales was merciless, and detailed descriptions of the horrors that awaited hunters if the Brazilian forces caught them abound in the communities. There are also many rumors regarding what may have happened to those hunters who disappeared on the "other" side. These stories and rumors ground a perception of the "other side of the river" as a "place of death," a place where on entrance one must kill or be killed. Some Yshiro hunters say that if they had not started to rely on fishing for subsistence, they all would likely have been killed. However exaggerated this view may seem, it does reflect the perception that the Yshiro have about hunting in Brazil: that it was a trap into which they were forced by the conditions imposed on them by the patronage system characteristic of the "hunting business." Necessity and indebtedness forced Yshiro hunters to hunt in Brazil despite its dangers, for Paraguayan *patrones* had at their disposal very effective instruments to coerce them into paying back their debts. Antonina, a female elder, recalled in an interview, "Until around 1979 it was a disaster. Like a slave they [whites] treated indigenous peoples. They tortured people. Ask Julio, he was tortured by the soldiers because he went to Asunción without paying his debt to his *patron*. . . . In those times you could do nothing because indigenous peoples were not recognized as persons. Indigenous peoples were like slaves, working just for an exchange of food. Enough to barely survive. If you complained, the *patrones* would beat you unconscious" (May 2000, tape recording).

From the late 1970s, and as the situation of indigenous peoples began to attract international attention, Paraguayan *patrones* saw themselves less and less able to use this kind of open coercion to pressure the Yshiro into the hunting business, more so after the end of the Stroessner regime. The emergence of the fishing economy was thus the last push that allowed the Yshiro to disengage from commercial hunting.

The shift from commercial hunting to commercial fishing was accompanied by a change in the "map" of natural-resources control and surveillance in Alto Paraguay. As commercial fishing grew, Brazilian and Paraguayan authorities quickly established fishing regulations. Yet, as local representatives of the Paraguayan state have consistently lacked the resources to effectively enforce those regulations, the Brazilian authorities have done so instead. Brazilian boat-patrols now confiscate the fishing nets of Yshiro fishermen, sometimes chasing them into Paraguayan territory. The patrols have even shot over the roofs of the Yshiro communities where fishermen sought refuge. Such incursions into Paraguayan territory never occurred while the "hunting economy" was dominant. Why this change?

While the fishing economy meant greater independence for the Yshiro in relation to Paraguayan *patrones*, it also meant the end of the hide-and-seek game in which the Yshiro played the role of pawns for the Brazilian and Paraguayan local authorities. The Yshiro and several former *patrones* now compete for the same resources, fish, and more generally "the environment." Moreover, Paraguayan "important people" (i.e., authorities) are pursuing joint ventures with Brazilian entrepreneurs in order to exploit the opportunities the region offers to the sport-fishing and tourist industries; former *patrones* in positions of authority are therefore less inclined to protect their former "employees" from the Brazilian authorities. For example, Benito, an Yshiro fisherman, complained to the military authorities because Brazilian authorities had crossed the river and entered into Paraguayan territory to confiscate his net. The Paraguayan officer to whom Benito talked responded, "Why are you trying to fish when is not the season?" He then threatened to fine him. In short, the Yshiro now have to face not only the Brazilian authorities, who have expanded their area of control, but also the Paraguayan authorities, who deny them protection and harass them in their economic activities.

The old and new layouts of natural-resources control and surveillance, as well as the struggles around them, constitute the background against which the events surrounding the establishment of the hunting program must be understood. Also factoring in is the fact that while commercial hunting was not new to the Yshiro, the way in which it was to be implemented within the framework of the Sustainable Hunting Program was entirely unprecedented. This was the first time for the Yshiro (and the entire region) that commercial hunting was to be done with the legal and technical backing of experts, in accordance with governmental regulations, and in partnership with rather than in subordination to other parties. Yet, in spite of its rhetoric about participation and autonomy, Prodechaco saw UCINY mostly as a link to translate the designs of the "experts" into action, rather than as an active partner in the design of the project. Hence, from the beginning there was only a weak connection between how "environmental sustainability" was discussed on the ground by the Yshiro and how it was conceived in the design boards of bureaucrats.

Conservation(s), Interests, and the Sustainable Hunting Program

While on a fishing trip with an Yshiro friend, I asked what he thought about the regulations on fishing and whether they would be useful at all to sustain the stocks of fish. As my friend looked at me utterly perplexed, I further explained my question by noting that the authorities claimed that restrictions were meant to protect the resource from disappearing. My friend said that this made no sense, for the amount of fish in the river had nothing to do with how much they were harvested, since fish come with the birds of rain (*Osasero*). As long as there is rain, there are fish. "Then why do you think that they make all these regulations," I asked. He responded,

> Don't you know? In the Bible it says that around the year 2000 the rich will laugh at the poor. Look at those tourists that come in their boats, they are all fat, they eat very well. Look at us [Yshiro], we are thin and our children sometimes cry because there is no food. Yet the government allows them [tourists and sport-fishermen] to take all the fish they want and does not allow us to work to feed our families. They are laughing at our poverty. (November 1999, field notes)

My friend's comment and his perplexity with regard to the idea that fishing regulations had something to do with conserving the stocks of fish underline a common perception among many Yshiro: that the abundance of animals is only indirectly connected to the way humans treat them. Thus, to understand how the hunting program's goal of sustainability was conceived in the Yshiro communities, one must take into account the assumptions that underlie what one may call "Yshiro conservation"—although to speak of "conservation" may be to indulge in a deceiving shortcut, for the practices that I describe under the banner of Yshiro conservation are not directly concerned with the objective of "conserving" fauna. Thus, conservation, if it occurs, can be considered almost as a "side effect" of those practices.

According to several Yshiro, but mostly elders, individual animals are the *abo* of an original specimen, the bahlut. Although for brevity the bahlut is usually described as the parent or the owner of the abo, a more detailed exegesis shows that the abo is an emanation of the bahlut (see Cordeu 1990: 167–69). In other words, an individual animal is a particular manifestation of the bahlut. Bahluts and humans sustain relations of reciprocity, most often mediated by konsaho. Bahluts give to the konsaho gifts that benefit the whole community, for example, the power to bring animals close to hunters, to cure diseases, or to make the bush fruitful. These gifts must be reciprocated by the konsaho in ritual ways that unavoidably involve the intervention of other humans. The incorporation of other humans into an expanding network of reciprocity that starts with the link between bahluts and konsaho is based on rules of reciprocity and sharing which are often shaped by the instructions of the bahlut. Disregard for these instructions may have negative results in the form of diseases, death, drought, floods, and, of relevance to the subject of hunting, the availability of the bahlut's abo, that is, animals (see also Susnik 1957b:33–34, 1995:55–61; Wilbert and Simoneau 1987:444–51; Cordeu 1989d).

From this perspective, the critical nexus between human behavior and the availability of animals is the reciprocity that must prevail in the network composed of both humans and bahluts.[2] Thus, if animals are not available, it means that at certain points in the network the flow of reciprocity is failing, usually in a human-to-human interface. This way of understanding the complex relations between humans and nonhumans is not shared or known in its details by everybody in the Yshiro communities. Yet I believe these ideas are lurking behind the general tendency of Yshiro commentators to look for the causes of fluctuations in the availability of wildlife first in the relations among humans. For example, most Yshiro insist that a diminishing population of animals is not primarily the result of the quantity of animals they hunt (or fish), but of the little return they obtain from trading their spoils from hunting (or fishing) activities. Those who are knowledgeable about the connections between reciprocity and the availability of animals argue that this amounts to an infraction of reciprocity that angers the bahlut, who withhold animals and fish. Those who do not know those connections or who do not believe in bahlut simply point out that since the Yshiro are paid little, they have to hunt and fish larger quantities, and thus

CHAPTER 9

the animal population decreases. Despite their differences, both arguments consider the issue of the availability of animals by primarily focusing on human-to-human relations.

Based on these assumptions, community members argued that conserving a sustainable animal population could not be achieved if the hunting program was organized according to the old system of the hunting business.[3] People pointed out that were the old system to operate again, animals would begin to hide or diminish as in the old times and the Yshiro would receive no benefits beyond filling their stomachs during the hunting season. At the basis of this evaluation of the challenges ahead was the idea that in order to ensure the availability of animals (i.e., the sustainability of the resource) the hunting program had to focus on the relevant connections, that is, human-to-human relations. Thus, it was proposed that UCINY adopt the role of broker between the hunters and the industry. In this role, UCINY could address what was essential to ensure "conservation," that is, that reciprocity among humans be balanced and widespread. The suggestion immediately raised questions about who should benefit from the hunting program. Experienced hunters with the necessary means (canoes and guns) would certainly benefit, but there remained the question of UCINY's responsibilities toward *all* those who had supported its creation, that is, almost everyone in the communities. Should not (the now grown-up baby) UCINY reciprocate them? These arguments, in turn, opened the way to more general arguments about reciprocity and duties toward others. For example, some elders pointed to the role of the bahlut and the konsaho in assuring a good hunting season, arguing that elderly konsaho should therefore be reciprocated even if they could not hunt. People asked how single mothers and widows would benefit from the hunting season. And what about the few Paraguayans living in the communities with their Yshiro partners? And the poor Paraguayan neighbors who had friends in the communities and who had shared with them tools and food in times of scarcity? "Shouldn't we act as good Christians and share with them now?" asked an Yshiro Pentecostal pastor. In one way or another, the issue of sustaining widespread reciprocity weighed heavily on how the Yshiro went about tackling the issue of sustainability.

Despite strong controversies, a consensus was gradually achieved that in order to ensure "sustainability" the benefits of the hunting season had to reach every single household in the Yshiro communities and even a few Paraguayan households outside those communities. The Yshiro communities prepared a preliminary proposal for how the hunting program had to be organized that pivoted around the demand that UCINY retain the exclusive right to act as a broker. This demand embodied the assumption that in this position UCINY could foster equitable sharing in the benefits of the hunting program and thus address the critical yet often weakest point in the yrmo to ensure the "conservation" of the animal population, that is, reciprocity among humans.

The Yshiro focus on the human-to-human interface in relation to "conservation" contrasts with what seems to be the primary focus of attention in bureaucratic and scientific conservation, that is, human-to-animal relations. In effect, governmental regulations seem to focus primarily on the number of animals that can be hunted or fished, their size or age, and the period during which they can be harvested. These regulations are based on "scientific studies" of animal behavior, patterns of reproduction, and the size of populations. Once these facts are established, the task of governmental regulations is to attune human behavior to them in order to achieve the goal of conservation. In this way of conceiving conservation and sustainability, regulations are organized around and anchored by scientific facts. However, "facts" (or accurate representations of reality) are not authorized in straightforward ways, but must somehow be accommodated along existing chains of equivalence.

Soon after UCINY and Prodechaco agreed to organize the hunting program, representatives of Prodechaco met with staff from CITES-Paraguay and NPD in order to give shape to the legal and technical aspects of the program. The news that a hunting season was soon to open quickly reached the processing industry and old hunting *patrones*, who initiated unofficial negotiations regarding quotas and conditions with NPD. The landowners association, ARP, also received news of the hunting program and informed NPD that their associates were worried about the potential intrusion of hunters onto their properties. Each of these parties attempted to shape the hunting program in a way that would suit their interests, which involved keeping free of disruption the chains of equivalences from which each of them emerged.

Prodechaco, partly echoing comments from the Yshiro leaders, insisted on making sure that the indigenous hunters be paid a fair price for animal skins and that the benefits of the program be directed mostly to them. However, always concerned with avoiding conflicts with the powerful landowners, Prodecho gave assurances to ARP that intrusions on private properties would be prohibited. CITES wanted the simplest and most transparent mechanism for impeding the laundering of illegally obtained hides through the program. Thus, in order to have fewer people to manage, CITES proposed to restrict permission for hunting to the Yshiro. The processing industry wanted NPD to establish a fixed number of hides that each company could buy and export; in that way they could avoid competition and raise the prices of the hides. Finally, the old *patrones* pressured NPD for a hunting season in the old style, open to whoever was able to benefit from it by hunting or brokering.

In March 2000, when Prodechaco had just started community formation through workshops that taught community members how to implement the diverse aspects of the hunting program, NPD passed a resolution regulating the program's technical and legal aspects.[4] While attending in part to the concerns of CITES and Prodechaco, the resolution misinterpreted UCINY's proposal and was clearly drafted to benefit the processing industry and the *patrones*. In effect, the resolution (NPD no. 19/00) spelled out the norms to be followed by the hunting program: in addition to setting the quota of animals that could be harvested, it established a minimum price for the skins; that the number of skins to be bought and exported by each industrial company was to be fixed; that rights to broker would be available to all those who applied for permits; that hunting was to be done with "traditional weapons"; that hunting permits were to be given only to residents of the Yshiro communities; and that hunting activities were to be carried out only on Yshiro lands, government lands, or the lands of those private owners who gave the Yshiro express permission for this. In this way, NPD responded to the different demands and relations of power between the parties involved in shaping the hunting program. Yshiro conservation and the demand for exclusive rights to broker were dismissed in favor of other more powerful interests. Yet, according to a NPD staff member with whom I later talked, setting a minimum price for the hides and restricting hunting permits to residents in the Yshiro communities were aimed at circumscribing the benefits of the season to the Yshiro, as Prodechaco had requested. CITES was also happy with this restriction, because a reduced number of hunters would ease the task of the inspectors. Moreover, the NPD staffer told me, they all agreed that "non-indigenous hunters are very destructive." This idea, in turn, grounded the norm that hunting should be done with "traditional weapons." According to the NPD staffer, the scientists from CITES had insisted that indigenous peoples' traditional weapons were better suited for "sustainable hunting." Why? My interlocutor could not remember if the scientists had given an explanation for this assertion.

Once UCINY learned of the shape that the project had taken, it began to pressure NPD to change the resolution. The struggle, which drew media attention, was long and complicated. The industrial lobby allied with *patrones* to keep the resolution intact as it was and through their contacts in the government were able to momentarily prevent any changes. In turn, UCINY gathered the support of a journalist, who kept the spotlight on the conflict throughout, and of Prodechaco, which found itself forced to side with UCINY. A couple of issues about these "alliances" help clarify how they unfolded.[5] First, the aforementioned journalist, Roque Gonzalez Vera, was interested in the conflict mainly as fodder for the editorial line of his newspaper, *ABC Color*, which was opposed to the government of unity created after the killing of Vice-President Argaña. Thus, Gonzalez Vera asserted that the key issue in the controversy revolved around the fact that Paraguayans (non-indigenous peoples) destroy the environment and indigenous peoples do not.[6] This made for a very appealing story involving the underdog, ecological Indians who care for the environment who were being harassed by the corrupt and careless Paraguayan government bureaucrats and entrepreneurs who have no concern for the environment. Second, Prodechaco was forced to side with UCINY because in a public press release previously circulated to explain the hunting program to the public and to quell environmentalists' concerns, Prodechaco had explicitly asserted that the sustainability of the program was ensured because UCINY would have the exclusive right to broker.[7] When the resolution that legally opened the hunting season was passed, UCINY publicly asked Prodechaco to withdraw support from the program, arguing that since UCINY had not obtained the exclusive right to broker, the sustainability of the program could not be guaranteed. Although members of the government pressured Prodechaco to stay in the project, the European staff were aware that they could not do so without risking a major scandal that would surely involve a strong environmental lobby in Europe, which could potentially achieve what the critical indigenistas had not been able to achieve: killing Prodechaco.[8]

Without Prodechaco, the hunting program could not be implemented, since NPD lacked the financial means to launch a hunting season with effective controls, and without such controls, the Paraguayan office of CITES could not tag the hides for legal international trade. Thus, the industrial lobby eventually held conversations with UCINY, came to an agreement about prices, and turned against the *patrones*. With this array of forces, NPD changed the regulations, making the right to broker exclusive for UCINY.

Given how the conflict unfolded and the focus of the media, UCINY's demand for exclusive rights to broker was narrowly understood in terms of economic interest. Hence, it was lost from sight that the Yshiro considered exclusive rights to broker as a means to ensure widespread reciprocity, not just as a way to get a greater share of the hunting program. However, "Yshiro conservation" was acceptable to the actors involved in the hunting program only to the extent that it was understood as economic interest. Yshiro demands were perceived as a problem of accommodating their (narrowly defined) interests along with those of other "stakeholders," rather than as a problem of articulating/translating different worlds. This "transactional" view of difference is characteristic of the multicultural approach associated with neoliberal agendas and embraced by Prodechaco. This approach assumes that cultural differences are mutually negotiable because they constitute nothing more than different "windows" onto a single reality, that common reality providing a common denominator that allows transactions across cultural differences. Who defines this "common reality" that operates as an unstated frame and how it is defined are not in question. Yshiro conservation profoundly disrupts the transactional view precisely because it questions this taken-for-granted common reality. Through the practices it grounded, Yshiro conservation brought to light the limits of the negotiable in a multicultural framework and, by extension, in modernity-cum-globality.

In July 2000, UCINY requested from NPD an extension of the hunting season, because the quotas were not yet filled. The conflict over rights to broker had delayed the start of the season until May, and ensuing floods had made it increasingly difficult to find animals. As the industrial lobby strongly supported the idea, NPD decided to grant the extension in spite of opposition from Prodechaco and CITES, which recommended that the hunting program be terminated as originally planned. The main concern raised by these institutions was the intrusion of "indigenous and Paraguayan hunters" onto private properties and into Brazilian territory. Moreover, the journalist Gonzalez Vera, who had found fodder for his attacks in the government's refusal to grant to the Yshiro exclusive rights to broker, now found new ammunition in the government's affirmative answer to the Yshiro's request for an extension of the hunting season.[9] He asserted that the hunting program had turned into an ecological disaster mostly because the Yshiro had sold quotas to Paraguayan hunters. He portrayed the hunting operations as "depredation" and "devastation" provoked by groups of indigenous and non-indigenous hunters who entered private properties and, worse, Brazilian territory, with the consequent risk of violent clashes with the policing forces there. Echoing the tourist operators in the area, Gonzales Vera wondered if it would not be better to have tourists pay to take pictures of the animals, rather than hunt them. He finally argued that to implement such an idea, a policing force just like the Brazilian forestales was needed in the area.[10]

How did this change of "alliances" among participants in the program come to occur?[11] To answer this, one must first understand how different interests and equivalences were at stake in the final shape of the hunting program. Once the industrial lobby had been assured an economic profit and *patrones* had been excluded from the hunting program, the other actors to which the hunting program had to respond, beside the Yshiro, were CITES and Prodechaco. CITES was interested in having only the "ecological Indians" participate in the hunting program. An overarching interest for Prodechaco was to avoid controversies with powerful landowners. And both Prodechaco and CITES operated within a frame in which the sanctity of private property and national jurisdictions remained undiscussed.

Prodechaco, as well as the other non-Yshiro participants involved in the hunting program, assumed that, as an expression of the Yshiro's (narrowly defined) interests, Yshiro conservation could be articulated with the interests of other participants. Yet "Yshiro conservation" contains a series of assumptions that are profoundly subversive of those dominant interests and equivalences. The first assumption, embodied in my friend's comment that the priority given to sport fishermen was an example of the rich laughing at the poor, is that given that all humans need to sustain themselves, they all have equal rights to natural resources—simple and "subversive." My friend signaled that if people need to "eat," they should not be denied the means to do it. Implicit in his critique of governmental regulations was that this basic idea should be the Archimedean point around which "natural resources use" should be organized. The second assumption, expressed in the communities' proposal that single women, elders, and poor Paraguayans be included in the hunting program, is that responsible relations between humans make inclusive, and not exclusive, the equal right to use natural resources for survival. That is, all humans in need are recognized. The third assumption is that nonhuman animals diminish or hide when there is a lack of attention to what constitutes responsible relations among humans; therefore, their availability depends in large proportion on how those responsibilities between humans are honored.

Following the logic of these assumptions to its ultimate consequences implies that Yshiro conservation is at the very least in conflict with, if not in outright contradiction of, private property, market values, and even international jurisdictions. However, other participants of the hunting program did not even suspect that these assumptions were at the root of UCINY's demands for exclusive rights to broker. On the contrary, it was assumed that once this issue had been agreed on, the Yshiro had become articulated in a relation of equivalence with the multiple interests and equivalences that shaped the hunting program. Nevertheless, people in the Yshiro communities acted without regard for this assumption and tended to dismiss regulations that seemed totally out of touch with the central issue in Yshiro conservation, that is, honoring relations of reciprocity among humans. The leaders found it difficult to explain to community members the meaning of certain norms, such as the restrictions on the participation of Paraguayan hunters, the spatial limitation of the hunt to Yshiro lands, and the need for obtaining the permission of private owners to hunt on their lands. In the end, they could only warn their community fellows that if these norms were not respected, the program could be suspended.

In spite of these warnings, hunters disregarded private property boundaries and national jurisdictions, and allowed Paraguayan hunters to participate. Hunters searched for animals wherever they could find them, which included private properties and Brazil.[12] It was impossible to expect a profitable hunt from only the short stretch of land that the Yshiro have along the river. The Yshiro also found a way to work around the norm which restricted participation in the program only to residents in the communities. Those Yshiro hunters without boats paired with Paraguayan hunters who had boats. Yshiro single mothers associated with Paraguayan hunters who would share the profits with the "owner" of the quota. All these arrangements were made between people who had longtime relations of collaboration and who trusted each other; thus, in no way did it involve the simple selling and buying of quotas, as the journalist Gonzalez Vera had asserted.

Since it was nearly impossible to sell hides without CITES certification, the Yshiro and the Paraguayan hunters did not hunt a single individual specimen beyond the quota. Yet their disregard for private property and national jurisdictions was characterized as environmental "depredation" and "devastation." This makes it clear that what appeared to be the core of the hunting program (i.e., scientific data about animal population) was actually articulated to a previously existing array of equivalences in a nondisruptive way. By depicting the Yshiro's disregard for private property and national jurisdictions as depredation and devastation, practices that challenged the current socioeconomic and political order (the existing array of equivalences) were cast as practices dangerous for the "environment." Instead of discussing why private property and national boundaries had come to constitute the limit within which the Yshiro were allowed to practice "their conservation" and to perform the yrmo, CITES and Prodechaco (as well as Gonzalez Vera) attacked the Yshiro for betraying the plan of conservation that had supposedly been produced with their own participation and thus supposedly represented their own "interests."

As Gonzalez Vera implicitly argued, such an example of bad faith could only be responded to with the establishment of a policing force that would instill in the Yshiro as much fear as the Brazilian forestales did. And, in 2001, the Paraguayan government created a secretary of the environment, established the office of the environmental prosecutor, and strengthened police vigilance in the Yshiro area. In this new map of natural-resources control and surveillance, an emerging "hegemonic coincidence" between environmental NGOs, policing forces, local landowners, and politicians-turned-tourist-operators has played a central role in shaping concerns for conservation in a way that disregards Yshiro conservation and the yrmo from which it emerges.

Multiculturalism and the Containment of the Pluriverse

Multiculturalism manages differences by framing them within dominant sets of values and visions of the world that are assumed to have universal applicability (Fish 1997; Povinelli 2001). Paraphrasing Bourdieu ([1977] 1997), one could say that multiculturalism is one way in which a system of dominance naturalizes its own arbitrariness, by turning the results of more or less stable chain of equivalences (i.e., imaginations) into "a world out there" that goes without saying. However, the assumptions embodied by multiculturalism are implicit in the practices of even those who repudiate neoliberalism, but who still conceive translation as the establishment of equivalences. Such was the case with the members of the School of Ecology (SOE), a Spanish NGO operating in the Yshiro area.

According to their own accounts, the two staff members of SOE, biologists by training, were active in the European environmental movement and strongly opposed to neoliberal ideas of "pricing the environment" and to neoliberalism in general. One of them even claimed to have been associated with the Zapatista support network in Spain. Among the objectives of SOE was the goal of fostering biodiversity by helping to preserve cultural diversity. Yet, when they noticed that UCINY was preparing the hunting program, they strongly opposed it. As soon as SOE staff learned of the hunting program, they started to comment in Bahía Negra how environmentally disastrous the program would be. In order to provide assurances to the contrary, the Yshiro leaders invited them to a meeting where the details of the hunting program were to be discussed. Although the SOE biologists participated in the meeting, their only question was whether the animal-population study that backed the decision to create the hunting program was "scientific" enough. For these environmentalists, it did not matter that for the Yshiro the sustainability of the project was assured by its focus on the "critical nexus" human to human; as long as there was no confirmation that this view would not contradict through its effect SOE's "scientific" understanding of nature, the sustainability of the hunting program would remain in doubt. They understood that the Yshiro had another *view of nature*, but its validity was dependent on its degree of equivalence with their scientific understanding of it. In other words, the Yshiro could *believe* whatever they wanted to believe about how the environment operates, but the actions prompted by these beliefs should not run counter to what the biologists *knew* about the environment.

As a result of their dissatisfaction with the scientific status of the hunting program, SOE ended up contributing to the hegemonic coincidence between landowners, tourist operators, and policing forces that is shaping the new map of natural-resources control and surveillance in the Yshiro area. This map of control and surveillance cannot be sustained without coercion, for there is no point of negotiation with the Yshiro. Given the (multicultural) assumption that nature preexists all views about it, those who do not even have "nature" as a referent will almost certainly be subordinated through the threat or the effective use of coercive force. While the multicultural framework, implicitly or explicitly adopted by neoliberalism and some of its opponents, argues against the use of coercion (effective or threatened) to secure a coincidence of views on reality, such restraint in practice applies only as long as indigenous peoples operate within the limits of what is reasonable and conceivable (Povinelli 2001); and these limits are defined by what is "real" and what goes without saying, the authorized imaginations taken to be reality "out there." Since the behaviors prompted by Yshiro conservation do not respond to dominant authorized imaginations, they are understood to be based at best in error, at worst in bad faith. Thus, today as before, Yshiro performances of the yrmo are disregarded or are taken to be anomalies that must be subjected to the disciplining power of coercion. In this way, coercion continues to be the "brutal epistemological guarantee" that the reality in which the Yshiro are forced to live will remain the same.

However, coercion and reality do not constitute each other symmetrically. Coercion is just one element that makes up reality. Indeed, without the mobilizing power of reality, it is difficult for coercion to be activated. No repressive system, no dictator makes use of coercion without reference to a certain reality to justify it, even when such reality may be illusory for other mortals. Reality, in contrast, does not always need coercion in its making, although it might need it to remain identical to itself. In effect, reality gets produced through the incessant processes by which imaginations articulate/translate each other in order to gain further (corpo)reality. Translation is necessary for imaginations to emerge out of indistinction. Translation is an ontological dynamic which does not need to be produced to happen. In contrast, keeping an imagination identical to itself does require coercion insofar as a direction and a limit is imposed on the ceaseless processes of articulation/translation. Yet this does not justify coercion, because it is the value one gives to the current state of being or imagination-reality that determines whether protecting it from change is justifiable. However, as long as reality is assumed to be out there, coercion can be seen as flowing from it, rather than as checking the forces that can change it. In this way, the value of reality or the current state of being is removed from discussion.

The dynamics between coercion and authorized imaginations seems to lead back to the late nineteenth century, when modernity began to be superimposed over the yrmo. Has nothing changed with globalization? Yes and no. The interplay between coercion and authorized imaginations is still a key principle of the modern regime of truth being reproduced in the global age by neoliberalism and modern forms of opposition to it. Yet the route that connects coercion and authorized imaginations is more circuitous and uncertain than before. In the nineteenth century, the imagination Indians already precluded the participation of the Indians in its authorization: being imagined as quasi-objects, Indians could not define themselves. In contrast, non-indigenous governmental institutions (including the academy) now need to involve indigenous peoples in their own processes of authorizing their imagination Indigenous Peoples. My own involvement with Yshiro intellectuals and the effects they have had on my telling of this story signals how hard it has become to disregard and neglect the pluriverse that manifests itself through other practices of reality-making (translations/articulations). It is true that coercion and the "framing" of these practices are used to shield dominant imaginations from being transformed in unwanted ways. Nevertheless, the more circuitous the connection between coercion and authorized imaginations, the more opportunities there exist to transform the latter before the former can protect them. This distance constitutes a window of hope, a window through which moderns can join in the task of translating/articulating a pluriverse that many nonmoderns have been contributing to perform since time immemorial.

In the final part of the story about the cannibal *anhet*, the boy-hero is being chased by the anhet when he calls the trees: "*Kole, kole* [grandmothers]! Trap the *anhet* and hold him tight so I can finish him." The trees then extend their branches, trapping the winged cannibal until the boy kills him. Among other things, the story tells of how humans and nonhumans mobilize their familial bonds to defend themselves against the threat of those who deny this all-encompassing sociality, of those who set themselves apart from it and attempt to sustain their existence without regard for the relations that tie them to others. One might very well understand what has taken place in the Yshiro-Ebitoso communities since 1986, and its resonances with other developments beyond the Paraguayan Chaco, in this key: nonhumans and some Ebitoso renewed bonds that had been weakened by the subordination of the yrmo to a modern world that denied reciprocity, attachment, and all-pervasive relationality in favor of contractual, objective, and detached relations. The consequences of the renewal of those relational bonds during the ensuing years have been far reaching and complex, but, ultimately, have lent further (corpo)reality to the yrmo and the pluriverse, contributing thus to disauthorize the modern myth.

The incorporation of the Chaco into the Paraguayan nation-state and the invisibilization of the yrmo were part of a process by which the pluriverse was rendered less (corpo)real. However, in the Yshiro case, the pluriverse never ceased to assert its presence, at least as "anomalies." In the last three decades a proliferation of anomalies has fueled the mutation of Indians, Nature, and Progress, three imaginations central to the modern myth, into

Indigenous Peoples, Environment, and Risk. While being genealogically related to the earlier ones, the new imaginations mark a shift in the way of conceiving and experiencing constitutive threads of the modern myth: linear time, the great divide, and the colonial difference. In effect, linear time is no longer associated with "progress ahead" but with "risks ahead," and the "others" of the modern society and the modern self (i.e., Nature and Indians) in principle stop being *so other* as they increasingly impose their presence (in the form of environmental crisis and the claim for self-representation and self-determination) as active subjects in the constitution of the various socionatural orders that constitute the pluriverse. The accumulation of anomalies (or, what is the same, the reassertion of the pluriverse) and the internal rearrangement of the modern myth (punctuated by the newly authorized imaginations) are being increasingly narrated as the coming of the global age or globality.

The stories of globalization enacted through diverse practices and agendas constitute different ways to face this (corpo)realizing state of affairs. The modernist story of globalization responds to the growing visibility of anomalies by reinstating the modern ontology as a metaframework expressed most visibly in governmental practices such as development projects in which, as with Prodechaco, "participation" and "autonomy" actually work to tame and discipline "others" (that is, to control anomalies) through ever subtler forms of coercion—although, when necessary, subtleties can be set aside. In any case, coercion remains fundamental to protect the (corpo)reality of modernity in the global age. Yet, for coercion to be activated, a "reality out there" must be invoked. This is a crucial move to protect the established order, a move that is continually reproduced by the modern knowledge practices of experts, whether sympathetic or not with the modernist story of globalization. As long as debates remain grounded on the assumption of a single "reality" and on a contest over who produces the most accurate representation of it (as is the case between different indigenistas), the very regime of truth that justifies the use of coercion to protect the status quo remains unshaken.

By shifting attention from competing knowledge claims in Paraguay to the regime of truth within which these claims make sense, I hope to have brought into view that the field of political intervention of someone located in the academy and linked to social movements involves much more than what may at first appear to be the immediate circumstances being addressed by such social movements. In effect, the very way in which one attempts to produce critical knowledge is an inescapable albeit little recognized component of those circumstances. "Knowing" in modernist terms and what I call "knowing as relating" enact different kinds of worlds. Modernity, with its inbuilt double drive toward colonizing difference and transmuting it into hierarchies, is a way of relating that produces a universe in which the negative potency of wozosh, expressed through the impoverishment of the pluriverse, is rampant. It is in order to avoid relating in modernist ways that I conceived this ethnography as storytelling, a performance which, along with other ways of relating (with) myself, the Yshiro, and the world, seeks to contribute to further (corpo)realizing that of which it speaks: globality as a pluriverse. In order to do this without falling back into the modern (i.e., objectivist) way of relating, I followed clues from Yshiro myth-history and from other academic works that led me away from the kind of performance that reenacts the modern myth.

The modern myth generates the modern enunciative position (and its associated moral stances) by performing that of which it speaks: a world of objects and subjects. And this world gets performed first and foremost by the denial of the performative character of modern knowledge in the form of claims that modern knowledge reflects a reality out there. In this way the modern myth becomes the never explicit frame sequestered from discussion and contestation. This is why in order to contest the modern regime of truth I first had to excavate its founding myth and trace its continuity beneath the changes brought about by the global condition. But in order to do this without rehearsing the same objectivist gesture I intended to undue, I told this story as a different sort of founding myth, one patterned after Yshiro myth-history.

What I have attempted is to verbalize and articulate what, to use Raymond Williams's words, one might call a "structure of feeling" that spans across sectors of the academy and contemporary social movements, and which has important points of contact with aspects of many indigenous peoples' struggles. In effect, the rupturist story of globalization reflects the intramodern recognition that shifts in the constitutive elements of the modern myth are symptoms of its bankruptcy and of the need to find alternatives to the regime of truth and domination that it founds. Parallel to the intramodern recognition of the problems with the modern regime is a growing visibility and intensity of the age-old extramodern contestation to this regime. Indigenous peoples' struggles for their worlds, aided by the enormous mobilizing power of nonhumans (most apparent in the form of what moderns perceive as environmental crises), unavoidably bring the pluriverse to the forefront, which in turn implies a challenge to modernity's universalism.

For the moment, the point of contact between these parallel developments seems to be what I call the global condition. But this point of contact is riddled with ambivalence and equivocations. In effect, while emerging global imaginations like Indigenous Peoples, Environment, and Risk provide platforms from where the pluriverse can be asserted, they do not fully make room for the pluriverse to flourish; rather, they can actually work to contain the pluriverse. A good example of the enabling possibilities offered by the new imaginations is the renewed contact between some Ebitoso and ukurb'deio (potent nonhumans), afforded in part by the existence of the imagination Indigenous Peoples, which prompted critical indigenistas to support the establishment of a "traditionalist" community. However, as with Prodechaco's attempt to shape "indigenous communities" in a way that would make them fit into its extending chain of equivalences, these imaginations also enable modernity to be reproduced as globality. Moreover, as exemplified by the events surrounding the creation of the Sustainable Hunting Program and its aftermath, there is a point at which the ambivalence of these imaginations ends, revealing the limit they imply for the pluriverse; they are, after all, the product of an asymmetrical articulation/translation that requires significant accommodation, or streamlining, from the subordinated term and little from the dominant one. In other words, they tame rather than welcome difference.

The taming of difference achieved by imaginations such as Indigenous Peoples and Environment is a paradoxical but central characteristic of the modern regime of truth, and it is therefore not surprising to find it in the performances of the modernist story of globalization. Modernity's embrace of multiculturalism, participation, and autonomy is just a more circuitous road to asserting its universalism under global conditions. But, as with the critical indigenistas, blindness to what is "other" in indigenous struggles compromises the rupturist story of globalization as well. And this problem, of course, goes further than the Paraguayan indigenistas. In January 2005, the young Yshiro leader Alejo Barras and I attended for the first time the World Social Forum (WSF) in Porto Alegre. The WSF motto, "Another World Is Possible," is intended precisely to counter the neoliberal mantra that however imperfect the market society may be, there is no world beyond it. Interestingly, the motto of the indigenous participants, "We Are Another World," spoke not to the neoliberal mantra, but to the WSF motto. Indeed, while meetings *about* indigenous peoples were held in central spaces of the conference area, the meetings *of* indigenous peoples were allocated the most marginal physical space. One could not avoid seeing that while the non-indigenous activists were searching for ways to imagine and make the world outside of the modern capitalist box, indigenous peoples were saying, "We are such a world, engage with us." Yet non-indigenous activists and intellectuals hardly engage with indigenous peoples as others, or, better, their "otherness" seems valuable only as an icon of the supposed newness of struggles that have a suspiciously familiar orientation.

This lack of open engagement precludes a border dialogue that might well be decisive for the project of performing "worlds and knowledges otherwise." This dialogue might put a mirror in front of us, making evident how even as we attempt to perform those worlds and knowledge otherwise, we actually contribute to performing globality as a continuation of modernity. This, in turn, might contribute to transform these performances so that they escape their self-contradicting tendency. Failing to engage in this dialogue, we just add another spin to the unceasing reproduction of modernity and its system of hierarchies and domination. Thus, a necessary (albeit not sufficient) condition for bringing into being a globality that is an alternative to modernity involves transforming the point of contact between the intra- and extramodern challenges to the modern myth into a bridge that allows for two-way communication. This implies that those experiencing the global condition from an intramodern position must take "anomalies" for what they are: manifestations of the pluriverse. In the Americas at least, this means making room for indigenous peoples' relational knowledge practices to flourish and to interpellate the often implicit modern assumptions of those of us who are lured by the rupturist story. In this way, perhaps our rupturist story would be transformed into the story of how we joined a struggle for the pluriverse that had been raging for much longer than our modern blinders allowed us to see.

It is no mere chance that it was an indigenous uprising that at the turn of the millennium galvanized the will to struggle of a wobbly Left. The Zapatista uprising of 1994 seemed to point toward a kind of politics that escaped many of the dichotomies and dead-ends of modernist traditions of struggle and thus became a referent for the emerging wave of antisystemic mobilization. Now, as the Zapatista spokesperson Subcomandante Marcos has repeatedly pointed out, the Zapatista political philosophy and praxis came out of a process through which the leftist ideology of a group of urbanite intellectuals and activists became thoroughly transformed by the Lacandon Maya's cosmologies (see Marcos 2001; also Lenkersdorf 2005). In other words, it was dialogical engagement with indigenous cosmologies that allowed these urbanite intellectuals and activists to think out of the modern box, which had become sterile. But what is peculiar about these indigenous cosmologies? Relationality. Indeed, many of the elements that make the Zapatista political imagination so compelling—the open-endedness of their proposal, their emphasis on the paramount importance of respecting differences, their insistent calls for dialogue and inclusivity, and a subjectivity predicated on an indissoluble relation between autonomy and interdependence, among others—are ubiquitous in Yshiro and other indigenous peoples' relational cosmologies (see Amawtay Wasy 2004; Cajete 2000; Waters 2004a; Descola and Pálsson 1996; Viveiros de Castro 2004; Lenkersdorf 2005; Fernandez-Osco forthcoming). Moreover, although it is not always easy to recognize, many indigenous peoples' ways of engaging the state, corporations, and other social movements have their roots in these relational cosmologies (see Blaser, Feit, and McRae 2004; Blaser et al. forthcoming).[1] There is much to learn from these cosmologies that is useful for addressing the challenges posed by the global condition.

I was for many years puzzled by the steadiness of Yshiro intellectuals' emotional investment in whatever (broadly political) issue we were dealing with. While I would swing between euphoria and depression according to the prospects for the success of our actions, they would remain in a steady mood zone. For a time I interpreted this attitude as a symptom of disinterest, yet this interpretation was clearly contradicted by the fact that the

CONCLUSION

Yshiro would continue to engage in these actions. Eventually, through conversation and by "connecting the dots," I started to perceive the foundations of their orientation and, by contrast, my own. While my Yshiro friends operated on the assumption of the coevalness of temporal stages (recall that puruhle, porowo, and azle are, above all, dimensions of reality "here and now") heavily imbued by notions of unending responsibility, I operated on the assumption of (modern) linear time heavily imbued by notions of a point of arrival (paradise or utopia). For me, the likelihood of realizing utopia (i.e., the objective sought) determined my mood and my willingness to engage in actions. For my Yshiro friends, the likelihood of achieving an objective was, if not irrelevant, at least nondetermining of their willingness to use eiwo in order to avert the negative aspect of wozosh. This is part of the unending collective task of sustaining Being. Yet sustaining Being does not imply eliminating the negative aspects of wozosh all together (that is, achieving something akin to utopia), for it is in the very nature of the yrmo that the negative aspects of wozosh will always be present. Thus, the task and responsibility of humans is to incessantly manage and restrain those negative aspects. By contrast, orienting political action in terms of linear time carries with it the perils of cyclical swings between hope and despair, which do seem to possess modern social movements, as utopian dreams rise only to be dashed by the stubborn tendency of "things" to somehow "go wrong."

The notion that the negative aspect of wozosh is an inherent part of life, which must be checked rather than eliminated, emerges from a conception of the yrmo as a web of relations. All entities or events (including those that may be valued negatively) are not self-contained and autonomous (and thus "foreign"); rather, they are manifestations of those relations. In this context, if the self (a manifestation of the cosmological web) were to behave toward an entity valued negatively (another manifestation of the cosmological web) as if the latter were a self-contained and autonomous entity, the ensuing dynamic would resemble that of a dog chasing its own tail without regard for the wider effects of this futile endeavor. Again, these unstated assumptions ground many Yshiro (and other indigenous) intellectuals' orientation to politics and sharply contrasts with the dominant one among those who try to contest modernity from a modern stance. For instance, this orientation is not focused on opposing something (the government, the indigenista NGOs, tourists, landowners, or, for that matter, neoliberal globalization), but rather is centered on pursuing life projects (Barras 2004; Blaser 2004b). Life projects entail what is considered a good life and include taking care of the responsibility to sustain the yrmo by checking the tendencies of some entities to manifest in negative ways. As exemplified by the way in which the Yshiro dealt with their internal differences to create UCINY, and later by how UCINY dealt with indigenistas, Prodechaco, and the Paraguayan government, this is seldom done by simply opposing those entities, but rather by trying to translate/articulate with them according to a logic in which the need of others to sustain their Being is recognized as relevant to the very process of translation/articulation. In this case, translation/articulation cannot be conceived of as the establishment of equivalences on the basis of an already existing common ground such as "reality out there"; here translation/articulation is about engaging others to construct partial common grounds. On this point, Yshiro performance come close to Latour's vision of what the rupturist story of globalization might have to offer.

Latour considers that we are nowadays confronted by challenges that require the abandonment of notions of a world out there that appear to guarantee a preexistent common ground while in fact obstructing the work of politics as the process of constitution of such common ground (Latour 2002, 2004). Latour longs for a unified common world that would be extracted from the pluriverse by the "due process" of gradual composition through cosmopolitics, which is contrasted to the modernist shortcut unification through the imposition of power under the guise of knowledge (Latour 2004:184–220). In this point a difference in orientation between Latour's project and that of the Yshiro (and, I will risk, other indigenous peoples) must be pointed out. Although Latour's "common world" would always be a receding horizon and vector informing the treatment of the pluriverse through "due process," it nevertheless orients conduct toward unification. In contrast, the horizon and vector that emerges from many indigenous relational cosmologies is coexistence; this implies an orientation geared toward constructing limited common grounds, or "partial connections" (Strathern 2004), in the various points of contact that arise among the diverse worlds that make the pluriverse, but also a concern for maintaining this diversity. In the Yshiro case, this orientation is based on a heightened awareness of the fundamental importance of recognizing and respecting the "otherness" of "others," not out of an abstract goodness, but out of the experiential knowledge that there is no other way to sustain the yrmo. This is often rendered in the form of songs and stories that stress the very specific responsibility that each and every one of the entities that exist have in sustaining the yrmo, and the importance of allowing those entities to fulfill their duties. Whether one knows which responsibility an entity has or does not have does not invalidate this tacit assumption (see also Arquette, Cole, and Akwesasne Task Force on the Environment 2004; McGregor 2004; Cajete 2000; Feit 2004).

One of the corollaries of this orientation is precisely that, in order to allow the space for the pluriverse to reproduce itself as such, one must remain open to the yet unknown positive potentials that other entities may have. This does not imply a naïve blindness to the tendencies of some entities to manifest in negative ways or a lack of will to check those tendencies; to the contrary, there is a disposition to act collectively to do the work of checking. And this might be one of the aspects of relationality that is more difficult for modern sensibilities to accept, for checking the negative tendencies of some entities and events in a relational world might imply intervening at points that appear far removed from the concern at hand. For example, how would a modern sensibility react to the idea that an individual's "right" to decide whether he or she wants to marry a given person can be denied because, for instance, the decision will impact the availability of animals for hunting? Keeping track of the complex relations that weave the world cannot but be a collective task, and this implies collective intervention in many areas that moderns have become used to thinking of as in the realm of individual decision-making. As many contemporary Yshiro assert, the discipline that the Yshiro porowo maintained to avert the negative aspects of wozosh was heavy indeed. A relational world is not paradise, and yet it seems better equipped than the modern one to exist and thrive on the basis of partial connections with other worlds forming the pluriverse. This is not to make of the Yshiro way of enacting a relational world a universal model, but rather to highlight the political possibilities that an orientation toward maintaining diversity opens up. While checking the negative tendencies of some entities or events might imply in some cases a heavy discipline by the collective, the orientation toward maintaining diversity within a relational world also implies not denying the potential that what has consistently manifested in negative ways might manifest in positive ways under other circumstances (see Deloria 2004). In turn, this implies a kind of politics that sharply contrasts with modern politics based on a contest about who is acting on the basis of the most accurate representation of a reality out there.

In a world of reality out there, the mutually constituting connections between entities that are assumed to be mutually independent disappear from sight, what exists appears already closured, and therefore politics cannot but be somehow exclusionary: "Reality/truth is one and we know it, they don't. You can be with us, with truth and reality, or against us. No other choices are available." Does this sound like the New Crusaders of our time? Certainly. And unfortunately, by all indications, as the pluriverse further manifests, these positions will become the more entrenched, in part because the exclusionary politics of the New Crusaders is also enacted by the self-defined progressive Left. It is on the basis of competing truths and realities that the latter constitutes itself and continuously breaks apart in smaller factions. For instance, many movements and organizations performing the rupturist story very hastily closure a "WE" by contrast to a "what we are against" by self-defining as being "one No and many Yeses" (Kingsnorth 2004). The idea is that while different peoples have different ideas of the world they want to live in, they share a common opposition to the capitalist globalization that impedes the realization of these visions. Yet this commonality quickly breaks down when one focuses on the relation between the multiple yeses and the single no and asks: Why do you say no to capitalist globalization? How does capitalism exactly impede the realization of your vision? In exploring these questions, it soon becomes evident that the hastily closured WE has put together "reformists," "radicals," "utopian freaks," and "sell-outs" who understand the "reality" of capitalism and its relation to their visions in quite different and often mutually exclusive ways. As a reaction to this tendency to split apart, strong countertendencies emerge to silence dissent and force homogenization. In this world of either/or, non-indigenous peoples, movements, and institutions cannot but see many indigenous peoples' responses to their interpellation (Are you going to fit in my chain of equivalences? Are you with us?) as anomalies. This is exemplified by the reactions of indigenistas to the creation of

UCINY: because the Yshiro conceive and perform translations as the progressive construction of common grounds that articulate differences rather than assuming an already given common ground (like a No), the indigenistas interpret their openness to dialogue and engagement as an anomaly that might indicate the potential of betrayal. In South America, where social movements have propelled "progressive" governments to power in the wake of the crisis of hegemony of neoliberalism, this "anomaly" might soon be violently contained. Conservative forces are responding to these advances in a way that reiterates Cold War antagonisms, and thus the perennial conflict between Right and Left threatens to again homogenize and dichotomize the field of social mobilization.[2] It is therefore essential to prevent this process by emphasizing that "anomalies" are symptoms of a pluriversality, which, while not free of conflicts, can nevertheless be indeed a livable political alternative to modern universalisms (from Right and Left).

Making evident that the pluriverse can be a livable alternative rather than a threat is a difficult task, part of which will be to demonstrate that the pluriverse is not synonymous with chaos, is not an ocean of arbitrariness and amoral relativism, but rather that, embraced, accepted, and dealt with appropriately, it might actually be the only viable way of Being. Notions of cosmopolitics and partial connections are vital to imagine ways of appropriately dealing with the pluriverse. The "cosmopolitical proposal" (Stengers 2005) invites us to remain open to the unforeseen and the unexpected, to refuse knowledge as closure. This does not mean refusing knowledge, but conceiving it in a different mode, as a hesitant gesture which can be stopped on its own track by the interpellation of others, thus opening up the interstice from which partial connections can be built. Partial connections (Strathern 2004), in turn, allow us to conceive the pluriverse as constituted by mutually related worlds yet lacking an overarching principle (which would then make it into a universe). Cosmopolitics thus works through the specificities of particular connections, seeking to enhance those that allow coexistence in the pluriverse and disrupting those that impoverish it.

In this work I have tried to do just this. On the one hand, I have tried to make evident that what from a modernist perspective appear to be anomalies that need to be contained are actually symptoms of the pluriverse. On the other hand, I have sought to contribute to making the pluriverse more (corpo)real as part of the project of producing worlds and knowledges otherwise. In a sense, and to use Boaventura de Sousa Santos' words (2004a, 2004b), I embarked on a project of countering the absence that modernity forcefully imposed on the yrmo and the pluriverse, and also of fostering their emergence by telling this story about the passage from modernity to globality in a way that has been contaminated by Yshiro intellectuals' knowledge practices. Yet this is a post facto project, for even before I conceived it in these terms I was taken up by the way in which Yshiro intellectuals perform the yrmo by articulating/translating new relations. Yshiro intellectuals articulated their efforts to sustain the yrmo with my vital trajectory, somehow transforming the latter profoundly. This, I believe, is not coincidence; rather, it is one of the ways in which they perform the yrmo. Being interpellated by Yshiro intellectuals' knowledge practices, I have been moved away from the modern enunciative position to tell my story of globalization, thus making the telling of this story part and parcel of the struggle it tells about. To put it plainly, I have told to a mostly academically informed audience a story of how the Yshiro have kept performing the yrmo in the face of encroaching modernity by echoing to some extent the knowledge practices through which they have done this, that is, through knowing as relating. This echoing is certainly a translation, but one that is not based on equivalences. Rather, the model could be that of musicians improvising together. Each one plays his or her own melody, seeking not equivalence with other players, but rather harmonious resonances that would amplify the effect of the performances through a collective effort. In this sense, my performance here can, and will, be evaluated by my Yshiro friends and acquaintances in terms of whether it resonated and amplified the strength of their performance of the yrmo or whether it actually interfered and forced it to move in directions they did not want. I hope to have been careful enough to avoid the second possibility.

I think that my Yshiro friends and acquaintances' performance of the yrmo does resonate with, and might amplify the effects of, the various "rupturist performances" to which this ethnography is indebted and "partially connected" (i.e., Modernity-Coloniality-Decoloniality, Actor Network Theory, ecofeminism, and experimental ethnography). As in any collective improvisation, while performing one must also remain aware and sensitive to the performances of others in order to engage them accord-

ingly. Thus, if what the rupturist story seeks is to foster worlds and knowledges otherwise, responding appropriately to other worlds and knowledges
is a key first step. I hope that my attempt to take this step will resonate with
other similar efforts performed by people operating both within and without the academy. If all these efforts get to resonate together through their
partial connections and amplify their collective effects, then perhaps the
chains of equivalences that compose modernity-cum-globality will start to
lose (corpo)reality, the coercion that guards the present state of affairs will
be harder to mobilize, and space for the pluriverse to flourish will open up.

Acronyms

ACIP: Apoyo a las Comunidades Indígenas del Paraguay (a Paraguayan indigenista NGO)

AIP: Asociación Indigenista del Paraguay (the first Paraguayan indigenista NGO)

ALA COMMITTEE: Asia and Latin America Committee, European Union

API: Asociación de Parcialidades Indígenas (an indigenous organization of national scope)

ARP: Asociación Rural del Paraguay (the landowners' association of Paraguay)

ASCIM: Asociación de Cooperation Indígena-Menonita (an association of Paraguayan Mennonite indigenistas)

CE: Council of Europe (one of the governing bodies of the European Union)

CITES: Convention on International Trade of Endangered Species

EC: European Commission (one of the governing bodies of the European Union)

EU: European Union

GOP: Global Operative Plan

INDI: Instituto Nacional del Indígena, Paraguay

NPD: National Parks Direction (Dirección de Parques Nacionales y Vida Silvestre), Paraguay

PRODECHACO: Programa de Desarrollo Sustentable del Chaco Paraguayo

SETA: (technical mission of consultants in charge of drafting initial parameters for Prodechacho)

SOE: School of Ecology (environmental NGO working in the Yshiro area)

Notes

Preface

1   The word *yrmo* has been transcribed differently by other ethnographers (Cordeu writes it *érmo* and Susnik *ïrmič*), but I follow the style increasingly adopted by the Yshiro themselves. The meaning of the word is expansive; it can refer to anything from the bush to all that exists.

2   "Significative differences" refers to differences in the context of a field of power, and not to the putative content of differences. These are the kind of differences that, as Donna Haraway pointed out, are not "playful" but "poles of world historical systems of domination" (1991: 160–61).

3   Actually, I should say "visible consequences," since only from a perspective that denies relationality can one seriously assume that not responding to others might have no consequences. I owe this point of clarification to Justin Kenrick.

Introduction   Worlds and Knowledges Otherwise

1   That there are other forms of conceiving dualism, with different effects, is evident if one thinks of the Chinese yin and yang or the Yshiro notions of *om* and *sherwo* as poles in a continuum. The practice of thinking through a pattern of poles in a continuum is one I use throughout this volume.

2   The "colonial difference" is the way in which the modern imaginary classifies the planet by transforming differences into values and, thus, into hierarchies (Mignolo 2000:13).

3   See Plumwood for a thorough analysis of Cartesian dualism as a logic of colonization and subordination (1993:41–68).

4   For general discussions of the role of expert knowledge in governmental practices, see contributors to Burchell, Gordon, and Miller 1991; and Barry, Osborne, and Rose 1996. For examples of expert knowledge in the context of development, see contributors to Marglin and Marglin 1990, 1996; Cooper and Packard 1997; Arturo Escobar 1995; Ferguson 1990; and Sachs 1992.

5   For a recent overview of the effects of the "self-reflexive turn" and its ramifications beyond anthropology, see Marcus 2007, 2008.

6   Place is understood here as "the experience of, and from, a particular location with some sense of boundaries, grounds, and links to everyday practices" (Arturo Escobar 2001:152). This experience is emergent and not a given; that is, place is a process of "embodied practices that shape identities" (see Gupta and Ferguson 1997). This perspective on place-making stresses the point that the immediate experiences of place and identity are inevitably constituted by larger sets of spatial relations. Thus, place is conceived not as a bounded and self-contained entity, but as a knot made of a particular mix of threads (i.e., links and connections), "including local relations 'within' the place and those many connections which stretch way beyond it" (Massey 1999:41).

7   For the notion of pluriverse in ANT, see Latour 2004:40–41; in MCD, see Mignolo 2000:311, 2007, although he most often uses the terms *diversality* and *mundialización* to refer to the pluriverse or pluriversality.

8   Although Callon and Latour (1981) recognized violence as part of the work of translation, it is probable that ANT's minimal interest in violence as a component of the performances of entities (actants, in its terminology) is due to its central focus on the performances of "scientific" entities. Nevertheless, it is notable that violence is given little to no consideration in Latour's story (1993) about how the "modern constitution" came into being.

9   The cited works provide overviews and analyses of these movements, but the reader must be warned that here the problem of invisibility emerges again. Indeed, while in these works, as in other studies of indigenous movements and revolt, there is an intention to understand the rationality behind mobilization, ultimately this rationality is translated through the filter of modern categories of linear time and oppositional dualisms. Hence, they produce what the Seminole scholar Anne Waters calls the "Eurocentric nonunderstandings . . . of precolonial ontology, rationality, beliefs, customs, and institutions of peoples indigenous to the Americas" (2004b:98). The use of terms like *millenarian* or *messianic* to describe nineteenth- and early-twentieth-century indigenous movements, when the idea neither of the millennium nor of the messiah had relevance for those movements, suggest how the distortion of one-way translations creates absences. In chapter 4 I discuss this in more detail, exploring how indigenous mobilizations fueled by a nondualist rationality are (mis)translated into oppositional politics.

10 *Language* is a shortcut term I use to refer to a certain conceptual universe and its ontological assumptions.

11 An exceedingly clear example of this "one way" translation is the relation between environmental movements and the indigenous movement, where the former's "story" defines not only what the struggle is about (i.e., conserving nature) but also what authentic indigenousness means (Conklin and Graham 1995; see also Mato 1996).

12 Note that according to most contemporary social sciences, networks appear merely as new objects to be accounted for by existing social theory (see, for example, Sonia E. Alvarez, Dagnino, and Escobar 1998; Castells 1996; Diani and McAdam 2003; Keck and

Sikkink 1998). In contrast, *networks* in this book refers to something much more expansive: it refers to an ontological condition and thus implies the need to rethink social theory from the ground up (Latour 1999). Indeed, the "simultaneity" of the "qualities" (natural, political, and discursive) of these networks means that moving sequentially from one aspect to another, as existing social theory does, is not enough—one must do away with the distinctions between "aspects" altogether.

13 For different ways in which indigenous peoples of the Americas conceive the world as networks or webs of relations, see Amawtay Wasi 2004; Arquette, Cole, and Akwesasne Task Force on the Environment 2004; Descola and Pálsson 1996; LaDuke 1999; McGregor 2004; Viveiros de Castro 2004; and Waters 2004a.

14 Recall the famous Bororo assertion, "We are parrots," and the anthropological fascination with the "mind" that could produce such a "counterfactual" utterance. Of course the great divide also made this "mind" and its "associated body" into objects on which moderns could apply the remedies they found suitable to free them from the *maladie* of categorical confusion.

15 How does the pluriverse, a possibly endless network of networks, generate distinctions, differences, and hierarchies within itself? Networks/worlds that connect with each other do not only extend each other but also establish stoppages or turning points for each other, thus creating the "borders" that make them distinguishable from one another (see Strathern 1996).

16 Partial connections here make reference to points of contact between different locations (or works) which, while mutually reinforcing, do not necessarily make a single whole (or universe). I will return to this concept and its role in cosmopolitics in the conclusion.

17 Examples of this kind of work are too many to enumerate here, but recent representative studies include Strathern 1992, 1999; Viveiros de Castro 2002; Ingold 2000; and Descola 2005.

18 See, among others, Cruikshank 2005; de la Cadena 2009; Gow 2001; Kenrick 2009; Kirsch 2006; Noble 2007; Poirier 2008; and Deborah B. Rose 2004.

19 I cannot claim a special authority predicated on my relations with some Yshiro, for many other Yshiro would probably disagree or completely deauthorize my "story." This does not mean that I disregard other sources of authority that escape my own will, such as my being part of networks connecting academia, states, and markets to the exclusion of other knowledges. However, I am trying to tell a story that remains open-ended and susceptible to transformation by its encounter with other stories.

20 For an English-language compilation of published works with stories that compose the Yshiro myth-history, see Wilbert and Simoneau 1987.

21 As I was finalizing this manuscript, John Law's *After Method* (2004) came to my attention. I was stricken by the many parallels between his depiction of "method assemblage" and my understanding of Yshiro storytelling as a knowledge practice. I was also gladly surprised by his reference to Australian aboriginal practices, which to some

extent confirmed a hunch I had early in this project: that ANT has a lot to gain from connecting with indigenous peoples, particularly with regard to the politics and ethics of operating in a relational ontology. In a similar vein, the problematic posed by Donna Haraway in *When Species Meet*—that is, how to "understand that human beings do not get a pass on the necessity of killing significant others, who are themselves responding, not just reacting" (2007:80)—is one about which indigenous peoples might have many insights to share.

22 Cordeu (1990:123–40) has provided a more detailed treatment of this term, although some of my interlocutors pointed out aspects of the concept that he did not address, for example, the "positive" aspect of wozosh when it is handled appropriately. Yet many other Yshiro interlocutors only recognized the most immediate meanings of this term: poison and putrefaction.

23 The term *actant* used by ANT is appropriate to name the entities that inhabit the yrmo, because in Yshiro myth-history all entities have agency and volition (see Cordeu and Braunstein 1974).

24 For a discussion of the meaning of the term *Anabsero*, see Cordeu 1991a:100–103. It is relevant to notice that the Anabsero are associated with animal species that inhabit the muddy bottom of the rivers or lagoons and the mud that remains under the dry surface of the soil during the dry season. Precisely because it is difficult to distinguish anything in it, this underworld constitutes a manifestation of the Yshiro puruhle state and thus signals a connection between the porowo and the puruhle dimensions.

25 This is the meaning that I give to the words *real* and *reality* throughout this book.

26 As I tell my story, the details of how imaginations are authorized will become clearer. In the meantime, the explanations I have heretofore provided should suffice to stress the notion that reality and ways of imagining reality are inextricably implicated with each other. This should guard against my being misinterpreted as committing either of the twin "distortions" of Cartesian dualism: the naive assumption that there is an extradiscursive, independent reality; and the nihilist pretension that for humans (at least) there is no other reality than the effects of language games.

27 According to Cordeu (1990:158–65), Yshiro "mythology" establishes the temporal horizon where contemporaneity begins after the events that the *Esnwherta au'oso* narrates. However, according to what I heard from many Yshiro, much of what happened after these events is now considered to be clearly part of the porowo times.

One Invisibilizing the Yrmo

1 For a critique of the Eurocentric notion of historicity embedded in the assumption that the contact with Europe sets the wheels of history in motion, see Gow 2001; Harris 1995; Hirsch and Stewart 2005.

2 Although for brevity the terms *bahlut* and *lata* are described as father and mother in relation to *abo* (children), a more detailed description renders the relation as one between an emanation (*abo*) and its source (*bahlut/lata*) (see also Cordeu 1990:167–69).

3 All translations from Yshiro, Spanish, or Italian sources (oral or written) are mine unless otherwise stated.

4 The term refers to people sharing a bond of reciprocity; in this case, this bond was created between the man who helped to bury the elder and the latter's relative.

5 In effect, racism and sexism draw their power to dictate interventions from "casting sexual, racial and ethnic differences as closer to the animal and the body [i.e., nature] construed as a sphere of inferiority" (Plumwood 1993:4; see also Haraway 1991; MacCormack and Strathern 1980; Merchant 1983; Yanagisako and Delaney 1995).

6 The masculinist tropes associated with the conquest of the "virgin lands" of the Chaco are ubiquitous in the records of the early settlers and explorers, and they clearly respond to the modern view that associates nature with femininity and passivity (see Merchant 1983).

7 In 1889, the Anglican South American Missionary Society began operations in the southern part of the Paraguayan Chaco, but did not reach the Yshiro area (Grubb [1925] 1993). The Catholic Church, because of financial problems, could not start operations until 1917, but from then on it established several missions along the Pilcomayo and Paraguay Rivers (Stunnenberg 1993:66–67; Fritz 1994; Heyn 1996).

8 The mission was a failure, and not until the 1950s were the Yshiro again targeted for systematic evangelization.

9 For Cancio, the leader of the expedition, the Ebitoso's fears were proof enough that everyone he encountered was at least an accomplice of the crime. Ultimately, he coerced an Yshiro man to confess to the crime and took him to Asunción, where he was arrested. After more than a year of claiming his innocence, the man was freed (Leigheb 1986:158–59).

10 The Tomaraho captives were usually adopted into the family and clan of the captors. While they usually had to perform the heavier chores, the differences between themselves and their adoptive siblings became less pronounced as they grew up.

Two Stabilizing Modernity

1 Also at issue was the right to decide the future of the Indians. Thus, since those times, different interested parties have invoked the poor treatment of the Indians as a justification for claiming rights to manage the Chaco. For an early version of these disputes, see Olmedo 1946 and Lopez Fretes 1946, which seem to contest each other point by point. On the one hand, Olmedo defends the civilizing role played by the tannin companies in Alto Paraguay. Lopez Fretes, in contrast, emphasizes the relentless exploitation that both indigenous and Paraguayan peoples suffered at the hands of the foreign personnel and owners of the tannin companies. For an informed reader, it is clear that, for the purposes of both arguments, indigenous peoples were just pawns in struggles that had little to do with their well-being.

2 Without ignoring that there are other uses of the term *indigenista* in the literature (see Diaz Polanco 1997:24; Ramos 1998:6–7), I intend mine to remain as close as possible

to the meaning most people give to it in Paraguay. There, *indigenista* is the label given to *non-indigenous* individuals, organizations, or institutions (governmental or not) concerned with indigenous peoples' issues.

3 For details on how the regime was organized and operated, see Barreto 1996; Hanratty and Meditz 1990; Lambert 1996; Lewis 1980; Nickson 1997; Roett and Sacks 1991; Yore 1992.

4 In 1992 the population of Alto Paraguay was 12,000, a figure well below the 17,000 inhabitants who in 1924 were counted around the tannin factories alone (see Klein-penning 1992:276; Dirección General de Estadística, Encuestas y Censos de Paraguay 1997:158).

5 Since the end of the nineteenth century, the Paraguay River has been a highly traveled waterway, with large boats carrying products north and south. Although with the end of the tannin boom the number of boats diminished, enough circulation remained to render exchanges and trade with people traveling in boats an important source of income for the Yshiro.

6 Between the 1950s and 1960s, feline skins were in high demand; between the 1970s and 1980s, alligator and caiman skins were sought after; and since the 1990s, fish have been a prized commodity. To the extent that hunting and making handicrafts were intertwined with the market, teaching and learning how to survive in the bush were in many cases focused only on those species that were more useful in the given context. This impoverishment of knowledge further reinforced the relative importance of the market for the subsistence of Yshiro families.

7 The exact date of arrival of the first NTM missionaries is not clear. The missionaries who lived in Diana until 2000 claimed that the mission began operations in 1955 (see Renshaw 1996:235); however, according to Borgognon's claim, written in 1963 and published in 1966, the approximate date seems to be 1951. Some Yshiro say that the missionaries were among them briefly seven years prior to taking up permanent residence, which would make 1944 the earliest possible date. In any case, NTM's official operations in Paraguay commenced simultaneously with the Cold War and growing U.S. aid for development in Latin America. Many analysts claim that this was not mere coincidence and argue that NTM, which is closely associated with the Summer Institute of Linguistics, was involved in counterinsurgent activities throughout Latin America (see Hvalkof and Aaby 1981; Stoll 1982; Colby and Dennett 1995:775–79).

8 In uxorilocal family arrangements, males move into the family households of their female partners.

9 It would be erroneous to understand conversion as merely a façade calculated to obtain benefits from these particular *patrones*. Although the people who felt coerced to convert to Christianity clearly narrate this experience as one of conscious accommodation to unfavorable circumstances, there are many others who describe their conversion as a heartfelt search for a way out of their predicaments, which included much more than addressing basic economic needs.

10 Both Susnik (1957b:6, 1995:40) and Renshaw (1996:236) mention these roles but without identifying the individuals who occupied them. After I asked people in Diana, it became clear that it was Cleto who occupied all these roles.

Three Modernity Unravels?

1 I will mention at several points critical and integrationist indigenistas, in most cases without providing further identifying details. I do so either because I agreed to respect anonymity or because, in consideration of concerns raised by Yshiro leaders and my close association with them, I cannot risk alienating institutions with which they need to coexist.

2 The literature on different aspects of the process by which indigenous peoples became constituted as subjects with rights is voluminous. For recent overviews in English, see, among others, Niezen 2003; Muehlebach 2003; Brysk 2000; Van Cott 2000; Assies, van der Haar, and Hoekema 2000; Postero and Zamosc 2004; Sieder 2002; and Yashar 2005.

3 I cannot expand on this here, but it is important to stress that Von Bremen made reference to the supposed mentality of peoples who by 1980s were subsisting on the basis of a mixed economy where wage-labor and several forms of agriculture were very important. For a thorough critique of Von Bremen's and other similar arguments applied to indigenous peoples living in the Chaco, see Gordillo 1993.

4 Renshaw's argument (1988, 1996) is similar, and it arrives at similar conclusions. The difference is that his focus is on the moral economy implicit in the hunter-gatherer mentality. This mentality ultimately leads development projects to failure because, by trying to incorporate indigenous peoples into activities with deferred return (i.e., agriculture), they interfere with those activities that indigenous peoples prefer for their immediate returns, which can be quickly incorporated into networks of reciprocity (i.e., wage labor, hunting-gathering).

5 More extended discussions of what the imagination Environment entails in political, economic, epistemic, and moral terms can be found in, among others, Arturo Escobar 1999; Haraway 1997; Franklin, Lury, and Stacey 2000; Takacs 1996; Hayden 2003. The blurring of nature and culture, and the consequent transposition of liberal concerns from one domain to the other, may be framed in different and even mutually opposing ways, as is evident in the contrasting images of "ecological modernization" (Hajer 1995) and the "cyborg" or "companion species" (Haraway 1991, 2003).

6 Agenda 21, preamble, available at the web site for the United Nations.

7 The salience of notions of risk to conceive development has only increased from the 1990s onward, as attested by the progressive merging of development and security concerns (see Duffield 2002; Beall, Goodfellow, and Putzel 2006).

8 Of course the agency of the imagination Environment is made intelligible through the environmental movement, which acts as its spokesperson. With this intermediation,

the environment reveals its needs and its limits. On the notion of spokesperson in this sense, and on its ambivalent yet necessary function, see Latour 2004:62–70.

9   The notion that modernity has changed the very fabric of reality is evident when Beck speaks of things being "no longer" the same, or of risk combining "what once was mutually exclusive" (nature and society).

10   Agenda 21, chaps. 26–27, available at the web site for the United Nations.

11   I claim not that the environment did not constitute a governmental preoccupation before the 1960s and 1970s, but that governing nature was not conceived in the same way as governing society was, that is, as a murky epistemological and ethical problem. Of course, there were disagreements about how to intervene in nature, but they centered on whether "man" could do so without regard for nature's laws (see Grove 1995:168–263; Drayton 2000:221–68); that man was entitled to intervene was unquestioned. Concerns about the effects that human activities have on nature were certainly articulated in ethical terms before the 1960s, but the mid- to late-twentieth-century environmental critique of anthropocentrism made an unprecedented push to the most powerful centers of decision-making, and on a scale never before attempted, the question of whether and under what conditions the rule of humankind over the environment was legitimate. Similarly, Indians had constituted a governmental preoccupation before, but until the 1960s there was little governmental concern about their autonomy, the dominant view being that they had to be integrated into modernity. As in the case of nature, voices were raised against this assumption, but they had little effect on governmental action before the 1960s.

12   In 1988, the World Bank estimated that traffic in contraband was equal to or larger than registered trade (see Nickson 1997:26).

13   For detailed discussions on the end of the Stroessner regime and the Paraguayan transition, see Carter 1992; Richer 1993; Abente 1999; Flecha and Martini 1994; Valenzuela 1997; Lambert and Nickson 1997b; Lambert 2000; Nickson and Lambert 2002; Nieto Neibuhr and Wall Enns 1998; Rivarola 2001.

14   For a general discussion of the chapters on indigenous peoples and the environment in the Paraguayan constitution, see Prieto and Bragayrac 1995; Horst 1998:397–407.

15   In several passages I qualify some leaders as "legal." By this I signal that in the Yshiro communities there are many leaders or influential individuals who do not have legal status. The distinction is important because while nonlegal leaders supposedly cannot carry out certain legal procedures, such as claiming lands or demanding aid from the state on behalf of a community, they nevertheless have the capacity to mobilize groups of supporters for different purposes, including the ousting of a legal leader. In addition, INDI officials often bypass legal leaders for whom they have no sympathy and attend to claims from these other individuals. In this way they erode the authority of "unfriendly" legal leaders.

16   Alberto Santa Cruz, the first president of API, was jailed for several months, then released and cleared of all charges (Alberto Santa Cruz, personal communication, November 1998).

17 The leader was quoted by the anthropologist Verena Regehr (personal communication, September 1999).

18 Indigenista institutions (from both sectors) were in charge of organizing a series of meetings in which indigenous leaders could discuss the issues that would be brought to the constitutional assembly. What this meant was that the discussions were held not by the communities but by those leaders that indigenista institutions chose to bring to Asunción for the meetings. Moreover, the constitutional assembly denied a petition from indigenous leaders who wished to participate directly as representative of their peoples. Only four leaders were allowed to participate in the debates, and even they were without the right to vote on the decisions (see Corte Suprema de Justicia del Paraguay 2003:82).

Four Enacting the Yrmo

1 The version of the events discussed in this chapter come from the juxtaposition of diverse versions told to me by direct participants. I have used written sources as available and cited them accordingly.

Five Taming Differences

1 Other theoreticians include Darcy Ribeiro, Stephano Varese, and Guillermo Bonfil Batalla (Nahmad 1997:240), all signatories of the Barbados Declaration.

2 The political consequences of both objectivist and constructionist analysis of indigenousness have produced a great deal of controversy in anthropological circles (see Briggs 1996; Mato 1996; Brosius 1999).

3 Technologies of government that respond to the logic of framing are proliferating in multiple domains and have been described under, among others, the labels of post-disciplinary technologies of control (Castel 1991; Donzelot 1991); technologies of "command-control-communication-intelligence" (Haraway 1991:164–65); "cultural control" (Nader 1997); "control of the surroundings" (Virilio 1999); distantiated relations of control (Nikolas S. Rose 1996:53–57); and actuarialism (O'Malley 1996). What these different technologies have in common is the appearance of respect for the autonomous "free will" of the object of intervention, which allows interventions to appear as non-interventions precisely because they operate by "framing."

4 I am indebted to my friend and colleague Rodrigo Villagra, who made me notice that by not recognizing that their practices are not only textual but also lived in relations, I had been enormously unfair with many critical indigenistas in previous versions of this manuscript, as well as in a previously published article (Blaser 2004a). In missing that recognition, and by contrast, I portrayed myself as the only one in Paraguay who has respectful relations with indigenous peoples, which is certainly not the case.

5 Keep in mind that, in a relational universe, differences are a function of location, not of essences. Ultimately, all that exists is the web of life.

6 Relational cosmologies are operative in different degrees (or not at all) in different indigenous movements; that is, indigenous and relational cosmologies must not be taken
to be synonymous. It is indisputable that many indigenous movements reveal in their
practices assumptions about the world that are quite modern, and so is the case with
some Yshiro individuals. However, such "modern stances" should not blind us to the
presence of relational stances, even when they might not be dominant in a specific indigenous movement or organization. In the Yshiro case, the weight of relational stances
have varied through time and according to circumstances.

Six Translating Neoliberalism

1 For example, several of the persons listed by Kidd (1995b:71) as being involved in controversies over land claims with indigenous peoples, either as landowners or as their
lawyers, were also listed by Richer (1993:14) as being involved in the "governability
pact" between Wasmosy and the opposition forces.

2 Letter dated 28 September 1994, from Mr. Woodham, the ALA committee's U.K. representative, to Stephen Kidd. Copy is on file with the author.

3 See Written Question E-563/95 by R. Howitt to the Commission and its answer (Official Journal of the Communities No C 179/36 13.7.95).

4 See various MEP Written Questions to the Commission and their answers (Official
Journal of the Communities No C 66/13 P-2470/95; No C 340/31 E-23333/95; No C 9/30
E-2334/95; No C40/31 E-2463/95).

5 The consortium was formed by the Natural Resources Institute and Halcrow Rural
Management. According to the project proposal, the EU technical assistance, which
was to be provided by the consortium, would include four Europeans acting as co-
director, anthropologist, forester, and an expert in participatory methodologies. Each
of these experts would have a Paraguayan counterpart. The European personnel would
report back to the South American Unit of the European Commission through the
consortium, while the Paraguayans would report back to the Paraguayan ministry of
agriculture (see European Commission and Gobierno del Paraguay 1995).

6 This becomes transparent in the public debate between critical indigenistas, the Paraguayan government, and EC representatives. See the newspapers *Ultima Hora* (9 March
1997) and *ABC* (17 March 1997), and the journal *Acción* (March 1997). Copies of letters
are on file with the author.

7 Copies of several letters between Prodechaco and diverse Paraguayan NGOs, dated between March and June 1997, are on file with the author.

8 Copy of letter from Prodechaco to several NGOs, dated 24 March 1998, is on file with
the author.

9 Copy of letter from several NGOs to ALA Committee, dated 21 April 1998, is on file with
the author.

10 Copy of e-mail between Survival International and a Paraguayan NGO, dated 29 July
1998, is on file with the author.

11 John Palmer, *Evaluación de Prodechaco: Informe sobre la situación de las reivindicaciones indígenas en el Chaco paraguayo* (1999), copy on file with the author.

12 Copy of e-mails from Survival International to a Paraguayan NGO, dated 24 May and 16 July 1999, is on file with the author.

13 Prodechaco, *Prodechaco Response to the Points Raised by Country Members' Delegations*, copy of Prodechaco internal document on file with the author.

14 Ibid.

Seven In which Many Worlds (Are Forced to) Fit

1 Intermediaries bought fish from the fishermen, froze or cooled it, stored, and transported it to urban markets.

2 After 1997, in three of the five Yshiro communities, Yshiro teachers with a steady income bought TV sets with satellite dishes or VCRs powered by small electricity generators.

3 I was not present at the workshop, but an Yshiro friend who did attend tape-recorded the meeting and later let me transcribe it.

4 Letter from several members of indigenous communities to Prodechaco co-directors, dated 17 August 1997, copy on file with the author.

5 Michael Holland, *The Importance of Prodechaco: A Personal View* (1998), a document internal to Prodechaco, copy on file with the author.

Eight Becoming the Yshiro Nation

1 Several young males have shown to me written prayers to the devil/Nemur that they keep in their pockets while visiting their female friends. It is said that this procedure will make the women fall in love with them. Asked if they are not afraid of praying to the devil, most youngsters affirm that these actions are "small things" that would not jeopardize their possibilities of entering into Heaven.

2 He was referring to rumors that the cultureros had orgies fueled by the widely known power of certain konsaho's songs to drive the men and women who hear them into a sexual frenzy.

3 Don Veneto was referring to the benefits a community receives by having a konsaha connected to the ukurb'deio (the nonhuman powers). This connection is made evident when the konsaha sings the songs the ukurb'deio, through visionary dreams, tell him or her to sing.

4 Note that this tolerant attitude is remarkably different from the one attributed to the Yshiro porowo. In effect, according to most Yshiro commentators the Yshiro porowo would have punished by death recurrent breaks with the *Esnwherta au'oso*.

5 He referred to the screams that are heard in the Pentecostal temple when the holy spirit descends over the congregation.

6 This refers to the *Anabser* who during the ritual goes from house to house throughout the community with a bag collecting food for the elders and the ill.

7 Instituto Nacional del Indígena, Memorandum PCN 182/99, copy on file with author.

8 Unión de las Comunidades Indígenas de la Nación Yshir, *Estatutos sociales de* UCINY (1999), copy on file with the author.

Nine Reality Check

1 Hunting on the Brazilian side of the river was more profitable because, in contrast to the Paraguayan side, which becomes very dry a few kilometers from the river, the Brazilian side is characterized by large swampy areas, where the most profitable species, caiman and anaconda, abound.

2 For similar (although not identical) indigenous conceptions of networks of sociality transcending the society-nature divide, see Feit 1995, 2001; Rival 1993; Descola and Pálsson 1996; Viveiros de Castro 2004.

3 For the present discussion, it is important to highlight that in the old hunting business *patrones* were in charge of stockpiling and transporting animal skins to the industrial factories that processed and exported them. Thus, the chain went from hunters to *patrones* to industries. The biggest share of the profits in this chain was taken by those operating as brokers (*patrones*).

4 Among the various "skills" to be developed with the help of Prodechaco were accounting, management of hunters' stores, and planning how to use the benefits derived from the hunting program. All these skills were geared to ensure the sustainability of the development process through time.

5 Some of the information regarding these issues was provided by "insiders," who requested I ensure their complete anonymity. Hence, the paucity of detail.

6 See, by Roque Gonzalez Vera, "Presión política y empresarial en torno a la caza en el norte," ABC *Color*, 6 April 2000, 24; "MAG habilita la caza en forma general en el Alto Paraguay," ABC *Color*, 7 April 2000, 20; "Presionan a indígenas para aceptar cacería comercial," ABC *Color*, 8 April 2000, 14; "MAG intenta rever postura de indígenas sobre la caza," ABC *Color*, 10 April 2000, 14; and "Indígenas solicitan acopio exclusivo de pieles silvestres," ABC *Color*, 11 April 2000, 15.

7 "Prodechaco, Solicitada—A la Opinion Publica," ABC *Color*, 6 April 2000, 6.

8 As the conflict unfolded, the Yshiro leaders let Prodechaco know that they were contacting representatives of CITES International to alert them to what was happening in Paraguay and that they would call into the conflict environmental NGOs if the project went ahead without UCINY.

9 See Roque Gonzalez Vera, "Cazadores invaden pantanal Brasileño," ABC *Color*, 30 July 2000, 18.

10 See, by Roque Gonzalez Vera, "Hasta cuando la caza en el Alto Paraguay?" ABC *Color*, 6 August 2000, 32; "Cazadores viven con la sombra de la Policía Florestal Brasileña," ABC *Color*, 4 August 2000, 20; and "Indígenas vendieron cupos a cazadores de Bahia Negra," ABC *Color*, 1 August 1 2000, 18.

11 The result of this new "controversy" shows the fluidity of alliances among powerful interests with capacity to lobby the Paraguayan government and the importance of the timing of their interventions. In this case, but only momentarily, the industrial lobby was able to impose its views against the landowners. In the long run a combination of landowners and other interests overcame the industrial lobby. Prodechaco, in turn, did not see any advantage in raising the stakes over its disagreement with NPD and UCINY. Nevertheless, Prodechaco would never again support a rerun of the hunting program, and after this experience it progressively delinked from UCINY.

12 Again, as in the past, necessity prevailed over the fear of crossing to Brazil. More so because, as the hunting program was backed by Prodechaco, the hunters assumed that they would have the protection of the Paraguayan government.

Conclusion *Eisheraho*/Renewal

1 There remains a whole work to be done exploring the many points of resonance between these cosmologies and the relational perspectives embraced by some feminists and ecologists (but see Plumwood 2002). Also, the focus of my argument here is specifically relationality, and not "indigeneity." That is, the promises and possibilities are inherent to the relational cosmologies that some indigenous movements reveal, and not to indigenous movements or peoples themselves. In other words, the argument is not about a new privileged historical subject, but rather about a different way of being or becoming.

2 The worldwide crisis of hegemony of neoliberalism following the 2008 financial crisis and the ascendancy of neo-Keynesian agendas might very well mean that this dichotomization and homogeneization spread on a world-wide scale adding another dimension to the rigidity of a political imagination already impoverished by the War on Terror.

Glossary

agalo: literally, "they eat together"; refers to pairs of people in a relation of reciprocity

agalio: advice

Anabsero (sing., Anabser): mythical beings whose story is narrated by the porowo narratives

azle: the temporal dimension of contemporaneity

bahlut or lata: the first individual of a species or kind, usually translated as "mother" or "father"

debylylta: the male initiation ritual

eiwo: the capacity to make distinctions and to reason

Esnwherta au'oso: literally, "the word of Esnwherta"; a narrative which structures debylylta

eisheraho: the coming generations, renewal

konsaha: (pl., *konsaho*): shaman

om: good, fresh; in connection with wozosh it refers to distinction and being

polotak: war leader

Porosht: God

porowo: the temporal dimension accessible to memory

puruhle: the temporal dimension accessible through dreams; the basic source of being

ukurb'deio: power, potency; a general term applied to various suprahuman entities

sherwo: chaotic, unpredictable; in connection with wozosh it refers to indistinction

weterak (sing., wetete): young initiated males

wozosh: the dynamic or energy which results in being and indistinction

yrmo: connotes both "bush" and "cosmos"

References

Abente, Diego. 1989. "Foreign Capital, Economic Elites and the State in
Paraguay during the Liberal Republic (1870–1936)." *Latin American Studies*
21, no. 1, 61–88.

———. 1999. "'People Power' in Paraguay." *Democracy* 10, no. 3, 93.

Abu-Lughod, Lila. 1990. "The Romance of Resistance: Tracing Transformations
of Power through Bedouin Women." *American Ethnologist* 17, no. 1, 41–55.

Adams, William. 1995. "Green Development Theory? Environmentalism and
Sustainable Development." *Power of Development*, ed. Jonathan Crush,
87–99. London: Routledge.

Alarcón y Cañedo, José, and Riccardo Pittini. 1924. *El Chaco paraguayo y sus
tribus*. Turin: Sociedad Editora Internacional.

Albanese, Denise. 1996. *New Science, New World*. Durham, N.C.: Duke University Press.

Albó, Xavier. 1999. "Andean People in the Twentieth Century." *South America:
Part 2*, ed. Frank Salomon and Stuart Schwartz, 765–869. Vol. 3 of *The Cam-
bridge History of the Native Peoples of the Americas*. Cambridge: Cambridge
University Press.

Alvarez, Serafina. 1995. "Modelos de desarrollo y economías indígenas." *Acción*
157, 22–23.

Alvarez, Sonia E., Evelina Dagnino, and Arturo Escobar. 1998. "Introduc-
tion: The Cultural and the Political in Latin American Social Movements."
*Cultures of Politics/Politics of Cultures: Re-Visioning Latin American Social
Movements*, ed. Sonia Alvarez, Evelina Dagnino, and Arturo Escobar, 1–29.
Boulder, Colo.: Westview.

Amawtay Wasi. 2004. *Sumak Yachaypi: Alli Kawasaypipash Yachakuna:
Aprender en la sabiduría y el buen vivir* (Learning wisdom and the good
way of life). Quito: Banco Central de Ecuador.

Appadurai, Arjun. 1996. *Modernity at Large: Cultural Dimensions of Globalization*. Minneapolis: University of Minnesota Press.

Arce, Alberto, and Norman Long, eds. 2000. *Anthropology, Development, and
Modernities: Exploring Discourses, Counter-Tendencies, and Violence*. London:
Routledge.

Arnold, David. 1996. *The Problem of Nature: Environment, Culture and European Expansion.* Cambridge, Mass.: Blackwell.

——. 2000. "'Illusory Riches': Representations of the Tropical World, 1840–1950." *Singapore Journal of Tropical Geography* 21, no. 1, 6–18.

Arquette, Mary, Maxine Cole, and Akwesasne Task Force on the Environment. 2004. "Restoring Our Relationships for the Future." *In the Way of Development: Indigenous Peoples, Life Projects, and Globalization,* ed. Mario Blaser, Harvey Feit, and Glenn McRae, 332–50. London: Zed / International Development Research Center.

Asad, Talal. 1973. *Anthropology and the Colonial Encounter.* London: Ithaca.

Asociación Indigenista del Paraguay. 1945. *Anales de la Asociación Indigenista Del Paraguay* 1, no. 1, 3–50.

Asociación Rural del Paraguay. 1994. *Tierras del chaco para indígenas y campesinos.* Asunción: Asociación Rural del Paraguay.

Assies, Willem, Gemma van der Haar, and Andre Hoekema. 1998. *The Challenge of Diversity: Indigenous Peoples and Reform of the State in Latin America.* Amsterdam: Thela Thesis.

Ayala, Elías. 1929. *Paraguay y Bolivia en el Chaco Boreal.* Asunción: Imprenta Nacional.

Baldus, Herbert. 1927. *Os Indios Chamacocos.* São Paulo: Separata do Tomo 15 Da Revista do Museu Paulista.

Barras, Bruno. 2004. "Life Projects: Development Our Way." *In the Way of Development: Indigenous Peoples, Life Projects, and Globalization,* ed. Mario Blaser, Harvey Feit, and Glenn McRae, 47–51. London: Zed / International Development Research Center.

Barreto, Raul A. 1996. "Institutional corruption, the public sector, and economic development: Institutional corruption and Paraguayan economic development." Ph.D. diss., Department of Economics, University of Colorado.

Barry, Andrew, Thomas Osborne, and Nikolas S. Rose, eds. 1996. *Foucault and Political Reason: Liberalism, Neo-Liberalism and Rationalities of Government.* Chicago: University of Chicago Press.

Bartolomé, Miguel. 1989. "Nación y etnias en Paraguay." *América Indígena* 49, no. 3, 407–18.

——. 1998. "Procesos civilizatorios, pluralismo cultural y autonomías étnicas en América Latina." *Autonomías étnicas y estados nacionales,* ed. Miguel Bartolomé and Alicia Barabas, 171–93. Mexico City: Consejo Nacional para la Cultura y las Artes / Instituto Nacional de Antropología e Historia.

Bauman, Zygmunt. 1993. "The Fall of the Legislator." *Postmodernism: A Reader,* ed. Thomas Docherty, 128–40. New York: Columbia University Press.

Beall, Jo, Thomas Goodfellow, and James Putzel. 2006. "Introductory Article: On the Discourse of Terrorism, Security and Development." *Journal of International Development* 18, no. 1, 51–67.

Beck, Ulrich. 1992. *Risk Society: Towards a New Modernity.* London: Sage.

——. 1994. "The Reinvention of Politics: Towards a Theory of Reflexive Modernization." *Reflexive Modernization: Politics, Tradition and Aesthetics in the Modern Social Order,* ed. Ulrich Beck, Anthony Giddens, and Scott Lash, 1–55. Stanford, Calif.: Stanford University Press.

———. 1999. *World Risk Society*. Cambridge: Polity.

Beck, Ulrich, Anthony Giddens, and Scott Lash, eds. 1994. *Reflexive Modernization: Politics, Tradition and Aesthetics in the Modern Social Order*. Stanford, Calif.: Stanford University Press.

Bejarano, Ramón. 1976. *Solucionemos nuestro problema indígena con el INDI*. Asunción: Centro de Estudios Antropológicos.

Belaieff, Juan. 1928. *Informe del Gral. Juan Belaieff*. Notas Reservadas Informes Sobre Movimiento de Tropas y Agentes Extranjeros, telegramas. Asunción: Archivos del Ministerio de Defensa Nacional de La Republica del Paraguay.

———. 1941. "Los indios del Chaco paraguayo y su tierra." *Revista de la Sociedad Científica del Paraguay* 5, no. 3, 1–47.

Bergonzi, Osvaldo. 2001. *Magnicidio en la diagonal*. Asunción: Imprenta Comuneros.

Blaser, Mario. 1992. "Y ya se es Ishir: Tradición e identidad en colonia Potrerito." *Actas del 1 Congreso Argentino de Americanistas*, 57–71. Buenos Aires: Liga Naval Argentina.

———. 1994. "El emerger de otras voces: Discursos globales y textos locales." *Runa* no. 21, 83–97.

———. 2004a. "Indígenas del Chaco paraguayo: ¿Proyectos de vida o proyectos de desarrollo?" *Suplemento Antropológico* 39, no. 1, 193–229.

———. 2004b. "Life Projects: Indigenous Peoples' Agency and Development." *In the Way of Development: Indigenous Peoples, Life Projects and Globalization*, ed. Mario Blaser, Harvey Feit, and Glenn McRae, 26–44. London: Zed / International Development Research Center.

———. 2009a. "The Threat of the Yrmo: The Political Ontology of a Sustainable Hunting Program." *American Anthropologist* 111, no. 1, 10–20.

———. 2009b. "Political Ontology: Cultural Studies without 'Cultures'?" *Cultural Studies* 23, no. 5–6, 873–96.

Blaser, Mario, Ravi DeCosta, Deborah McGregor, and William Coleman, eds. Forthcoming. *Indigenous Peoples and Autonomy: Insights for the Global Age*. Vancouver: University of British Columbia Press.

Blaser, Mario, Harvey Feit, and Glenn McRae, eds. 2004. *In the Way of Development: Indigenous Peoples, Life Projects, and Globalization*. London: Zed / International Development Research Center.

Blaut, James M. 1993. *The Colonizer's Model of the World: Geographical Diffusionism and Eurocentric History*. New York: Guilford.

Boccara, Guillaume. 2006. "The Brighter Side of the Indigenous Renaissance (Parts 1, 2 and 3)." *Nuevo Mundo Mundos Nuevos* no. 6, http://nuevomundo.revues.org/.

Bodley, John H. 1982. *Victims of Progress*. 2d edn. Menlo Park, Calif.: Benjamin Cummings.

Boggiani, Guido. 1894. *I Ciamacoco*. Roma: Societa Romana per l'Antropologia.

———. [1896] 1975. *Os Caduveos*. Sao Paulo: Livraria Itatiaia Editora.

———. 1900. *Compendio de etnografía paraguaya moderna*. Asunción: Revista del Instituto Paraguayo.

Borgognon, Juan. 1966. "El indio en el Chaco paraguayo." *El Gran Chaco paraguayo: Amparo de civilización y progreso: Estudio grafico de los aspectos mas resaltantes del pasado y presente de la región occidental*, ed. Natalicio Olmedo, 33–43. Asunción: El Grafico.

———. 1968. "Panorama indígena paraguayo." *Suplemento Antropológico* 2, no. 1, 341–71.

Borrini, Hector. 1997. *Poblamiento y colonización en el Chaco paraguayo (1850–1990)*. Resistencia, Chaco: Instituto de Investigaciones Históricas, Conicet.

Bourdieu, Pierre. [1977] 1997. *Outline of a Theory of Practice*. Cambridge: Cambridge University Press.

Bramwell, Anna. 1989. *Ecology in the Twentieth Century: A History*. New Haven, Conn.: Yale University Press.

Bravo, Francisco. 1879. *Oriente de Bolivia*. Buenos Aires: M. Biedma.

Briggs, Charles L. 1996. "The Politics of Discursive Authority in Research on the 'Invention of Tradition.'" *Cultural Anthropology* 11, no. 4, 435–69.

Brosius, Peter, ed. 1999. *Ethnographic Presence: Environmentalism, Indigenous Rights and Transnational Cultural Critique*. Newark, N.J.: Gordon and Breach.

Brysk, Alison. 1994. "Acting Globally: Indian Rights and International Politics in Latin America." *Indigenous Peoples and Democracy in Latin America*, ed. Donna L. Van Cott, 29–51. New York: St. Martin's.

———. 2000. *From Tribal Village to Global Village: Indian Rights and International Relations in Latin America*. Stanford, Calif.: Stanford University Press.

Burchell, Graham, Colin Gordon, and Peter Miller, eds. 1991. *The Foucault Effect: Studies in Governmentality*. Chicago: University of Chicago Press.

Burger, Julian. 1998. "Indigenous Peoples and the United Nations." *The Human Rights of Indigenous Peoples*, ed. Cynthia Price Cohen, 3–16. Ardsley, N.Y.: Transnational.

Cajete, Gregory. 2000. *Native Science: Natural Laws of Interdependence*. 1st ed. Santa Fe, N.M.: Clear Light.

Callon, Michel, and Bruno Latour. 1981. "Unscrewing the Big Leviathan: How Actors Macro-Structure Reality and How Sociologist Help Them to Do So." *Advances in Social Theory and Methodology: Towards an Integration of Micro and Macro-Sociology*, ed. K. Knorr-Cetina and A. Cicourel, 277–303. Boston: Routledge.

Carothers, Tom H. 1991. *In the Name of Democracy: U.S. Policy toward Latin America in the Reagan Years*. Berkeley: University of California Press.

Carter, Miguel. 1992. *El papel de la Iglesia en la caída de Stroessner*. Asunción: RP Ediciones.

Castel, Robert. 1991. "From Dangerousness to Risk." *The Foucault Effect: Studies in Governmentality: With Two Lectures by and an Interview with Michel Foucault*, ed. Graham Burchell, Colin Gordon, and Peter Miller, 281–98. Chicago: University of Chicago Press.

Castells, Manuel. 1996. *The Rise of the Network Society*. Cambridge, Mass.: Blackwell.

Castro-Gómez, Santiago. 2007. "The Missing Chapter of Empire." *Cultural Studies* 21, no. 2, 428–48.

Castro-Gómez, Santiago, Carmen Millán, and Oscar Guardiola Rivarola. 2001. *La reestructuración de las ciencias sociales en América Latina*. Bogota: Universidad Javeriana.

Chase-Sardi, Miguel. 1981. "La antropología aplicada en el Chaco paraguayo." *Suplemento Antropológico* 16, no. 2, 157–65.

———. 1987. *Derecho consuetudinario Chamacoco*. Asunción: RP Ediciones.

Chase-Sardi, Miguel, Augusto Brun, and Miguel A. Enciso. 1990. *Situación sociocultural, económica, jurídico-política actual de las comunidades indígenas en el Paraguay*. Asunción: Universidad Católica.

Chase-Sardi, Miguel, and Adolfo Colombres, eds. 1975. *Compilación del Proyecto Marandú: Documentos y testimonios*. Buenos Aires: Ediciones del Sol.

Clifford, James, and George E. Marcus, eds. 1986. *Writing Culture: The Poetics and Politics of Ethnography*. Berkeley: University of California Press.

Colby, Gerard, and Charlotte Dennett. 1995. *Thy Will Be Done: The Conquest of the Amazon: Nelson Rockefeller and Evangelism in the Age of Oil*. 1st edn. New York: HarperCollins.

Colombres, Adolfo. 1982. *La hora del "bárbaro": Bases para una antropología social de Apoyo*. 1st edn. Puebla, Mexico: Premiá Editora.

———. 1992. *Manual del promotor cultural*. Vol. 1, *Bases teóricas de la acción*. Buenos Aires: Editorial Humanitas / Ediciones Colihue.

Comitato Pro-Boggiani. 1903. *Alla ricerca di Guido Boggiani: Spedizione Cancio nel Ciaco Boreale (Alto Paraguay), relazioni e documenti*. Milan: Bontempelli Editore.

Conca, Ken, and Geoffrey D. Dabelko, eds. 2004. *Green Planet Blues: Environmental Politics from Stockholm to Johannesburg*. 3d edn. Boulder, Colo.: Westview.

Conklin, Beth A. 1997. "Body Paint, Feathers, and VCRs: Aesthetics and Authenticity in Amazonian Activism." *American Ethnologist* 24, no. 4, 711–37.

Conklin, Beth A., and Laura R. Graham. 1995. "The Shifting Middle Ground: Amazonian Indians and Eco-Politics." *American Anthropologist* 97, no. 4, 695–710.

Cooper, Frederick, and Randall M. Packard, eds. 1997. *International Development and the Social Sciences: Essays on the History and Politics of Knowledge*. Berkeley: University of California Press.

Cordeu, Edgardo. 1988. "Algunas características narrativas de los Tomaraxo y los Ebitoso del Chaco Boreal." *Suplemento Antropológico* 23, no. 2, 77–85.

———. 1989a. "Aishtuwente: Las ideas de deidad en la religiosidad Chamacoco (Parte 1)." *Suplemento Antropológico* 24, no. 1, 7–77.

———. 1989b. "Algunas focalizaciones semánticas y simbólicas de la mitología de los Tomaraxo del Chaco Boreal." *Scripta Ethnologica (Suplementa)* 8, 43–53.

———. 1989c. "Los Chamacoco o ishir del Chaco Boreal: Algunos aspectos de un proceso de desestructuración étnica." *América Indígena* 49, no. 3, 545–80.

———. 1989d. "Xoshyty: Una divinidad cazadora y los símbolos de la comida y el sexo en la mitología Ishir." *Cuadernos del Instituto Nacional de Antropología* 13, 33–43.

———. 1990. "Aishtuwente: Las ideas de deidad en la religiosidad Chamacoco (Parte 3)." *Suplemento Antropológico* 25, no. 1, 119–211.

———. 1991a. "Aishtuwente: Las ideas de deidad en la religiosidad Chamacoco (Parte 3 cont.)." *Suplemento Antropológico* 26, no. 1, 85–166.

————. 1991b. "Lo cerrado y lo abierto: Arquitectura cosmovisional y patrón cognitivo de los Tomaraxo del Chaco Boreal." *Scripta Ethnologica (Suplementa)* 11, 9–31.

————. 1991c. "Aishtuwente. Las ideas de deidad en la religiosidad chamacoco (Parte 4)." *Suplemento Antropológico* 26, no. 2, 145–233.

————. 1999. *Los relatos de Wolko*. Buenos Aires: Ciudad Argentina.

Cordeu, Edgardo, and Jose Braunstein. 1974. "Los aparatos de un shaman Chamacoco: Contribución al estudio de la parafernalia shamanica." *Scripta Ethnologica* 2, no. 2, 121–39.

Corte Suprema de Justicia del Paraguay. 2003. *Digesto normativo sobre Pueblos indígenas en el Paraguay (1811–2003)*. Asunción: International Work Group for Indigenous Affairs / Tierra Viva.

Costa, José M., and Oscar Ayala Bogarin. 1996. *Operación Gedeon: Los secretos de un golpe frustrado*. Asunción: Editorial Don Bosco.

Cruikshank, Julie. 2005. *Do Glaciers Listen? Local Knowledge, Colonial Encounters and Social Imagination*. Vancouver: University of British Columbia Press.

Dalton, Russell. 1993. "The Environmental Movement in Western Europe." *Environmental Politics in the International Arena: Movements, Parties, Organizations, and Policy*, ed. Sheldon Kamieniecki, 41–68. Albany: State University of New York Press.

Davis, Shelton H. 1977. *Victims of the Miracle: Development and the Indians of Brazil*. Cambridge: Cambridge University Press.

Dean, Mitchell. 1999. *Governmentality: Power and Rule in Modern Society*. London: Sage.

de la Cadena, Marisol. 2009. "Política indígena: Un análisis más allá de 'la política.'" *World Anthropologies Network Electronic Journal* 4, 140–72. http://www.ram-wan.net/html/journal.htm.

de Lauretis, Teresa. 1990. "Eccentric Subjects: Feminist Theory and Historical Consciousness." *Feminist Studies* 16, no. 1, 115–50.

Deloria Jr., Vine. 2004. "Philosophy and the Tribal Peoples." *American Indian Thought: Philosophical Essays*, ed. Anne Waters, 3–14. Malden, Mass.: Blackwell.

Delport, Jose. 1998. "Los indígenas angaité en las estancias." *Suplemento Antropológico* 33, nos. 1–2, 235–74.

Deruyttere, Anne. 1997. *Pueblos indígenas y desarrollo: El banco interamericano de desarrollo y los pueblos indígenas*. Documento de Trabajo: Presentación hecha ante el Foro de las Américas del Banco Interamericano de Desarrollo, 8 April. Washington: Unidad de Pueblos Indígenas y Desarrollo Comunitario / Departamento de Desarrollo Sostenible / Banco Interamericano de Desarrollo.

Descartes, René. 1993. *Discourse on the Method of Rightly Conducting One's Reason and Seeking Truth in the Sciences*. Project Gutenberg, http://www.gutenberg.org/.

Descola, Philippe. 1996. "Constructing Natures: Symbolic Ecology and Social Practice." *Nature and Society: Anthropological Perspectives*, ed. Philippe Descola and Gísli Pálsson, 82–102. London: Routledge.

————. 2005. *Par-delá nature et culture*. Paris: Gallimard.

Descola, Philippe, and Gísli Pálsson. 1996. *Nature and Society: Anthropological Perspectives*. London: Routledge.

Diani, Mario, and Doug McAdam, eds. 2003. *Social Movements and Networks: Relational Approaches to Collective Action*. New York: Oxford University Press.

Díaz Polanco, Héctor. 1997. *Indigenous Peoples in Latin America: The Quest for Self-Determination*. Boulder, Colo.: Westview.

Dirección General de Estadística, Encuestas y Censos de Paraguay. 1997. *Pueblos indígenas en el Paraguay*. Asunción: Dirección General de Estadística, Encuestas y Censos de Paraguay.

Dirlik, Arif. 2001. "Place-Based Imagination: Globalism and the Politics of Place." *Places and Politics in the Age of Globalization*, ed. Roxann Prazniak and Arif Dirlik, 15–51. Lanham, Md.: Rowman and Littlefield.

Docherty, Thomas, ed. 1993. *Postmodernism: An Introduction*. New York: Columbia University Press.

Donzelot, Jacques. 1991. "Pleasure in Work." *The Foucault Effect: Studies in Governmentality: With Two Lectures by and an Interview with Michel Foucault*, ed. Graham Burchell, Colin Gordon, and Peter Miller, 251–80. Chicago: University of Chicago Press.

Drayton, Richard H. 2000. *Nature's Government: Science, Imperial Britain, and the "Improvement" of the World*. New Haven, Conn.: Yale University Press.

Duffield, Mark. 2002. "Social Reconstruction and the Radicalization of Development: Aid as a Relation of Global Liberal Governance." *Development and Change* 33, no. 5, 1049–71.

Dussel, Enrique D. 1995. *The Invention of the Americas: Eclipse of "the Other" and the Myth of Modernity*. New York: Continuum.

————. 1998. "Beyond Eurocentrism: The World System and the Limits of Modernity." *The Cultures of Globalization*, ed. Fredric Jameson and Masao Miyoshi, 3–31. Durham, N.C.: Duke University Press.

Edwards, Michael, and David Hulme. 1996. "Introduction: NGO Performance and Accountability." *Beyond the Magic Bullet: NGO Performance and Accountability in the Post–Cold War World*, 1–20. West Hartford, Conn.: Kumarian.

Eisenstadt, Shmuel. 2002. *Multiple Modernities*. New Brunswick, N.J.: Transaction Publishers.

Ekins, Paul. 1993. "Making Development Sustainable." *Global Ecology: A New Arena of Political Conflict*, ed. Wolfgang Sachs, 91–103. London: Zed.

Ellen, Roy, and Holly Harris. 2000. "Introduction." *Indigenous Environmental Knowledge and Its Transformations: Critical Anthropological Perspectives*, ed. Roy Ellen, Peter Parkes, and Alan Bicker, 1–33. Amsterdam: Harwood Academic.

Elliott, John. 1970. *The Old World and the New: 1492–1650*. Cambridge: Cambridge University Press.

Escobar, Arturo. 1993. "The Limits of Reflexivity: Politics in Anthropology's Post-'Writing Culture' Era." *Anthropological Research* 49, no. 4, 377–92.

————. 1995. *Encountering Development: The Making and Unmaking of the Third World.* Princeton, N.J.: Princeton University Press.

————. 1999. "After Nature: Steps to an Antiessentialist Political Ecology." *Current Anthropology* 40, no. 1, 1–30.

————. 2001. "Culture Sits in Places: Reflections on Globalism and Subaltern Strategies of Localization." *Political Geography* 20, no. 2, 139–74.

————. 2003. "'Worlds and Knowledges Otherwise': The Latin American Modernity/ Coloniality Research Program." *Cuadernos el Centro de Estudios y Documentación Latinoamericanos* 16, 31–67.

————. 2004a. "Beyond the Third World: Imperial Globality, Global Coloniality and Anti-Globalisation Social Movements." *Third World Quarterly* 25, no. 1, 207–30.

————. 2004b. "Other Worlds Are (Already) Possible: Self-Organisation, Complexity, and Post-Capitalist Cultures." *The World Social Forum: Challenging Empires,* ed. Jai Sen, Anita Arnand, and Peter Waterman, 349–58. New Delhi: Viveka.

————. 2008. *Territories of Difference: Place, Movements, Life, Redes.* Durham, N.C.: Duke University Press.

Escobar, Ticio. 1999. *La maldición de Nemur: Acerca del arte, el mito y el ritual de los indígenas Ishir del Gran Chaco paraguayo.* Asunción: Centro de Artes Visuales / Museo del Barro.

Esteva, Gustavo. 1992. "Development." *The Development Dictionary: A Guide to Knowledge as Power,* ed. Wolfgang Sachs, 6–25. London: Zed.

Esteva, Gustavo, and Madhu S. Prakash. 1998. *Grassroots Post-Modernism: Remaking the Soil of Cultures.* London: Zed.

European Commission. 1994. *Proposal for a Financing Decision under Item B7–3010.* Brussels: Document VIII/152/94-EN South America Unit.

————. 1998. *Commission Working Document on Support for Indigenous Peoples in the Development Co-operation of the Community and the Member States.* Brussels: Document SEC 1998/0773 final.

European Commission and Gobierno del Paraguay. 1995. *Convenio de financiación del proyecto: Desarrollo duradero del Chaco paraguayo.* Brussel: Program ALA/93/40.

European Economic Community. 1992. *Framework Agreement for Cooperation between the European Economic Community and the Republic of Paraguay.* Brussels: Document 292A1030(01).

Fabian, Johannes. 1983. *Time and the Other: How Anthropology Makes Its Object.* New York: Columbia University Press.

Fals-Borda, Osvaldo. 1977. *El problema de como investigar la realidad para transformarla por la praxis.* Bogotá: Ediciones Tercer Mundo.

Feit, Harvey. 1995. "Hunting and the Quest for Power: The James Bay Cree and Whitemen in the Twentieth Century." *Native Peoples: The Canadian Experience,* ed. R. B. Morrison and C. R. Wilson, 181–223. Toronto: McClelland and Stewart.

—————. 2001. "Hunting, Nature and Metaphor: Political and Discursive Strategies in James Bay Cree Resistance and Autonomy." *Indigenous Traditions and Ecology: The Interbeing of Cosmology and Community*, 411–52. Cambridge, Mass.: Center for the Study of World Religions, Harvard Divinity School.

—————. 2004. "James Bay Crees' Life Projects and Politics: Histories of Place, Animal Partners and Enduring Relationships." *In the Way of Development: Indigenous Peoples, Life Projects and Globalization*, ed. Mario Blaser, Harvey Feit, and Glenn McRae, 92–110. London: Zed / International Development Research Center.

Ferguson, James. 1990. *The Anti-Politics Machine: "Development," Depoliticization, and Bureaucratic Power in Lesotho*. Cambridge: Cambridge University Press.

—————. 1997. "Anthropology and Its Evil Twin: 'Development' in the Constitution of a Discipline." *International Development and the Social Sciences: Essays on the History and Politics of Knowledge*, ed. Frederick Cooper and Randall M. Packard, 150–75. Berkeley: University of California Press.

Fernandez Osco, Marcelo. Forthcoming. "Ayllu: Decolonial Critical Thinking and Other Autonomy." *Indigenous Peoples and Autonomy: Insights for the Global Age*, ed. Mario Blaser, Ravi DeCosta, Deborah Mcgregor, and William Coleman. Vancouver: University of British Columbia Press.

Ferradás, Carmen A. 1998. *Power in the Southern Cone Borderlands: An Anthropology of Development Practice*. Westport, Conn.: Bergin and Garvey.

Finnemore, Martha. 1997. "Redefining Development at the World Bank." *International Development and the Social Sciences: Essays on the History and Politics of Knowledge*, ed. Frederick Cooper and Randall M. Packard, 203–27. Berkeley: University of California Press.

Fischer, Edward F. 2001. *Cultural Logics and Global Economics: Maya Identity in Thought and Practice*. 1st edn. Austin: University of Texas Press.

Fish, Stanley. 1997. "Boutique Multiculturalism, Or Why Liberals Are Incapable of Thinking about Hate Speech." *Critical Inquiry* 23, no. 2, 378–95.

Flecha, Victor, and Carlos Martini. 1994. *Historia de la transición: Pasado y futuro de la democracia en el Paraguay*. Asunción: Ultima Hora.

Foucault, Michel. 1973. *The Order of Things: An Archaeology of the Human Sciences*. New York: Vintage.

—————. 1980. *Power/Knowledge: Selected Interviews and Other Writings, 1972–1977*. New York: Pantheon.

Fox, Richard G. E. 1991. *Recapturing Anthropology: Working in the Present*. Santa Fe, N.M.: School of American Research Press.

Franklin, Sarah, Celia Lury, and Jackie Stacey. 2000. *Global Nature, Global Culture*. London: Sage.

Freire, Paulo. 1970. *Pedagogy of the Oppressed*. New York: Seabury.

Freres, Christian. 2000. "The European Union as a Global 'Civilian Power': Development Cooperation in EU–Latin American Relations." *Interamerican Studies and World Affairs* 42, no. 2, 63–85.

————, coord. 1998. *La cooperación de las sociedades civiles de la Unión Europea con América Latina.* Madrid: Asociación de Investigación y Especialización sobre Temas Iberoamericanos.

Fric, Pavel, and Yvonna Fricova, eds. 1997. *Guido Boggiani: Fotograf / fotografo / fotógrafo / photographer.* Prague: Nakladatelsvi Titanic.

Fritz, Miguel. 1993. "La changa: Opción de los indígenas nivacle de Campo Loa." *Suplemento Antropológico* 28, nos. 1–2, 43–106.

————. 1994."Nos han salvado": Misión: Destrucción o salvación?: Comienzos de una misión, entre etnocentrismo e inculturación.* Quito: Abya-Yala.

Gamble, Andrew. 1996. *Hayek: The Iron Cage of Liberty.* Boulder, Colo.: Westview.

Gaonkar, Dilip Parameshwar, ed. 2001. *Alternative Modernities.* Durham, N.C.: Duke University Press.

Giddens, Anthony. 1990. *The Consequences of Modernity.* Stanford, Calif.: Stanford University Press.

————. 1998. *The Third Way: The Renewal of Social Democracy.* Cambridge: Polity.

Giddens, Anthony, and Christopher Pierson. 1998. *Conversations with Anthony Giddens: Making Sense of Modernity.* Stanford, Calif.: Stanford University Press.

Gobierno del Paraguay. 1992. *Decreto 13423 por el que se crea la Comisión para a Elaboración de un Plan Maestro de Desarrollo Sustentable del Chaco Paraguayo.* Asunción: Imprenta Oficial.

Gómez-Perasso, José A. 1987. *Crónicas de cacerías humanas: La tragedia Ayoreo.* Asunción: El Lector.

Gordillo, Gaston. 1993. "La actual dinámica económica de los cazadores-recolectores del Gran Chaco y los deseos imaginarios del esencialismo." *Publicar* 2, no. 3, 73–96.

Gordon, Colin. 1991. "Governmental Rationality: An Introduction." *The Foucault Effect: Studies in Governmentality,* ed. Graham Burchell, Colin Gordon, and Peter Miller, 1–51. Chicago: University of Chicago Press.

Gow, Peter. 2001. *An Amazonian Myth and Its History.* Oxford: Oxford University Press.

Graeber, David. 2004. "The Twilight of Vanguardism." *The World Social Forum: Challenging Empires,* ed. Jai Sen, Anita Arnand, Arturo Escobar, and Peter Waterman, 329–35. New Delhi: Viveka.

Grillo, Ralph. 1985. "Applied Anthropology in the 1980s: Retrospect and Prospect." *Social Anthropology and Development Policy,* ed. Ralph Grillo and Alan Rew, 1–36. London: Tavistock.

Grossberg, Lawrence. N. d. "Cultural Studies in Search of Modernities." Unpublished ms.

Grove, Richard. 1995. *Green Imperialism: Colonial Expansion, Tropical Island Edens, and the Origins of Environmentalism, 1600–1860.* Cambridge: Cambridge University Press.

Grubb, William B. [1925] 1993. *Un pueblo desconocido en tierra desconocida.* Asunción: Biblioteca Paraguaya de Antropología.

Grunberg, Georg. 1997. "El Chaco sustentable y posible." *Acción* 171, 5–8.

Guha, Ramachandra. 2000. *Environmentalism: A Global History.* New York: Longman.

268

Guha, Ranajit. 1997. *Dominance without Hegemony: History and Power in Colonial India.* Cambridge, Mass.: Harvard University Press.

Gupta, Akhil, and James Ferguson. 1997. "Culture, Power, Place: Ethnography at the End of an Era." *Culture, Power, Place: Explorations in Critical Anthropology,* ed. Akhil Gupta and James Ferguson, 1–29. Durham, N.C.: Duke University Press.

Gutiérrez, Natividad. 1999. *Nationalist Myths and Ethnic Identities: Indigenous Intellectuals and the Mexican State.* Lincoln: University of Nebraska Press.

Hack, Henrick. 1978. "Indios y Menonitas en el Chaco paraguayo (1)." *Suplemento Antropológico* 13, nos. 1–2, 207–60.

————. 1979. "Indios y Menonitas en el Chaco paraguayo (2)." *Suplemento Antropológico* 14, nos. 1–2, 201–48.

————. 1980. "Indios y Menonitas en el Chaco paraguayo (3)." *Suplemento Antropológico* 15, nos. 1–2, 45–137.

Hajer, Maarten A. 1995. *The Politics of Environmental Discourse: Ecological Modernization and the Policy Process.* Oxford: Clarendon.

Halcrow Rural Management / Natural Resource Institute. 1995. *Propuesta técnica para proyecto de desarrollo sustentable del Chaco paraguayo.* Asunción: Archivo del Ministerio de Agricultura y Ganadería del Paraguay.

Hale, Charles. 2008. "Collaborative Anthropologies in Transition." *A Companion to Latin American Anthropology,* ed. Deborah Poole, 502–18. Malden, Mass.: Blackwell.

Hanratty, Dennis M., and Sandra W. Meditz, eds. 1990. *Paraguay: A Country Study.* Washington: Federal Research Division.

Haraway, Donna. 1991. *Simians, Cyborgs, and Women: The Reinvention of Nature.* New York: Routledge.

————. 1997. *Modest_Witness@Second_Millenium.FemaleMan©_Meets_OncoMouse™: Feminism and Technoscience.* New York: Routledge.

————. 2003. *The Companion Species Manifesto: Dogs, People, and Significant Otherness.* Chicago: Prickly Paradigm.

————. 2007. *When Species Meet.* Minneapolis: University of Minnesota Press.

Hardt, Michael, and Antonio Negri. 2000. *Empire.* Cambridge, Mass.: Harvard University Press.

————. 2004. *Multitude: War and Democracy in the Age of Empire.* New York: Penguin.

Harris, Olivia. 1995. "'The Coming of the White People': Reflections on the Mythologisation of History in Latin America." *Bulletin of Latin American Research* 14, no. 1, 9–24.

Harvey, David. 1996. *Justice, Nature, and the Geography of Difference.* Cambridge, Mass.: Blackwell.

Hayden, Corinne P. 2003. *When Nature Goes Public: The Making and Unmaking of Bioprospecting in Mexico.* Princeton, N.J.: Princeton University Press.

Hayek, Friedrich. 1973. "The Principles of a Liberal Social Order." *An Introduction to Moral and Social Philosophy: Basic Readings in Theory and Practice,* ed. Jeffrie G. Murphy, 248–63. Belmont, Calif: Wadsworth.

Herlitz, Lars. 1997. "Art and Nature in Pre-Classical Economics of the Seventeenth and Eighteenth Centuries." *Nature and Society in Historical Context,* ed. Mikuláš Teich, Roy Porter, and Bo Gustafsson, 163–75. New York: Cambridge University Press.

Heyn, Carlos. 1996. *Reseña histórica de las misiones salesianas del Chaco paraguayo 1917–1995.* Asunción: Don Bosco.

Hirsch, Eric, and Charles Stewart. 2005. "Introduction: Ethnographies of Historicity." *History and Anthropology* 16, no. 3, 261–74.

Hittman, Michael. 1997. *Wovoka and the Ghost Dance.* Expanded edn. Lincoln: University of Nebraska Press.

Hornborg, Alf. 1994. "Environmentalism, Ethnicity and Sacred Places: Reflections on Modernity, Discourse and Power." *Canadian Review of Sociology and Anthropology* 31, no. 3 (March), 245–67.

Horst, René H. 1998. "Authoritarianism, indigenous resistance and religious missions: Paraguay, 1958–1992." Ph.D. diss., Indiana University.

Hvalkof, Søren, and Peter Aaby, eds. 1981. *Is God an American? An Anthropological Perspective on the Missionary Work of the Summer Institute of Linguistics.* Copenhagen: International Work Group for Indigenous Affairs / Survival International.

Hymes, Dell H. 1974. *Reinventing Anthropology.* New York: Random House.

Ibarra, Carlos. 1930. "Bahía Negra: Un episodio olvidado." *Boletín de la Armada Nacional* 4, no. 72, 31–40.

Ingold, Tim. 2000. *The Perception of the Environment: Essays on Livelihood, Dwelling and Skill.* New York: Routledge.

Instituto Nacional del Indígena. 1981. *Censo y estudio de la población indígena del Paraguay.* Asunción: Instituto Nacional del Indígena.

———. 1998. *Ley 904/81: Estatuto de las comunidades indígenas.* Asunción: Instituto Nacional del Indígena.

International Work Group for Indigenous Affairs. 1971. *Declaration of Barbados.* Copenhagen: International Work Group for Indigenous Affairs.

Jobert, Bruno. 1994a. "Introduction: Le retour du politique." *Le tournant néo-libéral en Europe: Idées et recettes dans les pratiques gouvernementales,* ed. Bruno Jobert, 9–20. Paris: Harmattan.

———, ed. 1994b. *Le tournant néo-libéral en Europe: Idées et recettes dans les pratiques gouvernementales.* Paris: Harmattan.

Keck, Margaret E., and Kathryn Sikkink. 1998. *Activists beyond Borders: Advocacy Networks in International Politics.* Ithaca, N.Y.: Cornell University Press.

Kenrick, Justin. 2009. "The Paradox of Indigenous Peoples' Rights." *World Anthropologies Network Electronic Journal* 4, 12–55. http://www.ram-wan.net/.

Kidd, Stephen W. 1995a. "Development Failures among the Indigenous Peoples of the Paraguayan Chaco." Unpublished manuscript, copy on file with author.

———. 1995b. "Land, Politics and Benevolent Shamanism: The Enxet Indians in a Democratic Paraguay." *Latin American Studies* 27, 43–75.

————. 1997a. "Indigenous Peoples." *The Transition to Democracy in Paraguay*, ed. Peter Lambert and Andrew Nickson, 114–27. Houndmills, Basingstoke, Hampshire, England: Macmillan.

————. 1997b. *Report on the European Union's Project for Sustainable Development of the Paraguayan Chaco.* St. Andrews, U.K.: Centre for Indigenous American Studies and Exchange.

————. 1999. "The Morality of the Enxet People of the Paraguayan Chaco and Their Resistance to Assimilation." *Peoples of the Gran Chaco*, ed. Elmer S. Miller, 37–60. Westport, Conn.: Bergin and Garvey.

King, Thomas. 2003. *The Truth about Stories: A Native Narrative.* Toronto: House of Anansi.

Kingsnorth, Paul. 2004. *One No, Many Yeses: A Journey to the Heart of the Global Resistance Movement.* London: Free Press.

Kirsch, Stuart. 2006. *Reverse Anthropology: Indigenous Analysis of Social and Environmental Relations in New Guinea.* Stanford, Calif.: Stanford University Press.

Kleinpenning, Jan. 1988. "Política de desarrollo rural en el Paraguay desde 1960." *Suplemento Antropológico* 23, no. 1, 191–219.

————. 1992. *Rural Paraguay, 1870–1932.* Amsterdam: Centro de Estudios y Documentación Latinoamericanos.

Kleinpenning, Jan, and E. B. Zoomers. 1991. "Colonización interna como estrategia de cambio del sistema rural de un país: El caso de Paraguay." *Suplemento Antropológico* 26, no. 1, 43–63.

Kreimer, Osvaldo. 1998. "The Future Inter-American Declaration on the Rights of Indigenous Peoples: A Challenge for the Americas." *The Human Rights of Indigenous Peoples*, ed. Cynthia Price Cohen, 63–72. Ardsley, N.Y.: Transnational.

Kukathas, Chandran. 1989. *Hayek and Modern Liberalism.* Oxford: Clarendon.

Lackner, Thomas. 1998. *Algunas consideraciones sobre el "Informe sobre situación catastral de propiedades de comunidades indígenas en el Chaco paraguayo" de Prodechaco (ALA 93/40).* Asunción: Asociación Indigenista del Paraguay / Pan Para el Mundo / Global 2000.

LaDuke, Winona. 1999. *All Our Relations: Native Struggles for Land and Life.* Cambridge, Mass.: South End.

Lambert, Peter. 1996. "Mechanisms of Control: The Stroessner Regime in Paraguay." *Authoritarianism in Latin America since Independence*, ed. Will Fowler, 93–108. Westport, Conn.: Greenwood.

————. 2000. "A Decade of Electoral Democracy: Continuity, Change and Crisis in Paraguay." *Bulletin of Latin American Research* 19, no. 3, 379–96.

Lambert, Peter, and Andrew Nickson. 1997a. "The Regime of Alfredo Stroessner." *The Transition to Democracy in Paraguay*, ed. Peter Lambert and Andrew Nickson, 3–23. Houndmills, Basingstoke, Hampshire, England: Macmillan.

————, eds. 1997b. *The Transition to Democracy in Paraguay.* Houndmills, Basingstoke, Hampshire, England: Macmillan.

Lander, Edgardo, and Santiago Castro-Gómez, eds. 2000. *La colonialidad del saber: Euro-centrismo y ciencias sociales: Perspectivas Latinoamericanas.* 1st edn. Buenos Aires: Consejo Latinoamericano de Ciencias Sociales / UNESCO Unidad Regional de Ciencias Sociales y Humanas para América Latina y el Caribe.

Lange, Lynda. 1998. "Burnt Offerings to Rationality: A Feminist Reading of the Construction of Indigenous Peoples in Enrique Dussel's Theory of Modernity." *Hypatia* 13, no. 3, 132–45.

Lanthier, Isabelle, and Lawrence Olivier. 1999. "The Construction of Environmental 'Awareness.'" *Discourses of the Environment,* ed. Éric Darier, 63–78. Malden, Mass.: Blackwell.

Larmore, Charles E. 1996. *The Morals of Modernity.* Cambridge: Cambridge University Press.

Lash, Scott, Bronislaw Szerszynski, and Brian Wynne. 1996. *Risk, Environment and Modernity: Towards a New Ecology.* London: Sage.

Latour, Bruno. 1993. *We Have Never Been Modern.* Cambridge, Mass.: Harvard University Press.

———. 1999. *Pandora's Hope: Essays on the Reality of Science Studies.* Cambridge, Mass.: Harvard University Press.

———. 2002. *War of the Worlds: What about Peace?* Chicago: Prickly Paradigm.

———. 2003. "Is Re-modernization Occurring—And If So, How to Prove It? A Commentary on Ulrich Beck." *Theory, Culture and Society* 20, no. 2, 35–48.

———. 2004. *Politics of Nature: How to Bring the Sciences into Democracy.* Cambridge, Mass.: Harvard University Press.

Law, John. 2004. *After Method: Mess in Social Science Research.* London: Routledge.

Law, John, and John Hassard. 1999. *Actor Network Theory and After.* Oxford: Blackwell.

Law, John, and Annemarie Mol. 2002. *Complexities: Social Studies of Knowledge Practices.* Durham, N.C.: Duke University Press.

Leigheb, Maurizio. 1986. *Guido Boggiani: Pittore, esploratore, etnografo: La vita, i viaggi, le opere.* Ornavasso: Regione Piemonte.

Lenkersdorf, Carlos. 2005. *Filosofar en clave Tojolabal.* Mexico City: Miguel Angel Porrua.

Lewis, Paul H. 1980. *Paraguay under Stroessner.* Chapel Hill: University of North Carolina Press.

Leys, Colin. 2001. *Market-Driven Politics: Neoliberal Democracy and the Public Interest.* London: Verso.

Lins Ribeiro, Gustavo. 2001. "Commentary." *Current Anthropology* 42, no. 5, 669–70.

Liu, Lydia H. 1999. "The Question of Meaning-Value in the Political Economy of the Sign." *Tokens of Exchange: The Problem of Translation in Global Circulations,* ed. Lydia H. Liu, 13–41. Durham, N.C.: Duke University Press.

Locke, John. [1690] 1980. *Second Treatise of Government.* Indianapolis, Ind.: Hackett.

Lopez Fretes, R. 1946. *Lo que he bisto en el Alto Paraguay.* Asunción: Imprenta Nacional.

MacCormack, Carol P., and Marilyn Strathern. 1980. *Nature, Culture, and Gender.* Cambridge: Cambridge University Press.

MacKenzie, John M. 1997. *Empires of Nature and the Nature of Empires: Imperialism, Scotland and the Environment.* East Linton, Scotland: Tuckwell.

Macpherson, C. B. 1980. Introduction to *Second Treatise of Government.* Indianapolis, Ind.: Hackett.

Majavacca, José, and Juan Pérez Acosta. 1951. *El aporte italiano al progreso del Paraguay (1527–1930).* Asunción: Sociedad Científica del Paraguay.

Marcos, Subcomandante Insurgente. 2001. *Our Word Is Our Weapon: Selected Writings of Subcomandante Insurgente Marcos.* Foreword by José Saramago. Edited by Juana Ponce de León. New York: Seven Stories.

Marcus, George E. 1994. "Recapturing Anthropology: Working in the Present." *American Ethnologist* 21, no. 4, 927–29.

———. 2007. "Ethnography Two Decades after *Writing Culture*: From the Experimental to the Baroque." *Anthropological Quarterly* 80, no. 4, 1127–45.

———. 2008. "The End(s) of Ethnography: Social/Cultural Anthropology's Signature Form of Producing Knowledge in Transition." *Cultural Anthropology* 23, no. 1, 1–14.

Marglin, Frédérique A., and Stephen A. Marglin, eds. 1990. *Dominating Knowledge: Development, Culture, and Resistance.* Oxford: Clarendon.

———. 1996. *Decolonizing Knowledge: From Development to Dialogue.* New York: Clarendon.

Martinez Cobo, José R. 1986. *Study of the Problem of Discrimination against Indigenous Populations.* New York: United Nations.

Massey, Doreen. 1999. "Imagining Globalization: Power-Geometries of Time-Space." *Global Futures: Migration, Environment, and Globalization,* ed. Avtar Brah, Mary J. Hickman, and Mairtin Mac an Ghaill, 27–44. Houndmills, Basingstoke, England: St. Martin's.

Mato, Daniel. 1996. "On the Theory, Epistemology, and Politics of the Social Construction of 'Cultural Identities' in the Age of Globalization: Introductory Remarks to Ongoing Debates." *Identities* 3, nos. 1–2, 61–72.

McGregor, Deborah. 2004. "Traditional Ecological Knowledge and Sustainable Development." *In the Way of Development: Indigenous Peoples, Life Projects, and Globalization,* ed. Mario Blaser, Harvey Feit, and Glenn McRae, 72–91. London: Zed / International Development Research Centre.

Meadows, Donella H., Dennis L. Meadows, Jørgen Randers, and William W. Behrens III. 1975. *The Limits to Growth: A Report for the Club of Rome's Project on the Predicament of Mankind.* 2d edn. New York: New American Library.

Mendoza, Marcela. 2004. "Western Toba Messianism and Resistance to Colonization, 1915–1918." *Ethnohistory* 51, no. 2, 293–316.

Merchant, Carolyn. 1983. *The Death of Nature: Women, Ecology, and the Scientific Revolution.* San Francisco: Harper and Row.

Mignolo, Walter. 2000. *Local Histories/Global Designs: Coloniality, Subaltern Knowledges, and Border Thinking.* Princeton, N.J.: Princeton University Press.

————. 2007. "Coloniality of Power and De-Colonial Thinking: Introduction." *Cultural Studies* 21, nos. 2–3, 155–67.

Mignolo, Walter, Freya Schiwy, and Michael Ennis, eds. 2002. *Knowledges and the Known: Andean Perspectives on Capitalism and Epistemology*. Special dossier, *Nepantla* 3, no. 1.

Miller, Elmer S. 1989. "Argentina's Toba: Hunter-Gatherers in the City." *Crossroads* (June), 636–45.

Millones, Luis, ed. 1990. *El retorno de las Huacas: Estudios y documentos sobre el Taki Onqoy: Siglo 16*. Lima: Instituto de Estudios Peruanos / Sociedad Peruana de Psicoanálisis.

Mol, Annemarie. 1999. "Ontological Politics: A Word and Some Questions." *Actor-Network Theory and After*, eds. John Law and John Hassard, 74–89. Boston, Mass.: Blackwell.

————. 2002. *The Body Multiple: Ontology in Medical Practice*. Durham, N.C.: Duke University Press.

Momaday, N. Scott. 1989. *House Made of Dawn*. 1st Perennial library edn. New York: Harper and Row.

Mora, Frank O. 1998. "The Forgotten Relationship: United States–Paraguay Relations, 1937–89." *History* 33, no. 3, 451–73.

Muehlebach, Andrea. 2003. "What Self in Self-Determination? Notes from the Frontiers of Transnational Indigenous Activism." *Identities: Global Studies in Culture and Power* 10, no. 2, 241–68.

Muñoz, H. 2001. "Good-Bye U.S.A.?" *Latin America in the New International System*, ed. Joseph S. Tulchin and Ralph H. Espach, 73–90. Boulder, Colo.: Lynne Rienner.

Münzel, Mark. 1973. *The Aché Indians: Genocide in Paraguay*. Copenhagen: International Working Group for Indigenous Affairs.

————. 1974. *The Aché: Genocide Continues in Paraguay*. Copenhagen: International Working Group for Indigenous Affairs.

Nader, Laura. 1997. "Controlling Processes: Tracing the Dynamic Components of Power." *Current Anthropology* 38, no. 5, 711–38.

Nahmad, Salomon. 1997. "Mexican Applied Anthropology: From Founder Manuel Gamio to Contemporary Movements." *The Global Practice of Anthropology*, ed. Marietta L. Baba and Carole E. Hill, 229–44. Williamsburg, Va.: Department of Anthropology, College of William and Mary.

Narvaez Arza, Federico. 1998. *Lino Oviedo: Más allá del golpe*. Asunción: Instituto para la Nueva Republica.

Nickson, Andrew. 1997. "Corruption and the Transition." *The Transition to Democracy in Paraguay*, ed. Peter Lambert and Andrew Nickson, 24–44. Houndmills, Basingstoke, Hampshire, England: Macmillan.

Nickson, Andrew, and Peter Lambert. 2002. "State Reform and the 'Privatized State' in Paraguay." *Public Administration and Development* 22, no. 2, 163–74.

Nieto Niebuhr, Atilio, and Melita Walls Enns. 1998. *La reforma del Estado Paraguayo: Descentralización política y administrativa*. Asunción: Don Bosco.

Niezen, Ronald. 2003. *The Origins of Indigenism: Human Rights and the Politics of Identity.* Berkeley: University of California Press.

Noble, Brian. 2007. "Justice, Transaction, Translation: Blackfoot Tipi Transfers and WIPO's Search for the Facts of Traditional Knowledge Exchange." *American Anthropologist* 109, no. 2, 338–49.

Notes from Nowhere. 2003. *We Are Everywhere: The Irresistible Rise of Global Anticapitalism.* London: Verso.

Olmedo, Natalicio. 1946. *Vida y actividades en el Alto Paraguay: Historia / Critica / Relato De hechos desconocidos / Descripción fiel de las poblaciones industriales / Ilustraciones interesantes.* Asunción: El Grafico.

———. 1966. *El Gran Chaco paraguayo: Amparo de civilización y progreso.* Asunción: El Grafico.

O'Malley, Pat. 1996. "Risk and Responsibility." *Foucault and Political Reason: Liberalism, Neo-Liberalism and Rationalities of Government,* ed. Andrew Barry, Thomas Osborne, and Nikolas S. Rose, 189–207. Chicago: University of Chicago Press.

Oviedo, Lino. 1997. *El golpe que no existió: Raíces y razones.* Asunción: Unión Nacional de Colorados Eticos.

Pastore, Carlos. 1972. *La lucha por la tierra en el Paraguay.* Montevideo: Editorial Antequera.

Patzi, Félix. 2004. *Sistema comunal: Una propuesta alternativa al sistema liberal: Una discusión teórica para salir de la colonialidad y del liberalismo.* La Paz: Comunidad de Estudios Alternativos.

Pels, Peter. 1997. "The Anthropology of Colonialism: Culture, History, and the Emergence of Western Governmentality." *Annual Review of Anthropology* 26, 163–83.

Phelan, Shane. 1993. "Intimate Distance: The Dislocation of Nature in Modernity." *In the Nature of Things: Language, Politics and the Environment,* ed. Jane Bennett and William Chaloupka, 44–62. Minneapolis: University of Minnesota Press.

Plett, Rudolf. 1979. *Presencia Menonita en el Paraguay: Origen, doctrina, estructura y funcionamiento.* Asunción: Instituto Bíblico.

Plumwood, Val. 1993. *Feminism and the Mastery of Nature.* London: Routledge.

———. 2002. *Environmental Culture: The Ecological Crisis of Reason.* London: Routledge.

Poirier, Sylvie. 2008. "Reflections on Indigenous Cosmopolitics: Poetics." *Anthropologica* 50, no. 1, 75–85.

Postero, Nancy G., and León Zamosc. 2004. *The Struggle for Indigenous Rights in Latin America.* Brighton, England: Sussex Academic.

Povinelli, Elizabeth. 2001. "Radical Worlds: The Anthropology of Incommensurability and Inconceivability." *Annual Review of Anthropology* 30, 319(16)–35.

Prieto, Esther, and Enrique Bragayrac. 1995. *Legislación indígena/legislación ambiental en el Paraguay.* Asunción: Ministerio de Agricultura y Ganadería / Centros de estudios Humanitarios.

Prodechaco. 1998a. *Plan Operativo Global.* Vol 2., *Informe principal.* Asunción: Prodechaco / Archivo del Ministerio de Agricultura y Ganadería de Paraguay.

———. 1998b. *Plan Operativo Global.* Vol. 3, *Anexos y consultorías.* Asunción: Prodechaco / Archivo del Ministerio de Agricultura y Ganadería de Paraguay.

Puccini, Sandra. 1999. *Andare lontano: Viaggi ed etnografia nel secondo Ottocento.* Rome: Carocci.

Quijano, Aníbal. 2000. "Colonialidad del poder, Eurocentrismo y América Latina." *La colonialidad del saber: Eurocentrismo y ciencias sociales: Perspectivas Latinoamericanas,* ed. Edgardo Lander and Santiago Castro-Gómez, 201–46. Buenos Aires: Consejo Latino-americano de Ciencias Sociales / UNESCO Unidad Regional de Ciencias Sociales y Humanas para América Latina y el Caribe.

Rahnema, Majid. 1992. "Participation." *The Development Dictionary: A Guide to Knowledge as Power,* 116–31. London: Zed.

Ramos, Alcida R. 1998. *Indigenism: Ethnic Politics in Brazil.* Madison: University of Wisconsin Press.

Rappaport, Joanne. 2005. *Intercultural Utopias: Public Intellectuals, Cultural Experimentation, and Ethnic Pluralism in Colombia.* Durham, N.C.: Duke University Press.

Ratzlaff, Gerhard. 1993. *Inmigración y colonización de los Mennonitas en el Paraguay Bajo la ley 514.* Asunción: Comité Social y Economico Mennonito.

Redekop, Calvin W. 1980. *Strangers Become Neighbors: Mennonite and Indigenous Relations in the Paraguayan Chaco.* Scottdale, Penn.: Herald.

Regehr, Walter. 1984. "Teorías del desarrollo y autogestión indígena." *Suplemento Antropológico* 19, no. 1, 89–95.

Renshaw, John. 1988. "Property, Resources and Equality among the Indians of the Paraguayan Chaco." *Man* 23, no. 2, 334–52.

———. 1996. *Los indígenas del Chaco paraguayo: Economía y sociedad.* Asunción: Intercontinental Editora.

Richer, H. 1993. *Reforma del estado, neoliberalismo y crisis política.* Asunción: Base Investigaciones Sociales.

Riles, Annelise. 2000. *The Network Inside Out.* Ann Arbor: University of Michigan Press.

Rist, Gilbert. 1997. *The History of Development: From Western Origins to Global Faith.* Atlantic Highlands, N.J.: Zed.

Rival, Laura. 1993. "The Growth of Family Trees: Understanding Huaorani Perceptions of the Forest." *Man* 28, no. 4, 635–52.

Rivarola, Marcos. 2001. *Marzo paraguayo: Una lección de democracia.* Asunción: Ultima Hora.

Robbins, Wayne. 1984. "Proyectos de desarrollo y comunidades indígenas." *Suplemento Antropológico* 19, no. 1, 71–79.

———. 1999. *Etnicidad, tierra y poder.* Asunción: Comisión Nacional de Pastora Indígeno / Centro de Estudios de Antropologia de la Universidad Cataliea.

Roett, Riordan, and Richard S. Sacks. 1991. *Paraguay: The Personalist Legacy.* Boulder, Colo.: Westview.

Rojas, Esther. 1996. "Economía indígena y economía alternativa de desarrollo." *Suplemento Antropológico* 31, nos. 1–2, 251–73.

Romero, Carlos. 1913. *Repatriación: Anexo, la explotación de los montes fiscales.* Asunción: Imprenta Nacional.

Romero, Luis A. 1977. "El ciclo del tanino en Argentina." *Revista Paraguaya de Sociología* 14, no. 38, 157–80.

Rosaldo, Renato. 1989. *Culture and Truth: The Remaking of Social Analysis.* Boston: Beacon.

Rose, Deborah B. 2004. *Reports from a Wild Country: Ethics for Decolonisation.* Sydney: University of New South Wales Press.

Rose, Nikolas S. 1996. "Governing 'Advanced' Liberal Democracies." *Foucault and Political Reason: Liberalism, Neo-Liberalism and Rationalities of Government,* ed. Andrew Barry, Thomas Osborne, and Nikolas S. Rose, 37–64. Chicago: University of Chicago Press.

Sachs, Wolfgang. 1992. *The Development Dictionary: A Guide to Knowledge as Power.* London: Zed.

Sahlins, Marshall. 1999. "What Is Anthropological Enlightenment? Some Lessons of the Twentieth Century." *Annual Review of Anthropology* 28, i–xxiii.

Sanders, Douglas E. 1977. *The Formation of the World Council of Indigenous Peoples.* Copenhagen: International Working Group for Indigenous Affairs.

———. 1998. "The Legacy of Deskaheh: Indigenous Peoples as International Actors." *The Human Rights of Indigenous Peoples,* ed. Cynthia Price Cohen, 73–88. Ardsley, N.Y.: Transnational.

Santos, Boaventura de Sousa. 2004a. "The World Social Forum: Toward a Counter-Hegemonic Globalisation (Part 1)." *The World Social Forum: Challenging Empires,* ed. Jai Sen, Anita Anand, Arturo Escobar, and Peter Waterman, 235–45. New Delhi: Viveka.

———. 2004b. "The World Social Forum: Toward a Counter-Hegemonic Globalisation (Part 2)." *The World Social Forum: Challenging Empires,* ed. Jai Sen, Anita Anand, Arturo Escobar, and Peter Waterman, 336–43. New Delhi: Viveka.

———. 2006. *The Rise of the Global Left: The World Social Forum and Beyond.* London: Zed Books.

Schelling, Vivian. 2000. *Through the Kaleidoscope: The Experience of Modernity in Latin America.* London: Verso.

Scott, James C. 1990. *Domination and the Arts of Resistance: Hidden Transcripts.* New Haven, Conn.: Yale University Press.

Scott, Joan W. 1992. "Experience." *Feminists Theorize the Political,* ed. Judith Butler and Joan W. Scott, 22–40. New York: Routledge.

Scott, John, and Gordon Marshall. 2005. *A Dictionary of Sociology.* Oxford: Oxford University Press.

Seelwische, J. 1984. "Los valores culturales de un pueblo y sus proyectos de desarrollo." *Suplemento Antropológico* 19, no. 1, 57–64.

Sen, Jai, Anita Arnand, and Peter Waterman, eds. 2004. *The World Social Forum: Challenging Empires.* New Delhi: Viveka.

SETA (Foundation for Political, Economic and Social Research). 1992. *Desarrollo sostenible del Chaco paraguayo: Protección de los bosques y del hábitat de los indígenas.* Informe Provisional Pedido de Prestación no CC/ALA/MISION 8069/PARAGUAY. Asunción: Archivo Ministerio de Agricultura y Ganadería de Paraguay.

Shore, Chris, and Susan Wright. 1997. "Colonial Gaze to Critique of Policy: British Anthropology in Policy and Practice." *The Global Practice of Anthropology*, ed. Marietta L. Baba and Carole E. Hill, 139–54. Williamsburg, Va.: Department of Anthropology, College of William and Mary.

Sieder, Rachel. 2002. *Multiculturalism in Latin America: Indigenous Rights, Diversity, and Democracy.* Basingstoke, Hampshire, England: Palgrave.

Silko, Leslie Marmon. 1977. *Ceremony.* New York: Viking.

Smith, Linda T. 1999. *Decolonising Methodologies: Research and Indigenous Peoples.* New York: Zed.

Sosa Gaona, E. 1996. *Orígenes de la misión salesiano del Chaco paraguayo: 1920–1930.* Asunción: Don Bosco.

Stahl, Wilhem. 1993. "Antropología de acción entre indígenas Chaqueños." *Suplemento Antropológico* 28, nos. 1–2, 25–42.

Stengers, Isabelle. 2005. "The Cosmopolitical Proposal." *Making Things Public: Atmospheres of Democracy*, ed. Bruno Latour and Peter Weibel, 994–1003. Cambridge, Mass.: MIT Press.

Stengers, Isabelle, and Mary Zournazi. 2003. "'A Cosmopolitics': Risk, Hope, Change: A Conversation with Isabelle Stengers." *Hope: New Philosophies for Change*, ed. Mary Zournazi, 244–71. New York: Routledge.

Stirrat, Roderick. 2000. "Cultures of Consultancy." *Critique of Anthropology* 20, no. 1, 31–46.

Stoll, David. 1982. *Fishers of Men or Founders of Empire? The Wycliffe Bible Translators in Latin America.* London: Zed.

Strathern, Marilyn. 1992. *After Nature: English Kinship in the Late Twentieth Century.* Cambridge: Cambridge University Press.

———. 1996. "Cutting the Network." *Journal of the Royal Anthropological Institute* 2, no. 3, 517–35.

———. 1999. *Property, Substance, and Effect: Anthropological Essays on Persons and Things.* London: Athlone.

———. 2004. *Partial Connections.* Updated edn. Walnut Creek, Calif.: AltaMira.

Stunnenberg, P. 1991. "Sedentarizacion de los indígenas del Chaco paraguayo." *Suplemento Antropológico* 25, no. 1, 23–42.

———. 1993. *Entitled to Land: The Incorporation of the Paraguayan and Argentinean Gran Chaco and the Spatial Marginalization of the Indian People.* Saarbrücken: Verlag Breitenbach.

Suarez Arana, Cristian. 1919. *Exploraciones en el oriente Boliviano.* La Paz: Gonzales y Medina Editores.

Susnik, Branislava. 1957a. *Estructura de la lengua Chamacoco-Ebitoso.* Asunción: Museo Etnográfico Andrés Barbero.

————. 1957b. *Estudios Chamacoco*. Asunción: Museo Etnográfico Andrés Barbero.

————. 1995. *Chamacocos 1: Cambio Cultural*. Asunción: Museo Etnográfico Andrés Barbero.

Susnik, Branislava, and Miguel Chase-Sardi. 1995. *Los Indios del Paraguay*. Madrid: Editorial MAPFRE.

Swepston, Lee. 1998. "The Indigenous and Tribal Peoples Convention (no. 169): Eight Years after Adoption." *The Human Rights of Indigenous Peoples*, ed. Cynthia Price Cohen, 17–36. Ardsley, N.Y.: Transnational.

Szerszynski, Bronislaw. 1996. "On Knowing What to Do: Environmentalism and the Modern Problematic." *Risk, Environment and Modernity: Towards a New Ecology*, ed. Scott Lash, Bronislaw Szerszynski, and Brian Wynne, 104–37. London: Sage.

Takacs, David. 1996. *The Idea of Biodiversity: Philosophies of Paradise*. Baltimore: Johns Hopkins University Press.

Thorndahl, Marie. 1997. "Terrains de chasse et chasses gardees du development: Indigenisme et conflits fonciers dans le Chaco paraguayen." Diplome de Recherche thesis, Institut Universitaire d'Études du Développement, Geneva.

Tomasevski, Katerina. 1993. *Development Aid and Human Rights Revisited*. New York: Pinter.

Tomlinson, Jim. 1990. *Hayek and the Market*. London: Pluto.

Valenzuela, Arturo. 1997. "Paraguay: The Coup that Didn't Happen." *Democracy* 8, no. 1, 43.

Van Cott, Donna L. 1994. *Indigenous Peoples and Democracy in Latin America*. New York: St. Martin's / Inter-American Dialogue.

————. 2000. *The Friendly Liquidation of the Past: The Politics of Diversity in Latin America*. Pittsburgh: University of Pittsburgh Press.

Varese, Stefano, Guillermo Delgado, and Rodolfo Meyer. 2008. "Indigenous Anthropologies beyond Barbados." *A Companion to Latin American Anthropology*, ed. Deborah Poole, 375–98. Malden, Mass.: Blackwell.

Velasco del Real, Octavio. 1892. *Viaje por la América del Sur: Impresiones y recuerdos*. Barcelona: R. Molinas.

Venuti, Lawrence. 1998. *The Scandals of Translation: Towards an Ethics of Difference*. London: Routledge.

Virilio, Paul. 1999. *La inercia polar*. Madrid: Trama Editorial.

Viveiros de Castro, Eduardo. 2002. *A inconstância da alma selvagem e outros ensaios de antropologia*. São Paulo: Cosac and Naify.

————. 2004. "Exchanging Perspectives: The Transformation of Objects into Subjects in Amerindian Ontologies." *Common Knowledge* 10, no. 3, 463–84.

Vizenor, Gerald R. 1994. *Shadow Distance: A Gerald Vizenor Reader*. Hanover, N.H.: Wesleyan University Press.

Von Bremen, Volker. 1987. *Fuentes de caza y recoleccion modernas: Proyectos de ayuda al desarrollo destinados a los indígenas del Gran Chaco (Argentina, Paraguay, Bolivia)*. Stuttgart: Servicios de Desarrollo.

REFERENCES

————. 1994. "La significación del derecho a la tierra para los pueblos tradicionalmente no-sedentarios del Chaco paraguayo." *Suplemento Antropológico* 29, nos. 1–2, 143–62.

————. 2000. "Dynamics of Adaptation to Market Economy among the Ayoreode of Northwest Paraguay." *Hunters and Gatherers in the Modern World: Conflict, Resistance, and Self-Determination*, ed. Peter P. Schweitzer, Megan Biesele, and Robert K. Hitchcock, 273–86. New York: Berghahn.

Vysokolan, Oleg. 1983. "Panorama del indigenismo en 1982, en la Republica de Paraguay." *Suplemento Antropológico* 18, no. 1, 31–43.

————. 1992. *La traición de Papa Réi: 500 años de resistencia.* Asunción: Cabichui.

Wallerstein, Immanuel M. 2004. *The Modern World-System in the Longue Durée.* Boulder, Colo.: Paradigm.

Walsh, Catherine E., Freya Schiwy, and Santiago Castro-Gómez. 2002. *Indisciplinar las ciencias sociales: Geopolíticas del conocimiento y colonialidad del poder: Perspectivas de lo Andino.* 1st edn. Quito: Universidad Andina Simón Bolívar.

Warren, Harris G. 1978. *Paraguay and the Triple Alliance: The Postwar Decade, 1869–1878.* Austin: Institute of Latin American Studies, University of Texas, Austin.

Warren, Kay B. 1998. *Indigenous Movements and Their Critics: Pan-Maya Activism in Guatemala.* Princeton, N.J.: Princeton University Press.

Warren, Kay B., and Jean E. Jackson. 2002. *Indigenous Movements, Self-Representation, and the State in Latin America.* 1st edn. Austin: University of Texas Press.

Wasmosy, Juan C. 1998. *La respuesta de la democracia.* Asunción: RP Ediciones.

Waters, Anne. 2004a. *American Indian Thought: Philosophical Essays.* Malden, Mass.: Blackwell.

————. 2004b. "Language Matters: Nondiscrete Nonbinary Dualism." *American Indian Thought: Philosophical Essays*, ed. Anne Waters, 97–115. Malden, Mass.: Blackwell.

Weaver, Frederick S. 2000. *Latin America in the World Economy: Mercantile Colonialism to Global Capitalism.* Boulder, Colo.: Westview.

Whigham, Thomas L., and Barbara Potthast. 1999. "The Paraguayan Rosetta Stone: New Insights into the Demographics of the Paraguayan War, 1864–1870." *Latin American Research Review* 34, no. 1, 174–86.

Wilbert, Johannes, and Karin Simoneau. 1987. *Folk Literature of the Chamacoco Indians.* Los Angeles: UCLA Latin American Center Publications, University of California, Los Angeles.

Williams, John H. 1979. *The Rise and Fall of the Paraguayan Republic, 1800–1870.* Austin: Institute of Latin American Studies, University of Texas, Austin.

Wilmer, Franke. 1993. *The Indigenous Voice in World Politics: Since Time Immemorial (Violence, Cooperation, Peace).* Newbury Park, Calif.: Sage.

World Commission on Environment and Development. 1987. *Our Common Future.* Oxford: Oxford University Press.

Worster, Donald. 1977. *Nature's Economy: A History of Ecological Ideas.* Cambridge: Cambridge University Press.

————. 1993. *The Wealth of Nature: Environmental History and the Ecological Imagination.* New York: Oxford University Press.

Wright, Robin M. 1988. "Anthropological Presuppositions of Indigenous Advocacy." *Annual Review of Anthropology* 17, 365–90.

Yanagisako, Sylvia J., and Carol L. Delaney. 1995. *Naturalizing Power: Essays in Feminist Cultural Analysis.* New York: Routledge.

Yashar, Deborah J. 2005. *Contesting Citizenship in Latin America: The Rise of Indigenous Movements and the Postliberal Challenge.* Cambridge: Cambridge University Press.

Yehia, Elena. 2006. "De-colonizing Knowledge and Practice: A Dialogic Encounter between the Latin American Modernity/Coloniality/Decoloniality Research Program and Actor Network Theory." *Journal of the World Anthropology Network* 1, no. 2, 91–108.

Yore, Fatima. 1995. *La dominación stronista, origen y consolidación: Seguridad nacional y represión.* Asunción: BASE-IS.

Youngblood Henderson, James (Sákéj). 2000. "The Context of the State of Nature." *Reclaiming Indigenous Voice and Vision,* ed. Marie Battiste, 11–37. Vancouver: University of British Columbia Press.

————. 2004. "Exchanging Perspectives: The Transformation of Objects into Subjects in Amerindian Ontologies." *Common Knowledge* 10, no. 3, 463–84.

Index

Skills, 184, 186; translation of, 151–52, 225; UCINY and, 206–7

INDI. *See* Instituto Nacional del Indígena

Indians, 247n1; acculturated Ebitoso views of, 176–77; imagination of, 54–55, 57–58, 126–27

Indigenista field, 65, 91

Indigenistas, indigenismo, 91, 115, 124, 247n2, 249n1, 251n4, 251n18; factions of, 98–100; knowledge production by, 127–34; Law 904/81 and, 96–98; opposition to, 134–35; positions of, 83–84; projects among, 81–82; on traditional and acculturated groups, 116–17; and UCINY, 203, 236–37

Indigenist movements, 81–82, 87, 244n10

Indigenous peoples, 2, 7, 35, 64, 140, 146, 232, 249nn3–4; advocacy network on behalf of, 128–29; autonomy of, 91–92, 101–2; development projects and, 159–64; entrepreneurial, 175–77; European concepts and treatment of, 54–57; indigenistas and, 98–99, 251n18; land rights of, 96–98, 101; liberation of, 127–28; moralities of, 130–31; movements of struggle concerning, 14–15; natural resources and, 178–79; nature and, 85–86; organization of, 188–91; patronage networks and, 173–74; Prodechaco and, 166–68, 180–86; respect for, 129–30; rights of, 80–81, 101

Indigenous People's National Trust, 69

Initiation ritual (debylylta), 30, 42, 71, 75, 191, 253n6; missionary interference with, 73, 74; religious factions and, 192–93, 197; revival of, 123–24; Tomaraho practice of, 72, 115, 116

Instituto Indigenista Inter-Americano, 69

Instituto Nacional del Indígena (INDI), 82, 83, 110, 188, 204; API and, 99–100; land rights and, 97–98

Integrationists: Law 904/81 and, 98

Intellectual others, 16–17

Intellectuals, 127, 129, 238; emotional investment of, 232–33; among Yshiro, 23–26, 33–34, 145, 187

Inter-American Development Bank, 66

Inter-American Foundation: and Marandú, 81–82

International Conference of Americanists: on human rights violations, 80–81

International League for the Rights of Man (New York), 82

International Work Group for Indigenous Affairs (IWGIA), 80–81, 82, 128

Interventionism, 135, 251n3; Chacoan development and, 68–75; political, 228–29; of state, 64–65

IWGIA. *See* International Work Group for Indigenous Affairs

Karcha Bahlut (Puerto 14 de mayo), 44–45, 52, 142; cultureros in, 192–94; initiation ritual at, 123–24; land claims for, 118–19

Keiwe (Ebitoso elder), 43

Kinship, 114, 119; leadership and, 108, 109–10, 198; patronage and leadership systems and, 76–79

Knowledge, 16, 29, 72, 140, 228; modern, 5–6; ontological conflict and, 3–4; performance of, 19, 21; production of, 127–34, 141–42; relationships and, 144–45; traditional, 118–19; uncertainty of, 137–38

Knowledge practices, 7–8, 35, 238; in ethnography, 21–22; storytelling as, 27, 31, 245n21

Konsaho (shamans), 29, 60, 214, 253nn2–3

Lacandon Maya, 232

Lamberto (Yshiro leader), 177

Land; land claims, 107, 160, 175, 252n1; ARP opposition to, 134–35, 159; indigenous rights to, 70, 97–98, 101, 178–79; in Karcha

Land (*cont.*)

Bahlut, 118–19; Law 904/81 and, 96–98; Prodechaco and, 165–69, 181; Tomaraho rights to, 115–16; whites' taking of, 46–47

Landowners, 134

Landscape: intellectual, 114

Law 904/81, 84; and land rights, 96–98, 107–8, 134

Leadership, 118, 250n15; among Ebitoso, 76–77, 107–8; community factions and, 192–98; reciprocity and, 198–202; and UCINY, 202–5, 208; unified, 189–91; in Ynishta, 109–10, 175–77

Legislation, 35; about indigenous rights, 84, 96–97

Liberalism: Progress, 49–50

Literacy, 108, 110, 112

Loans, 94

Locke, John: *Second Treatise of Government*, 3

Logging camps: in Chaco, 51, 52, 59–60; indigenous people and, 55, 59, 72

Logging companies: Tomaraho and, 74–75

Looting: by whites, 61

Lopez family (Paraguayan ruling family), 50

Marandú (indigenous organizational effort), 81–82, 84, 100, 128

Marcos, Subcomandante, 232

Market, 135; neoliberalism and, 136–38

Market goods: access to, 67–68

Market society: neoliberalism and, 136–37

Martinez, Candido, 203, 205

Martinez, Modesto, 178–79; on cultureros, 194–95

Mbya-Caduveo, 46

MCD. *See* Modernity/Coloniality and Decolonial thinking

Medicine, 60; missionaries and, 73, 74

Mennonites, 63, 159; agroindustrial development and, 66–67

Mercosur (South American regional economic bloc), 94, 154, 164, 172

Missionaries, 54–55, 57, 71, 247n7; attitudes of, 72–73; impacts of, 73–74, 191; patronage systems and, 75–79; traditional myth-history and, 25, 31

Missions, 247n8; New Tribes Mission, 71, 78, 108, 248n7

Modernity, 1–2, 4–5, 35, 88, 230, 250n9; colonialism and, 11–12; globalization and, 9–10, 228, 238; pluriverse and, 102–3

Modernity/Coloniality and Decolonial (MCD) thinking, 10, 11–13, 15, 16–17

Modernization, 88, 92

Moralities, 35, 111, 126, 145; of indigenous peoples, 130–31; situated, 110, 115

Moral logic, 110, 143; Cartesian vs. relational, 111, 124–25; relational, 112–14, 115, 145–46, 207; of traditionalists, 117–18

Multiculturalism, 139, 223, 224

Munzel, Mark, 82

Myth, 3; modern, 227–28, 229; modernity and, 4–5

Myth-history, 246n27; contact with whites in, 43–46; *Esnwherta au'oso* as, 41–42; social rules in, 42–43; storytelling and, 26–33; variations of, 25–26

Nationalism, 64

National Parks and Wildlife Direction (NPD), 209; Yshiro hunting and, 216, 217–18, 219, 220, 255n11

Natural resources, 155, 224; access to, 178–79; conservation of, 213–14; reciprocity of, 214–15

Natural rights, 49

Nature, 4, 12, 89, 247n6, 250n11; Chaco as, 53–54; civil government and, 48–49; environmental activism and, 87–88; indigenous peoples and, 85–86; progress and, 49–50; relativism vs. universalism in, 149–50

Nemur (Anabsero survivor), 42, 191, 192, 253n1

Neoliberalism, 91, 95, 255n2; autonomous decision-making and, 138–39; streamlining and, 153–54; environmentalism and, 223, 224; land rights and, 96–97; market and, 135–38; Prodechaco project and, 35–36; sustainable development and, 154–55

Networks, 244n12, 245n15; sharing, 114–15; world, 18, 21

New Policy Agenda, 154

New Tribes Mission (NTM), 71, 78, 108, 248n7; missionary attitudes and, 72–73

Nongovernmental organizations (NGOs), 112, 203; environmentalism and, 223–24; indigenista, 115, 116, 128; and Prodechaco, 166–69, 180–81, 183, 185, 186; sustainable development proposals and, 156–58, 160–61, 163; traditionalist projects and, 118–19

Nonhumans, 35; relations with, 120–23, 227

NPD. See National Parks and Wildlife Direction

NTM. See New Tribes Mission

Objectivity: of anthropology, 129–30

Ontological conflicts, 1–2; knowledge and, 3–4

Organization of American States, 82

Other: Chaco as, 53–54

Our Common Future (WCED), 89–90

Oviedo, Lino, 164, 188

Ozuna, Babi, 197

Paraguay, 7, 223; commercial fishing in, 211–12; commercial hunting in, 210–11; constitution of, 95–96; development politics in, 166–69; government of, 94–95; nineteenth-century, 50–51

Paraguayans, 64; and Europeans in Chaco, 55–56; Tomaraho and, 71–72; violence against Yshiro by, 58–59; Yshiro hunting program and, 220, 222

Paraguay River, 41, 51, 60, 248n5; hunting on, 209, 210; protection of, 210–11

Patronage system, 99, 164; Colorado Party and, 65–66; indigenous peoples and, 173–74, 179–80; leadership and, 198–99; market goods and, 67–68; missionaries and, 75–79; Paraguayan economy and, 172–73; in Ynishta, 108–10

Patronato Nacional de Indígenas, 69

Patrones, 178, 254n3; Ebitoso views of, 58–59, 70–71; fishing, 172–73, 176; leadership and, 76–78; market goods and, 67–68; in Ynishta, 108–9

Payá, Teresa, 176, 177, 205

Pentecostals, 253n5; vs. cultureros, 192–98; UCINY and, 202–5

Performance, 35, 144; of knowledge, 19, 21; of yrmo, 35–36, 145–46, 238–39

Philanthropy, 69–70

Philosophy of passivity, 85–86

Pitiantuta (Tomaraho settlement site), 123

Pluriverse, 21, 144, 227, 230, 237–38, 245n15; modernity and, 102–3

Politics, 236; Paraguayan, 94–96

Polotaks (person in charge; Ebitoso elder/ leader), 76

Porowo narratives, 27, 235, 253n4; inflexibility of, 29–30; social rules and, 42–43

Poverty, 183, 185

Power: differential, 16–17; of stories, 28–29

Prestige: market goods and, 75–76

Privatization, 95

Prodechaco, 35–36, 161, 163–64, 170, 254n4; chain of equivalences in, 171–72; community representation in, 183–87; development and, 165–69, 227; hunting programs and, 209–10, 212–13, 216–23, 255nn11–12; proposal development, 180–82; UCINY and, 204–5, 206; Yshiro organization and, 189–91

Work, 47; in logging camps, 60–61

World Bank, 66

World Commission on Environment and Development (WCED): *Our Common Future*, 89–90

World Economic Forum, 160

Worlds, 3, 18

World Social Forum (WSF), 14, 231

Worldviews, 3–4

Wozosh, 233, 246n22; management of, 42–43, 235; in myth-history narratives, 27, 29

WSF. *See* World Social Forum

Wututa (Ebitoso, Tomaraho settlement site), 116; conflicts in, 122–23; social rules in, 117–20

Ylhirta (Ebitoso settlement site), 71, 72, 107

Ynishta (Puerto Esperanza), 52; cooperative store in, 109–10; Ebitoso land in, 107–8; entrepreneurs in, 175–77; on initiation ritual in, 192–98; patronage system in, 108–9; Tomaraho in, 115–16, 128

Yrmo (Yshiro reality/world), 23, 57, 187, 227, 243n1; degradation of, 33–34; modern world and, 34–35; myth-history and, 27, 29; performance of, 35–36, 145–46, 238–39; remaking of, 30, 70; as web of relations, 233–34

Yshiro. *See* Ebitoso; Tomaraho

Yshiro Nation, 191, 205

Zapatista uprising, 232

Mario Blaser is the Canada Research Chair in Aboriginal Studies,
Memorial University of Newfoundland.

Library of Congress Cataloging-in-Publication Data

Blaser, Mario, 1966–
Storytelling globalization from the Chaco and beyond / Mario Blaser.
p. cm.—(New ecologies for the twenty-first century)
Includes bibliographical references and index.
ISBN 978-0-8223-4530-5 (cloth : alk. paper)
ISBN 978-0-8223-4545-9 (pbk. : alk. paper)
1. Chamacoco Indians—Paraguay.
2. Ethnology—Chaco Boreal (Paraguay and Bolivia)
3. Globalization—Economic aspects—Chaco Boreal (Paraguay and Bolivia)
4. Globalization—Social aspects—Chaco Boreal (Paraguay and Bolivia)
I. Title. II. Series: New ecologies for the twenty-first century.
F2230.2.C5B53 2010   989.2'2—dc22   2010006793